Marine Diesel Basics 1

Maintenance

Lay-up

Winter Protection

Tropical Storage

Spring Recommission

Written and Illustrated by
Dennison Berwick

Marine Diesel Basics

visual guides to marine diesel systems on sail, power & canal boats

Voyage Press

Voyage Press

7B Pleasant Blvd ., Unit 1045
Toronto, Ontario Canada M4T 1K2

www.marinedieselbasics.com

Marine Diesel Basics 1 2nd edition 2022
ISBN   978-0-9811233-5-6

Catalogue Information

Berwick, Dennison, 1956-, author, illustrator Maintenance, lay-up, winter protection, tropical storage, spring recommission / written and illustrated by Dennison Berwick.

(Marine diesel basics ; 1) Includes index.

Issued in print and electronic formats.

ISBN   978-0-9811233-5-6   (softcover)

ISBN   978-0-9811233-7-0   (hardcover)

ISBN   978-0-9811233-4-9   (spiral bound)

ISBN   978-0-9811233-6-3   (HTML)

Marine diesel motors--Maintenance and repair.

Marine diesel motors--Maintenance and repair--Pictorial works. I. Title. II. Series: Berwick, Dennison, 1956- . Marine diesel basics ; 1

Books in the Marine Diesel Basics series:

Maintenance eLogbook - fillable form pdf for iPads, tablets and desktops

Maintenance Logbook - softcover, hardcover, spiral bound

Forthcoming Titles:

MDB2 How Things Work + Installation Guidelines - *summer 2022*

MDB3 Troubleshooting – identifying and fixing problems, not symptoms
MDB4 Marine Mechanic's Know-How – advanced techniques etc.

Table of Contents

Introduction to Second Edition   **xi**

Disclaimer..xi

Using This Book...xii

Value of the Maintenance Logbook 1

Purpose of Maintenance - Reliable and Robust 1

1   Maintenance – Engine Essentials   **2**

  Main Concerns..2

  Task List..2

  1   Visual Engine Room Inspection................................3

  2   Check Engine Oil Level...4

  3   Check Belt Tension 4

  4   Check Coolant/Antifreeze & Top Up if Needed 6

  5   Check Transmission Fluid Level................................7

  6   Inspect Hoses and Hose Clamps 7

  7   Fit & Inspect Chafe Protection.................................8

  8   Inspect Wires and Wiring Terminals 9

  9   Inspect Belts - Alternator, Coolant & Raw Water Pump 11

  10   Inspect Pulleys (Sheaves) 12

  11   Check Alignment of Belts & Pulleys 13

  12   Adjust Pulley Alignment...15

  13   Tighten Alternator and Water Pump Belts 16

  14   Inspect & Repair Sound Insulation........................17

  15   Start Engine Procedure 17

  Cautionary Tale 18

2   Maintenance – Diesel Fuel   **19**

  Main Concerns..19

  Task List..19

  Importance of Very Clean Fuel................................19

  3 Ways to Contaminate Diesel Fuel & Tanks 20

  Preventing Fuel Contamination 21

  1   Inspect Fuel Deck Fill Fitting.................................21

  2   Add Biocide to the Fuel Tank(s)..............................22

  How Small is Small? 23

  Diesel Fuel Primary Fuel Filter 23

  3   Change the Primary Fuel Filter...............................24

4   Change the Secondary Fuel Filter 26

5   Bleed the Diesel System.. 29

Release a Locked-up Mechanical Fuel Pump 29

Three Sections of the Fuel Supply Circuit 30

6   Check Diesel Tank(s) for Contamination 33

Check for Water in a Keel Fuel Tank or Tank with No Drain 34

7   Inspect Injection Pump and Injectors 34

Cautionary Tale 35

3 Maintenance – Lubrication   36

Main Concerns.. 36

Task List.. 36

Keeping the Lubrication System Happy 37

Oil Is An Engine's Life Blood.. 37

1   Check Engine Oil Level..38

2   Dipstick Diagnostics – Engine Oil...38

3   Check Transmission Fluid Level 41

4   Dipstick Diagnostics – Transmission Fluid 41

Turbocharger Best Practices 44

5   Change the Engine Oil & Filter 45

Oil Filter Buyer's Guide.. 45

Oil Change Procedure - follow these simple steps 46

Warm Oil Flows More Easily 46

6   Change the Transmission Fluid (Engine Oil)............................. 52

Turbocharger 52

7   Grease the Control Cable Ends and Engine Mount Threads........ 54

8   Lubricate Ignition Key Slot 55

9   Check Injection Pump & Governor Dipsticks 55

Cautionary Tale 56

4 Maintenance – Raw Water Cooling   57

Main Concerns.. 57

Task List.. 57

Heat of Combustion.. 57

Water Words 58

Indirect Cooling (Fresh Water Cooled) 58

Direct Cooling...59

Keel Cooling 60

1   Clean Thruhull of Anti-Foul Paint and Marine Growth 61

2   Check Emergency Plug Tied to Every Seacock 61

3   Check Seacock Opens/Closes Smoothly 62

4   Inspect Raw Water Strainer 62

5   Service Raw Water Pump & Impeller 63

Anode(s) 68
  6   Check and Change Heat Exchanger Anode(s) 68
  7   Flush and Clean the Syphon Break 69
Cautionary Tale 71

5 Maintenance – Coolant/Antifreeze   72
Main Concerns 72
Task List 72
Ethylene Glycol Coolant/Antifreeze 72
Critical Functions of Coolant/Antifreeze 73
  1   Check Coolant/Antifreeze Level in Header Tank or Overflow Bottle 73
  2   Inspect Condition of Coolant 74
  3   Drain and Replace Worn-out Coolant/Antifreeze 74
Disposal of Ethylene Glycol Coolant/Antifreeze 75
Cautionary Tale 76

6 Maintenance – Breathing   77
Main Concerns 77
Task List 77
Why Clean the Air Filter? 77
  1   Clean the Air Filter 78
  2   Check the Crankcase Breather and Filter 79
Good Engine Room Ventilation 80
  3   Check Adequate Air Flow Through Engine Room 80
  4   Inspect & Repair Sound Insulation 81
Cautionary Tale 81

7 Maintenance – Electrical   82
Main Concerns 82
Task List 82
Sulphation 82
  1   Keep Lead Acid Battery(s) Charged 83
Trickle Charging Lead Acid Batteries 83
  2   Check Battery Open Circuit Voltage with a Multimeter 84
  3   Keep Battery Terminal Connections Tight 84
  4   Clean Battery Tops & Terminals 85
Maintaining Lithium-Iron (LiFePo4, LFP) Batteries 85
  5   Check the Electrolyte Levels of Wet-Cell Batteries 87
  6   Add Water to Unsealed Wet-Cell Battery 89
  7   Check Specific Gravity of a Wet-Cell Battery 90
  8   Load Testing a 12 Volt Battery 92
Adjust Specific Gravity Readings for Temperature 92
Understanding Battery Load Test Results 93

Cables or Wires, Cabling or Wiring? 94
Cautionary Tale 94

8 Maintenance – Drive Train 95
Main Concerns...95
Task List...95
1 Check Coupling Between Transmission & Prop Shaft............................95
2 Inspect the Propeller Shaft...97
3 Inspect the Stern Gland (Stuffing Box)..98
4 Inspect the Strut 101
5 Inspect the Cutlass Bearing... 102
6 Inspect the Propeller Anode 103
7 Clean the Propeller, Strut & Shaft.. 103
8 Inspect the Propeller 104
9 Inspect the Propeller Nuts and Cotter Pin 104
10 Inspect a Folding Propeller 105
11 Inspect the Anode on a Feathering Propeller 105
12 Grease a Feathering Propeller... 105
Cautionary Tale 107

9 Saildrives – Maintenance, Lay-Up & Recommission 108
Main Concerns.. 108
Task List... 108
Saildrive Oil Seals 109
1 Check Gear Oil Level & Top Up... 109
2 Change the Saildrive Gear Oil 109
3 Burp Air from Saildrive Gear Oil Dipstick.................................. 112
Watertight Seal (boot, bladder, foot sealing membrane) 113
4 Inspect Exterior Rubber Fairing Flange 113
5 Inspect Interior Rubber Sealing Ring & Water Sensor Alarm 114
6 Inspect Saildrive Anodes 115
7 Inspect and Repair Paint Protection.. 116
8 Clean Raw Water Intakes 116
9 Inspect the Propeller 117
10 Grease a Feathering Propeller 117

Saildrive Lay-up Task List 117
1 – 9 Lay-up Tasks... 117
10 Drain Raw Water from Saildrive.. 117
11 (In Water) Protect Lower Unit from Marine Growth 118

Saildrive Recommission Task List 119
1 Check Level of Gear Oil 119
2 Inspect Interior Rubber Sealing Ring & Water Sensor Alarm 119

3   Inspect Exterior Rubber Fairing Flange 119

4   Inspect and repair paint protection 119

Vessel Laid-up in the Water..120

5   Remove Covering from Propeller and Shaft 120

6   Inspect Saildrive Anodes 120

7   Inspect and repair paint protection 120

8   Clean Raw Water Intake.. 120

Lay-Up – Winter Protection & Tropical Storage   121

Main Concerns...121

10 Lay-Up – Engine Essentials   122

Main Concerns... 122

Task List... 122

1   Change Engine Oil & Filter... 122

2   Change Transmission Fluid 122

3   Slacken Tension Off Belts 123

4   Clean the Bilge 124

5   Wipe Down the Engine..125

6   Grease Engine Mounts 125

7   Write Up Good Notes in Maintenance Logbook.......................125

11 Lay-Up – Diesel Fuel   126

Main Concerns... 126

Task List... 126

1   Add Biocide to Last Fuel Fill 126

2   Check Deck Fill Fuel Cap is Closed 126

3   Change Primary Fuel Filter 126

Condensation and Filling the Fuel Tank(s)................................ 126

4   Bleed Fuel System 127

5   Close All Fuel Valves – Supply & Return 127

6   Check Fuel Vent Cannot Back Flood...127

12 Lay-Up – Lubrication   128

Main Concerns... 128

Task List... 128

1   Change Engine Oil & Filter... 128

2   Change Transmission Fluid 128

3   Grease Control Cable Ends & Engine Mount Threads 128

4   Lubricate Ignition Key Slot 128

5   Check Injection Pump & Governor Dipsticks (if fitted) 128

6   Fill the Transmission with ATF (or Engine Oil) 128

13 Lay-Up – Raw Water Cooling   129

Main Concerns... 129

Laying-up the Raw Water Cooling Circuit 129

Indirect Cooling Task List 130

Direct Cooling Task List 131

  1   Inspect Hoses and Hose Clamps 131

  2   Drain Raw Water from the Engine Block....................................... 132

  3   Check and Change Engine Block Anode(s) 133

  4   Remove the Engine Thermostat 134

  5   Fill the Block with Propylene Glycol Antifreeze............................ 135

  6   Re-install the Engine Thermostat 136

  7   Add Propylene Glycol Antifreeze to Header Tank.......................... 137

  8   Add Propylene Glycol Antifreeze to Raw Water Circuit 137

  3 Ways to Add Propylene Glycol Antifreeze 138

  9   Run Engine to Flush Raw Water Circuit.. 139

  10 Drain Raw Water Hoses 139

  11 Drain the Raw Water Strainer.. 140

  12 Service Raw Water Pump & Impeller 140

  13 Drain the Heat Exchanger(s) 141

  14 Check Heat Exchanger Anode 142

  15 Protect Raw Water Thruhull from Marine Growth 142

  16 Service the Exhaust Riser.. 143

  17 Clean the Raw Water Syphon Break 145

  18 Drain the Water-Lift Muffler 145

Cautionary Tale 145

14 Lay-Up – Coolant/Antifreeze   **147**

Main Concerns..147

Task List...147

  1   Check Coolant Level in Header Tank or Overflow Bottle.................147

  2   Drain and Replace Coolant/Antifreeze 147

  3   Test Frost Protection of Coolant/Antifreeze 147

  Freezing Point of Ethylene Glycol Coolant/Antifreeze................... 148

  Testing Coolant/Antifreeze with Hydrometer............................... 148

15 Lay-Up – Breathing   **149**

Main Concerns.. 149

Task List... 149

  1   Clean Air Filter/Air Intake 149

  2   Seal Air Intake with Plastic.. 149

  3   Disconnect Exhaust Riser & Hose from Exhaust Manifold.............. 150

  4   Drain Water-Lift Muffler.. 150

  5   Prevent Rodents Entering via Exhaust Thruhull 151

16 Lay-up – Electrical 152

Main Concerns...152

Task List...152

Battery Self Discharge 152

Wet Cell Battery State of Charge and Electrolyte Freezing 153

Lead Acid Battery Freezing 153

1 Clean Battery Top and Terminals 153

2 Check Electrolyte Levels...153

3 Add Water to Unsealed Wet-Cell Battery 153

4 Charge Battery(s)..153

5 Load Test a Questionable Battery 153

6 Trickle Charge Battery...154

7 Disconnect Terminals from Battery 154

Where to Store Lead Acid Batteries 154

Lay-Up Lithium-Iron Batteries (LFP batteries) 154

17 Lay-Up – Drive Train 155

Main Concerns...155

Task List...155

1 Check Coupling Between Transmission & Prop Shaft 155

2 Inspect the Propeller Shaft...155

3 Inspect the Stern Gland..155

Dripless Shaft Seals in Severe Freezing Conditions 156

4 Inspect the Strut 156

5 Inspect the Cutlass Bearing...156

6 Inspect the Propeller Shaft Anode 156

7 Clean the Propeller, Strut and Shaft 156

8 Inspect the Propeller 156

9 Inspect the Propeller Nuts & Cotter Pin 156

10 Inspect a Folding Propeller 156

11 Inspect the Anode of a Feathering Prop 156

12 Grease a Feathering Propeller 157

13 Lay-Up a Traditional Stuffing Box In Water 157

14 Protect the Propeller & Shaft from Marine Growth 158

Recommissioning 159

Main Concerns...159

18 Recommission – Engine Essentials 159

Main Concerns...159

Task List...159

1 Visual Engine Inspection..159

2 Check Hoses and Hose Clamps 159

3   Inspect Wires and Wiring Terminals 160
4   Check Pulley and Belt Alignment 160
5   Tighten Alternator and Water Pump Belts 160

19   Recommission – Diesel Fuel   160

Main Concerns 160
Task List 160
1   Check Diesel Tank(s) for Contamination 160
2   Open Fuel Valve(s) 160

20   Recommission – Lubrication   161

Main Concerns 161
Task List 161
1   Rotate Engine Without Starting 161
2   Drain Transmission Fluid to Maximum Level on Dipstick 162

21   Recommission – Raw Water Cooling   163

Main Concerns 163
Task List 163
1   Check Seacocks Open/Close Smoothly 163
2   Check the Raw Water Strainer 163
3   Check Engine and Heat Exchanger Anodes 164
4   Re-Install the Raw Water Pump Impeller & Face Plate 164
6   Remove Plugs from Exhaust & Raw Water Intake Thruhulls 166
5   Open Raw Water Seacock for Engine 166

22   Recommission – Coolant/Antifreeze   167

Main Concerns 167
Task List 167
1   Check Coolant Level in Header Tank or Overflow Bottle 167

23   Recommission – Breathing   168

Main Concerns 168
Task List 168
1   Open Engine Room Ventilators 168
2   Unseal Air Intake on Engine 168
3   Re-Connect Exhaust Riser and Hoses 169
4   Close Drain on Water-Lift Muffler or Reconnect Hose 169
Cautionary Tale 170

24   Recommission – Electrical   171

Main Concerns 171
Task List 171
1   Check Exterior Condition of Battery – Signs of a Frozen Battery 171
2   Top-up Battery Water Levels (unsealed wet-cell only) 171

3   Charge Battery(s)..172

4   Load Test a 12 Volt Battery 172

5   Reconnect Battery Terminals (Lugs) 172

25 Recommission – Drive Train   173

Main Concerns..173

Task List...173

1   Check Control Cables are Securely Attached to Levers 173

2   Check Throttle Cable Movement..........................174

3   Check Transmission Control Cable 174

Single Lever Dual Action 174

4   Check Stop Cable or Stop Solenoid Button.........175

5   Grease Rubber Cup on Dripless Shaft Seal.........176

6   Hand Tighten & Lock Packing Gland on Traditional Stuffing Box 177

7   Check Hose(s) on Dripless Shaft Seal 177

26 Recommission – In Water   178

Main Concerns..178

Task List...178

1   Remove Wrap Around Propeller and Shaft 178

2   Prime Raw Water Strainer 179

3   Start Engine Procedure 180

4   Check Raw Water Being Expelled with Exhaust.....180

5   Burp Raw Water Strainer to Release Trapped Air.....181

6   Check Oil Pressure Is Normal 181

8   Check Seacocks, Raw Water Strainer & Exhaust for Leaks 182

7   Check Alternator is Charging 182

9   Check Vessel Moves in Gear.................................183

10 Re-adjust Packing in Traditional Stuffing Box 184

11 Burp Air from Dripless Shaft Seal........................185

Task Lists   187

Tools & Supplies Required   203

Acknowledgements   205

MDB Series   206

About the Author   207

Index   208

Introduction to Second Edition

I created this book, and the Marine Diesel Basics project, five years ago to try to de-mystify diesel systems because, too often, boatowners, skippers and crews can become passengers on their own boats; intimidated by a system we are relying on, yet may not properly understand. I hoped simple drawings and clear text could help.

Since then, support for this book, and for the full MDB project, has been very energizing and gratifying - it *is* something of a marathon to produce the many 100s of drawings, and I am encouraged and grateful for all the generous reviews and kind words from readers around the world. I'm delighted other sailors are finding the MDB books and workshop materials of value. Lots more to come!

This Second Edition is a small update, with several new topics, some clearer drawings and removal of a few typos that inevitably got past all the checking. The layout is much the same. The Index has been re-edited to be more useful. This edition is available in paperback, wire spiral bound, hardcover and ebook.

What is the Value of this Book?

This book shows, with over 350 illustrations, how to complete:

•   all basic maintenance tasks of the marine diesel system – fuel, lubrication, cooling, breathing, electrical, and drive train from transmission to propeller
•   all the tasks to lay-up the complete diesel system of a vessel for winter (freezing conditions) and for tropical storage (high heat and humidity)
•   all the tasks to recommission the diesel system before a vessel is relaunched

Time and effort invested in routine maintenance, and proper lay-up and recommissioning help prevent sudden breakdowns, and accelerated wear. The book treats marine diesel propulsion as a single system in which all the components need to work together to reliably move a vessel in all conditions.

Disclaimer

A conscientious effort has been made to verify and double-check the accuracy of all the information in this book. However, equipment designs and models, installation and conditions on different types and ages of vessels vary enormously. The author and publisher assume no responsibility for any personal injury, damage to property, or other loss of any sort suffered from any actions taken based on or inspired by information or advice in this book. Ensure that equipment and procedures are understood before beginning any work. If unsure, contact a professional marine mechanic. Use of this book implies your acceptance of this disclaimer.

CAUTION: This book does NOT cover gasoline engines, potable water or sewage systems, electronics or other equipment or systems which may be on a vessel.

Contact me via marinedieselbasics.com, or hail me if you see *Oceans Five* in an anchorage or harbour. Meanwhile, I wish you fair winds and a reliable diesel!

Dennison Berwick
SV Oceans Five, Tanga Yacht Club, Tanzania, March 2022

Using This Book

The book is laid out in three sections. Each section is divided into chapters, covering the different parts of the marine diesel system. All the necessary tasks for each part are listed in a table at the front of each chapter. Where tasks are repeated, (eg. Check Engine Oil under Maintenance is repeated under Recommission) the page reference to the relevant drawings is given in the table.

These symbols warn when attention needs to be made because of specific situations:

Risk of damage in freezing conditions. These precautions must be taken if there is any risk of temperatures falling below 0°C (32°F). A complete list of tasks for Winter Protection is given on pages 191 – 192.

These precautions are especially important in locations of high humidity or high temperatures (ie. tropics). Protect components against accelerated aging (eg. rusting) See pages 192 –193.

Technical Word Lists - illustrated lists of all the technical words used in this book are available free:

- Dutch
- French
- German
- Italian
- Portuguese (BRZ)
- Russian
- Spanish

www.marinedieselbasics.com

Words - Canadian, American, Australian & British Equivalents

Spellings follow Canadian conventions, also common in the English-speaking world outside the United States (eg. colour, rather than color). Different words are used for a few tools and components across the English-speaking world. Equivalents are listed below, included in chapters where relevant. Common equivalents include:

Tools

Allen key	hex key	Phillips screwdriver	crosshead screwdriver
box end wrench	ring spanner		
flare nut wrench	crow's foot spanner	utility knife	boxcutters
tube wrench		vice grips	mole grips
flashlight	torch	wrench	spanner

Engine & Component Parts

circlip	snap ring	set screw	grub screw
crankcase sump	drip pan	tachometer	rev counter
grease nipple	Zerk fitting	transmission	gearbox
idle	tickover		

Supplies

cotter pin	split pin	hose clamp	jubilee clip
gasket sealant	jointing compound	steel wool	wire wool

Purpose of Maintenance - Reliable and Robust

The purpose of all work we do on our marine diesel engine and its ancillary components is to make the whole system reliable and robust – so that we can enjoy our boat for all the reasons we bought her. Simple, regular maintenance is the easiest, quickest and cheapest way to avoid problems and accelerated engine wear. Most expensive repairs start from a lack of basic maintenance or ignoring small warnings:

• trust yourself. Maintenance is not complicated; it just needs to be done!

• know your boat. Take full responsibility. Don't assume that because something was installed by a previous owner or the boatbuilder that it's correct or correctly installed. Some boatbuilders, as well as owners, have been known to cut corners.

• can you afford *cheap*? Quality components rarely fail suddenly (unless the boat hits something). Using quality parts and supplies, and doing the job right the first time, usually saves money in the long run as well as potentially saving the vessel! Pay now or pay later.

• cultivate vigilance as a habit. Take heed of a warning that something is not right – a new sound, less water in the exhaust, a nut or washer found under the engine. A keen eye goes a long way to being able to spot potential problems before they become trouble.

• the "diesel engine" is a system. All the parts need to work together and to be in balance. Problems arise when they're not. Neglecting one area (perhaps because it's too hard to reach) may well have effects that show up somewhere else.

Value of the Maintenance Logbook

One of the most important, and easiest, ways to ensure the health and longevity of all mechanical equipment on a boat is keep a Maintenance Log. The more comprehensive and detailed, the more useful the logbook becomes over time:

A Maintenance Log has four main functions:
1. recording details of work done and equipment serviced, when and by whom
2. system history – what was installed, model & serial numbers etc.
3. time and details of any changes in performance, new sounds etc.
4. early warning of potential problems. Most problems develop slowly and are often simple to correct if caught early

Maintenance eLogbook
• iPad, tablet and desktop
• tap and edit
• 196-pages, 6 sections
• 19 inspections in detailed drawings
• inventory, checklists, logbook etc.
• live calculator for measures & units
• uses "fillable forms" free pdf app
• $7.99 fillable form pdf
• also hardcover and spiral bound

1 Maintenance – Engine Essentials

Main Concerns
- neglecting maintenance leads to breakdowns and premature aging of the engine
- making small omissions or errors can have serious consequences
- lack of good record-keeping often allows problems to develop unnoticed

Task List

	Description	Frequency	Page
1	visual engine room inspection	daily	3
2	check engine oil level	daily	4
3	check belt tension	daily	4
4	check coolant/antifreeze & top up as needed	daily	6
5	check transmission fluid	weekly	7
6	inspect hoses and hose clamps	weekly	7
7	fit & inspect anti-chafe protection	weekly	8
8	inspect wires & terminals	weekly	9
9	inspect belts(s)	weekly	11
10	inspect pulleys (sheaves)	weekly	12
11	inspect alignment of belts & pulleys	monthly	13
12	adjust pulley alignment	monthly	15
13	tighten alternator & water pump belts	as needed	16
14	inspect & repair sound insulation	as needed	17
15	follow engine start procedure		17

The frequency of tasks generally depends on engine hours, though tasks should not be ignored just because the engine is not being used, unless the vessel has been laid-up. Filters may have to be changed often if fuel becomes contaminated. See page 187 for all the Task Lists.

A plain notebook makes a simple Maintenance Logbook. Divide each double page spread into four columns:
- date/time – monitoring a developing problem over time
- item – which component (eg. oil filter, alternator etc.)
- notes – write down the details
- follow-up – what further action needs to be taken?

1   Visual Engine Room Inspection

Taking a quick look around – at belts, wires, engine block and the bilge etc. – every time the engine compartment is opened is an easy and important habit that can help detect problems before they become serious.

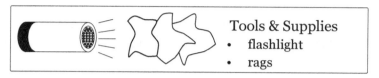

Tools & Supplies
- flashlight
- rags

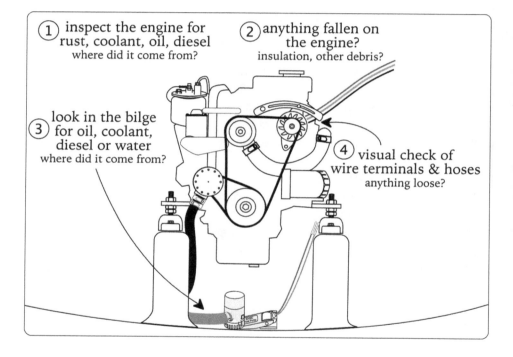

① inspect the engine for rust, coolant, oil, diesel
where did it come from?

② anything fallen on the engine?
insulation, other debris?

③ look in the bilge for oil, coolant, diesel or water
where did it come from?

④ visual check of wire terminals & hoses
anything loose?

2 Check Engine Oil Level

Tools & Supplies
- rags
- engine oil
- funnel

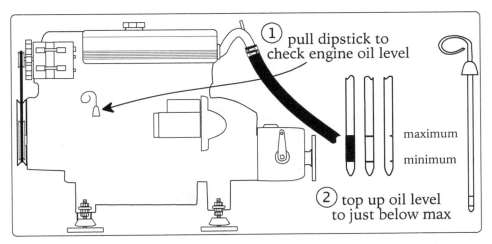

① pull dipstick to check engine oil level

maximum

minimum

② top up oil level to just below max

3 Check Belt Tension

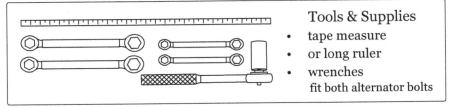

Tools & Supplies
- tape measure
- or long ruler
- wrenches
  fit both alternator bolts

Apply "firm" thumb pressure mid-way between pulleys

distance between pulleys		belt deflection	
cm	inches	mm	fraction
30	12	2 mm	3/16"
35	14	5 mm	1/4"
40	16	6.5 mm	1/4"
45	18	7.5 mm	9/32"

Check Belt Tension

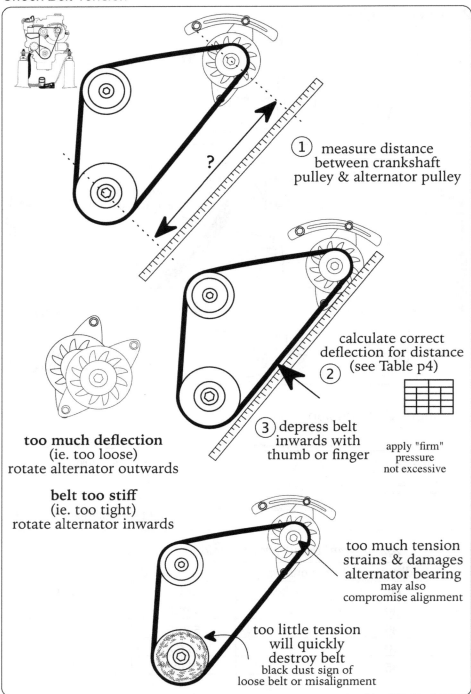

① measure distance between crankshaft pulley & alternator pulley

calculate correct deflection for distance (see Table p4)

②

③ depress belt inwards with thumb or finger

apply "firm" pressure not excessive

too much deflection
(ie. too loose)
rotate alternator outwards

belt too stiff
(ie. too tight)
rotate alternator inwards

too much tension strains & damages alternator bearing
may also compromise alignment

too little tension will quickly destroy belt
black dust sign of loose belt or misalignment

To adjust belt tension, see *"Tighten Alternator and Water Pump Belts"* on page 16

4 Check Coolant/Antifreeze & Top Up if Needed

Check the level in the header tank or overflow bottle before every engine start and top up if needed. The *ethylene glycol* coolant flows in a closed loop between engine and heat exchanger and should rarely need topping up, unless there is a leak. Note any amount added in the Maintenance Logbook – this will help identify abnormal consumption, such has a small, persistent leak.

Do not mix different types or brands of coolant/antifreeze. Many bottles of coolant/antifreeze are sold to consumers pre-mixed 50/50, giving frost protection down to -37°C (-35°F). Full strength coolant/antifreeze should be diluted with water. Though distilled or de-ionized water are best, these are not always available and alternatives may be used. The aim is to minimize dissolved minerals and salts which can react with chemicals in the coolant to precipitate deposits, thus removing these chemicals from active circulation and protection of the engine.

To promote full mixing, always pre-mix coolant/antifreeze with water before adding to the header tank or overflow bottle.

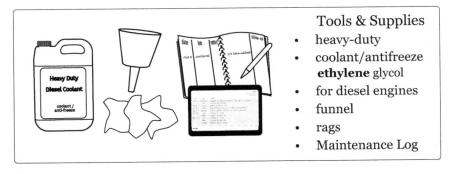

Tools & Supplies

- heavy-duty
- coolant/antifreeze **ethylene** glycol
- for diesel engines
- funnel
- rags
- Maintenance Log

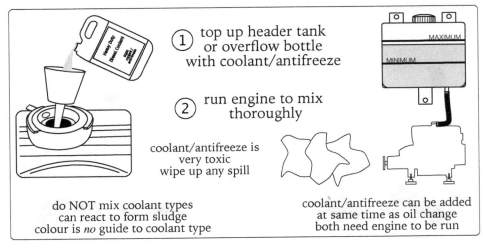

① top up header tank or overflow bottle with coolant/antifreeze

② run engine to mix thoroughly

coolant/antifreeze is very toxic wipe up any spill

do NOT mix coolant types can react to form sludge colour is *no* guide to coolant type

coolant/antifreeze can be added at same time as oil change both need engine to be run

5 Check Transmission Fluid Level

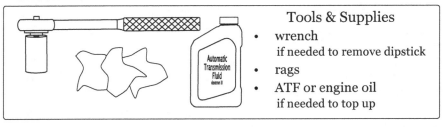

Tools & Supplies

- wrench
  if needed to remove dipstick
- rags
- ATF or engine oil
  if needed to top up

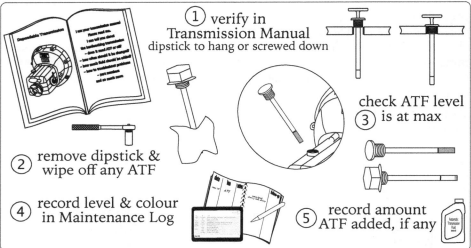

① verify in
Transmission Manual
dipstick to hang or screwed down

③ check ATF level
is at max

② remove dipstick &
wipe off any ATF

④ record level & colour
in Maintenance Log

⑤ record amount
ATF added, if any

6 Inspect Hoses and Hose Clamps

No hose or hose clamp lasts for ever; they can be degraded by age, diesel fuel, oil, ATF fluid, greases, acids, heat, UV light and vibration. Best practice is to make a quick inspection of hoses every time the engine compartment is opened and to replace them at the first sign of deterioration – a failed oil line or raw water hose can have serious and expensive consequences, far outweighing the cost of a new quality hose and hose clamps.

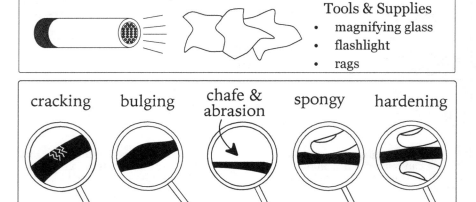

Tools & Supplies

- magnifying glass
- flashlight
- rags

cracking   bulging   chafe &
                       abrasion   spongy   hardening

Inspect Hose Clamps (Jubilee Clips)

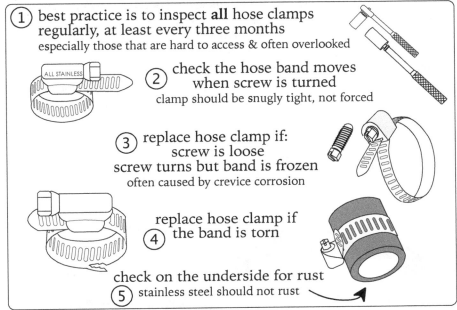

(1) best practice is to inspect **all** hose clamps regularly, at least every three months
especially those that are hard to access & often overlooked

ALL STAINLESS

(2) check the hose band moves when screw is turned
clamp should be snugly tight, not forced

(3) replace hose clamp if:
screw is loose
screw turns but band is frozen
often caused by crevice corrosion

(4) replace hose clamp if the band is torn

(5) check on the underside for rust
stainless steel should not rust

7   Fit & Inspect Chafe Protection

Rubber hoses chafe easily against metal objects or against other hoses, because of engine vibration and the vessel's motion. Best practice is to fit protection everywhere a hose might rub or touch another hose, the vessel hull or stringers, engine block etc. Old hose, cut into sections and split lengthways, makes excellent, cheap anti-chafe protection. Allow 2.5 – 5 cm (1" - 2") extra hose on each side beyond the "rub zone".

Tools & Supplies
- old hose
- utility knife
- cable ties (2 per hose)

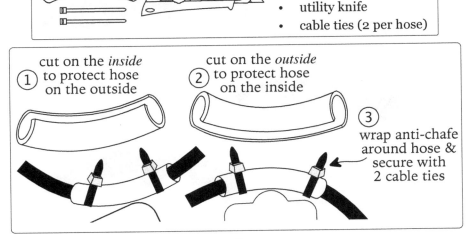

(1) cut on the *inside* to protect hose on the outside

(2) cut on the *outside* to protect hose on the inside

(3) wrap anti-chafe around hose & secure with 2 cable ties

8   Inspect Wires and Wiring Terminals

Just like hoses, wires and wiring terminals can be degraded by age, diesel fuel, engine oil, ATF fluid, greases, acids, heat, UV light and vibration. In addition water and salt spray can accelerate corrosion causing electrical problems. Best practice is to make a quick visual inspection to ensure:

- wires and terminals are clean of contaminants
- terminals are fastened tight – securing nuts which can vibrate loose
- wires are secured together with cable ties – single wires not hanging loosely

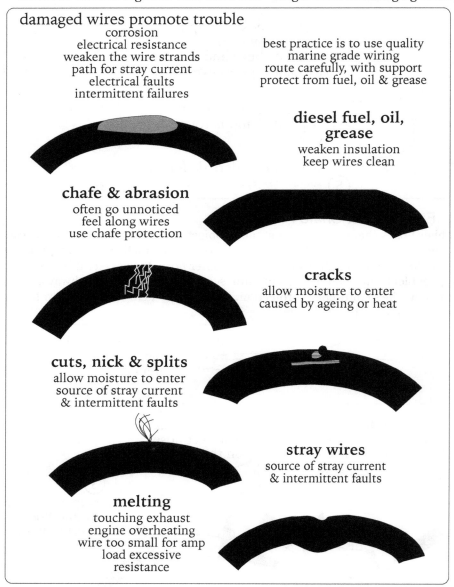

damaged wires promote trouble
corrosion
electrical resistance
weaken the wire strands
path for stray current
electrical faults
intermittent failures

best practice is to use quality
marine grade wiring
route carefully, with support
protect from fuel, oil & grease

diesel fuel, oil, grease
weaken insulation
keep wires clean

chafe & abrasion
often go unnoticed
feel along wires
use chafe protection

cracks
allow moisture to enter
caused by ageing or heat

cuts, nick & splits
allow moisture to enter
source of stray current
& intermittent faults

stray wires
source of stray current
& intermittent faults

melting
touching exhaust
engine overheating
wire too small for amp
load excessive
resistance

Inspect Wiring Terminals

9 Inspect Belts - Alternator, Coolant & Raw Water Pump

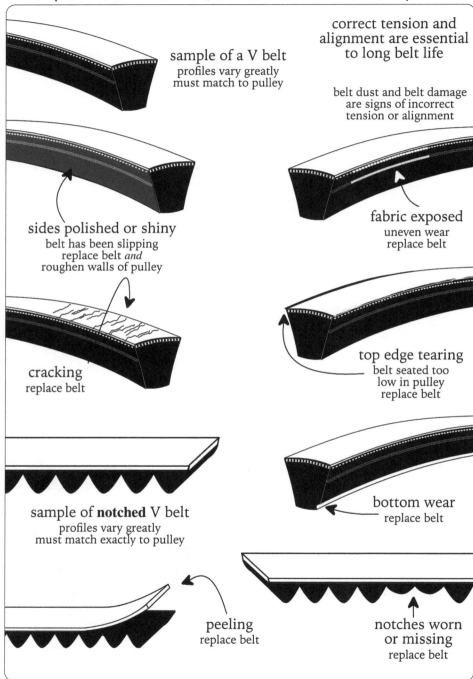

sample of a V belt
profiles vary greatly
must match to pulley

correct tension and
alignment are essential
to long belt life

belt dust and belt damage
are signs of incorrect
tension or alignment

sides polished or shiny
belt has been slipping
replace belt *and*
roughen walls of pulley

fabric exposed
uneven wear
replace belt

cracking
replace belt

top edge tearing
belt seated too
low in pulley
replace belt

sample of **notched** V belt
profiles vary greatly
must match exactly to pulley

bottom wear
replace belt

peeling
replace belt

notches worn
or missing
replace belt

10 Inspect Pulleys (Sheaves)

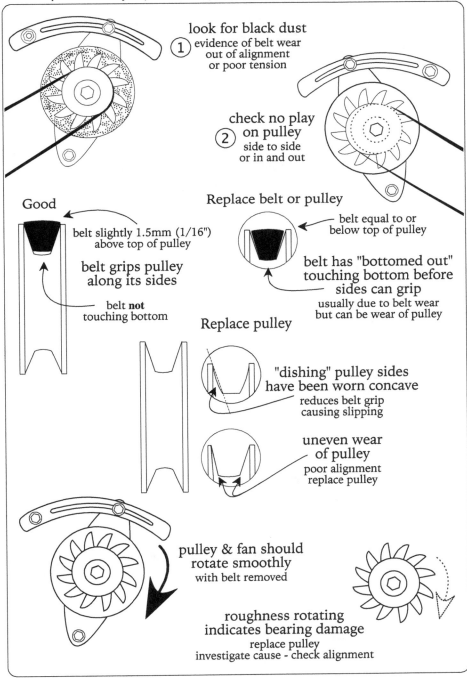

look for black dust
(1) evidence of belt wear
out of alignment
or poor tension

check no play
(2) **on pulley**
side to side
or in and out

Good

belt slightly 1.5mm (1/16")
above top of pulley

**belt grips pulley
along its sides**

belt **not**
touching bottom

Replace belt or pulley

belt equal to or
below top of pulley

belt has "bottomed out"
touching bottom before
sides can grip

usually due to belt wear
but can be wear of pulley

Replace pulley

**"dishing" pulley sides
have been worn concave**

reduces belt grip
causing slipping

**uneven wear
of pulley**

poor alignment
replace pulley

**pulley & fan should
rotate smoothly**
with belt removed

**roughness rotating
indicates bearing damage**
replace pulley
investigate cause - check alignment

11   Check Alignment of Belts & Pulleys

Alignment will need to be re-checked every time a belt is replaced, tightened or if there is black belt dust or other evidence of belt or pulley wear.

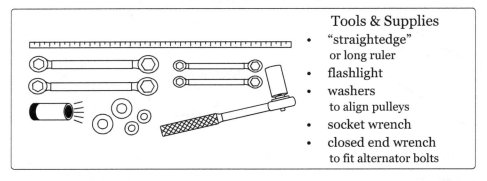

Check Pulley and Belt Alignment A

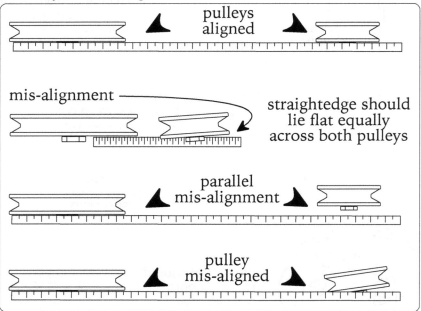

Check Pulley and Belt Alignment B

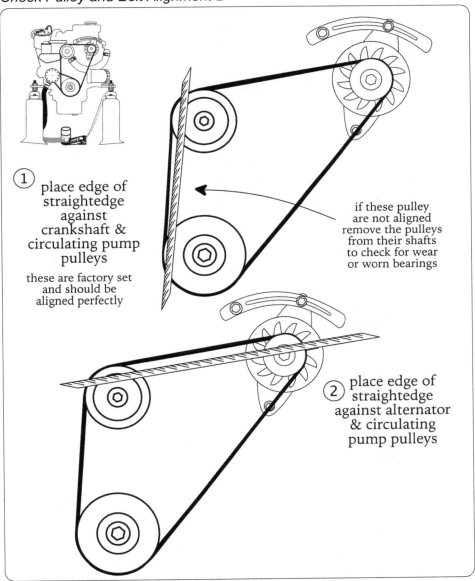

1 place edge of straightedge against crankshaft & circulating pump pulleys

these are factory set and should be aligned perfectly

if these pulley are not aligned remove the pulleys from their shafts to check for wear or worn bearings

2 place edge of straightedge against alternator & circulating pump pulleys

12 Adjust Pulley Alignment

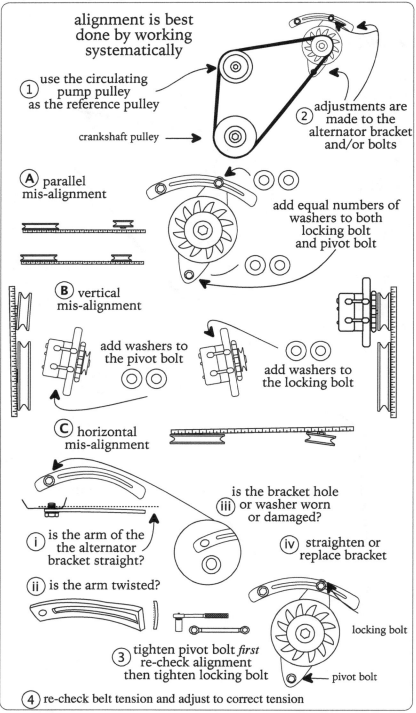

13   Tighten Alternator and Water Pump Belts

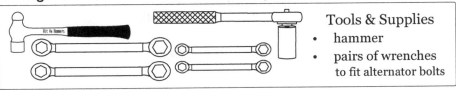

Tools & Supplies
- hammer
- pairs of wrenches
  to fit alternator bolts

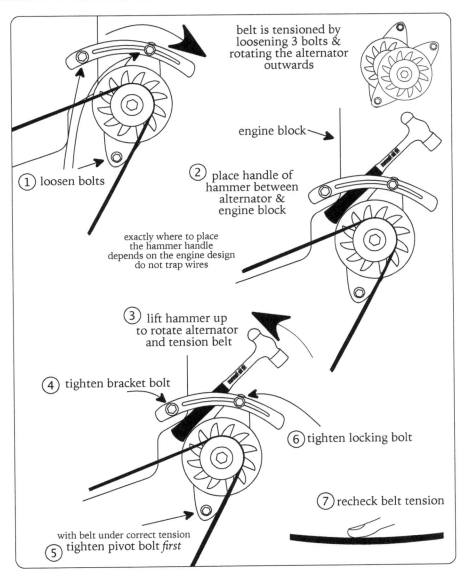

belt is tensioned by
loosening 3 bolts &
rotating the alternator
outwards

engine block

(1) loosen bolts

(2) place handle of
hammer between
alternator &
engine block

exactly where to place
the hammer handle
depends on the engine design
do not trap wires

(3) lift hammer up
to rotate alternator
and tension belt

(4) tighten bracket bolt

(6) tighten locking bolt

(7) recheck belt tension

with belt under correct tension
(5) tighten pivot bolt *first*

14 Inspect & Repair Sound Insulation

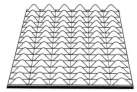

Disintegrating foam sound insulation can be a major source of contamination in air filters. Insulation is easily damaged, especially in a cramped engine compartment.

See page 81, Maintenance – Breathing

15 Start Engine Procedure

The engine should start almost immediately if the Start battery is fully charged and in good condition. In cooler weather or where the engine is cold (even if the day is warm), use glow plugs to warm the pre-combustion chamber or the air intake heater heating incoming air into the cylinders in a direct injection engine:

- do not crank for more than 15 seconds
- if the engine does not start, find out why not - fuel, air supply, exhaust blockage
- allow the Starter to cool for one minute before cranking the engine again
- CAUTION: raw water is being pumped into the water-lift muffler all the time an engine is being cranked. This can fill the muffler, because the engine is not expelling exhaust gases; water can back up into the engine's exhaust manifold. This is an easy way to drown a marine diesel engine!
- CHECK water is being expelled from the exhaust, once engine has started

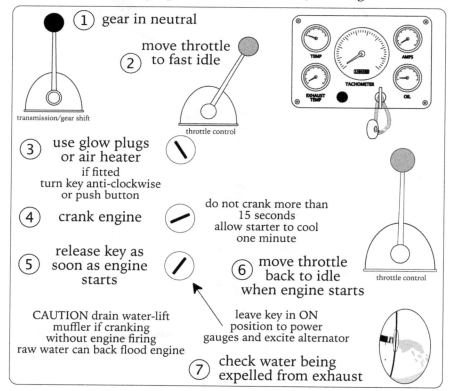

Cautionary Tale

Everything was set to be a perfect day on the water in the new motor boat. The novice skipper had diligently checked the raw water impeller, coolant level, belts and batteries and had spares aboard. He'd reached around the engine as best he could to check hoses and hose clamps; two hoses were too difficult to reach, but one of them was on the fresh water supply line to the head so a leak there would not be critical.

All went well leaving the dock and transiting the marina entrance. Weather conditions were ideal – blue sky, not much wind and a gentle swell coming off the ocean – as the skipper and two friends motored towards a bay a few miles along the coast.

Hours later, after swims and a snooze, they raised the anchor and headed back towards the marina. The first sign of trouble came when one friend appeared suddenly in the companionway. "Smoke!" he shouted.

The boat was half a mile offshore, with no other vessels around. The skipper shut down the engine and let the boat drift (lie ahull) while he went below to investigate. His friends stood in the cockpit, one of them already trying to raise help on his phone.

The smoke smelled of diesel. The skipper found the engine compartment full of engine exhaust and water in the bilge. He remembered advice given by someone on the dock – "if you find water, taste it". He dipped his finger and licked it – warm salt water.

He opened up all the hatches to clear the toxic fumes, then went on deck to clear his lungs and to reassure his friends that there was no fire.

With the engine shut down, the skipper could not see where the smoke and water had been coming from. So he restarted the engine – over the objections of his friends – took a deep breath and went down below. Eventually he found the problem. The exhaust hose at the back of the engine compartment had slipped off the water-lift muffler allowing engine exhaust and raw water to expel inside the boat. The skipper had to empty one of the cockpit lazarettes, then climb down inside to be able to reach the muffler. Then he quickly pushed the hose back onto the barb and secured it with an extra hose clamp.

They motored back to the marina with no further problems, the cabin eventually cleared of the smell of fumes, and the skipper manoeuvred his new boat smoothly into her slip. He was pleased he'd been able to solve the problem easily, but he could see his friends were still shaken by the incident. He promised himself that, in future, he'd always take the extra few minutes to make check everything *thoroughly* before leaving the dock.

2 Maintenance – Diesel Fuel

Main Concerns
- growth of HUM (bacteria, fungi and yeasts)
- water leak into tank(s)
- fuel hose leak, potentially causing tank to drain or syphon out in the bilge

Task List

	Description	Frequency	Page
1	inspect fuel deck fill	3 monthly	21
2	add biocide to the fuel tank(s)	on fill	22
3	change the primary fuel filter	yearly	24
4	change the secondary fuel filter	yearly	26
5	bleed the fuel system	as needed	29
6	check diesel tank(s) for contamination	yearly	33
7	inspect injection pump & injectors	monthly	34

The frequency of tasks generally depends on engine hours, though tasks should not be ignored just because the engine is not being used, unless the vessel has been laid-up. Filters may have to be changed often if fuel becomes contaminated. See page 187 for all the Task Lists.

Importance of Very Clean Fuel

Very clean fuel is essential for a diesel engine to perform well and operate trouble-free for hundreds, if not thousands, of hours. Diesel fuel can be made from natural gas, coal, animal fats, even plant matter. Rudolph Diesel used peanut oil to run his engine at the World's Fair in Paris in 1911.

There's rarely any choice about what diesel to buy – it's what's available at the pump or at the dock. Ultra Low Sulphur Diesel (ULSD) is sold in North America and Europe, and many countries are steadily reducing the sulphur content of diesel fuels. On a boat, what matters is that the fuel is not contaminated by any water, HUM or dirt.

In more remote places, diesel may be sold out of steel drums. These are often left exposed in all weathers and are prone to contamination with rain water. Problems can often be avoided if the fuel is left standing overnight in jerrycans, to allow water and sediments to settle out, before adding to a vessel's fuel tanks.

3 Ways to Contaminate Diesel Fuel & Tanks

1) Water

Water in any form – vapour or droplets – is harmful to a diesel engine. Even tiny amounts of water in the injection pump or injectors can cause significant damage. Potential damage caused by water in the fuel includes:

•   abrasion – water is not a lubricant; it displaces oil and diesel, exposing engine surfaces to metal to metal friction

•   etching – water + sulphur (in the fuel) produces acid which "eats" into metal surfaces

•   cavitation – collapsing water vapour bubbles cause metal fatigue and pitting

•   spalling – water forced into cracks causes microscopic flaking

•   steam – water turns into steam with explosive force if it reaches the hot injectors and can do serious damage

Water can get into a fuel tank through several sources:

•   fuel from a filling station's contaminated tanks

•   missing or damaged o-ring in fuel deck filler cap or failure to tighten

•   poor fuelling practices (eg. avoid fuelling in the rain or with spray)

NOTE: condensation in the tank is rarely a source of any significant water

2) Bacteria, Fungi & Yeasts

 Bacteria, fungi and yeasts – collectively known as "HUM" (Hydrocarbon Utilizing Microorganisms) – can all thrive in diesel tanks under the right conditions:

•   microbes live in the fuel/water interface and can grow very fast in warm conditions

•   single cell weighing 1/1,000,000 of a gram can multiply to 10 kilograms within 12 hours under "ideal" conditions

•   HUM can grow up to 10 times faster in biodiesel than hydrocarbon-based diesel

•   microbes feed on the carbon in diesel, producing sludge, acids and other by-products

•   forms long strings or mats of slime on the walls of the tank and in the fuel

•   often misnamed as "algae" (algae need sunlight to live and grow, not available in a tank)

•   smell of rotten eggs (hydrogen sulphide) is confirmation of a badly contaminated fuel tank

•   low pH value of fuel (eg. pH4, acidic) is indication of HUM; normal pH of diesel is 6 – 8

•   biocides kills HUM and prevent their growth, but the dead microbes can still clog filters – which will need to be changed, and hoses cleaned after a bad infection

3) Grit, Sand & Dirt

- any particles can block the nozzle of a fuel injector causing rough running and other problems (See *How Small is Small?* on page 23)
- keep fuel lines and filters clean, always wipe away dirt before servicing
- cover disconnected fuel hose ends or opened filter housing when servicing

Preventing Fuel Contamination

- avoid buying fuel within 3 hours of a fuel delivery (allows water to settle out)
- check deck fuel fitting o-ring and close completely. Take extra care if the fuel fill fitting is located in the cockpit floor or side deck – likely to be immersed when heeled or flooded by rainwater
- use a biocide – add biocide maintenance dose when refuelling
- drain water and any sludge from the bottom of the tank(s)
- use 10 & 2 micron elements for primary and secondary fuel filters and change regularly
- beware of fuel vent back-flooding, eg. on side deck when heeling
- pre-filter through a filter funnel before adding to fuel tank

1   Inspect Fuel Deck Fill Fitting

This screw-top fitting in the first defence to keep water out of the fuel tank. Ensuring the diesel deck fill o-ring is in place and in good condition is cheap insurance. Check that the deck fill is closed correctly and snug tight. A damaged or missing o-ring or unsecured deck fill plate will allow water to enter the fuel tank.

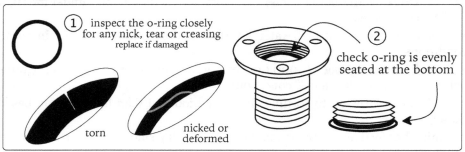

(1) inspect the o-ring closely for any nick, tear or creasing
replace if damaged

torn

nicked or deformed

(2) check o-ring is evenly seated at the bottom

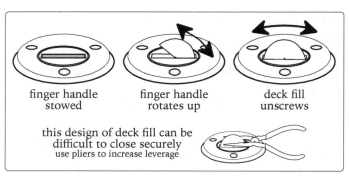

finger handle stowed

finger handle rotates up

deck fill unscrews

this design of deck fill can be difficult to close securely
use pliers to increase leverage

2   Add Biocide to the Fuel Tank(s)

Prevention is much, much easier and cheaper than cure. Best practice is to add a maintenance dose of biocide each time the fuel tank is refilled in all but the coldest locations where temperatures are too low for HUM to grow.

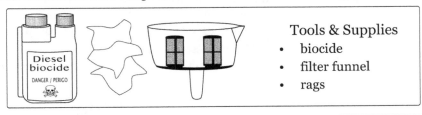

Tools & Supplies
- biocide
- filter funnel
- rags

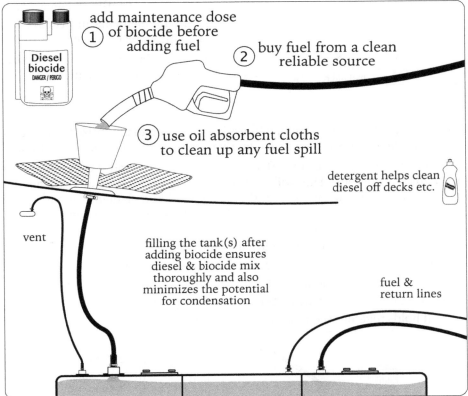

① add maintenance dose of biocide before adding fuel

② buy fuel from a clean reliable source

③ use oil absorbent cloths to clean up any fuel spill

detergent helps clean diesel off decks etc.

vent

filling the tank(s) after adding biocide ensures diesel & biocide mix thoroughly and also minimizes the potential for condensation

fuel & return lines

Filter Funnel

An inexpensive filter funnel is one of the best tools to keep water and dirt *out* of the diesel tank. Pre-filtering fuel does slow down the refuelling process but, especially where quality is suspect, it can save tanks from serious contamination and helps prolong filter life in the diesel fuel system.

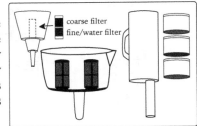

coarse filter
fine/water filter

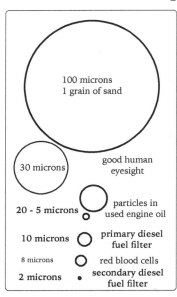

How Small is Small?

Easy to be fooled into thinking that because a diesel filter looks clean, it doesn't need to be replaced. This can be a dangerous and expensive mistake, potentially causing engine failure at a critical time (eg. entering a harbour in adverse conditions) or damaging the injector pump or injectors:

* best practice is to change filter elements on a regular schedule

* do not trust to human eyesight – we cannot see microscopic particles with the naked eye

* use 10 & 2 micron elements in primary and secondary fuel filters respectively

* 1000 microns (μ) in one millimetre (0.001 mm) or 25,400 microns in one inch

Diesel Fuel Primary Fuel Filter

Best practice is to change both fuel filters before lay-up to minimize the presence of HUM in the fuel system – any contamination will only get worse over time.

The primary filter (off the engine) should be 10 microns and the secondary (on the engine) 2 microns. This will ensure that only *very* clean fuel reaches the injection pump. (Tests have shown that using 2 micron elements in both filters clogs the primary filter sooner and is not as effective as using a combination of 10 and 2 micron filter elements).

Four designs of primary fuel filter are in common use:

A. filter element held in place by lid with screw-down handle
B. large knob secures metal band clamping together lid and assembly
C. spin-on filter element is inside a screw-on disposable metal can
D. bolt holds together sections of the fuel filter

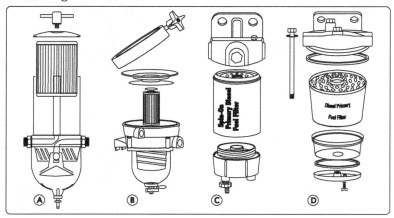

3. Change the Primary Fuel Filter

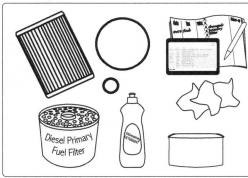

Tools & Supplies
- new fuel filter 10 μ
  2 micron too fine
- o-rings for filter
- Maintenance Log
- container
  for used filter & fuel
- rags
- detergent for clean up

Change the Primary Fuel Filter A

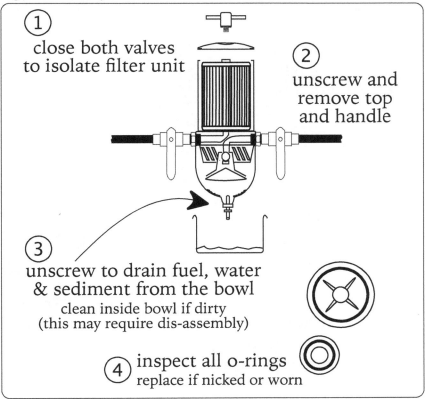

① close both valves
to isolate filter unit

② unscrew and
remove top
and handle

③ unscrew to drain fuel, water
& sediment from the bowl
clean inside bowl if dirty
(this may require dis-assembly)

④ inspect all o-rings
replace if nicked or worn

Change the Primary Fuel Filter B

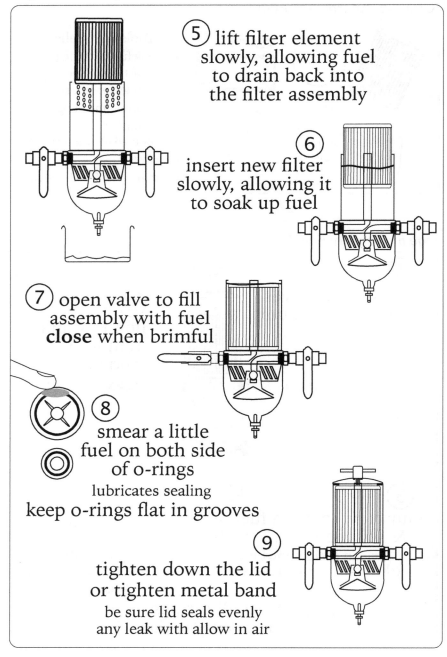

⑤ lift filter element slowly, allowing fuel to drain back into the filter assembly

⑥ insert new filter slowly, allowing it to soak up fuel

⑦ open valve to fill assembly with fuel **close** when brimful

⑧ smear a little fuel on both side of o-rings
lubricates sealing
keep o-rings flat in grooves

⑨ tighten down the lid or tighten metal band
be sure lid seals evenly
any leak with allow in air

4   Change the Secondary Fuel Filter

The secondary filter is the last defence against dirt getting into the injection pump and/or the injectors, which can cause rough running, stop the engine, or cause serious and expensive damage. The secondary filter is almost always located on the engine, immediately before the injection pump. The filter element may be a spin-on canister (like a small oil filter) or a disposable element inside a screw-on metal cup (like most primary filters). Unfortunately, the canister type rarely state the micron size; most often, it is larger than 2 microns, the recommended size for the secondary filter.

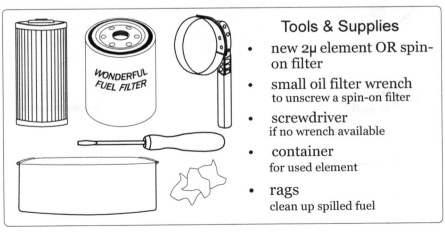

Tools & Supplies

- new 2µ element OR spin-on filter

- small oil filter wrench
  to unscrew a spin-on filter

- screwdriver
  if no wrench available

- container
  for used element

- rags
  clean up spilled fuel

Change a Canister-type Secondary Fuel Filter

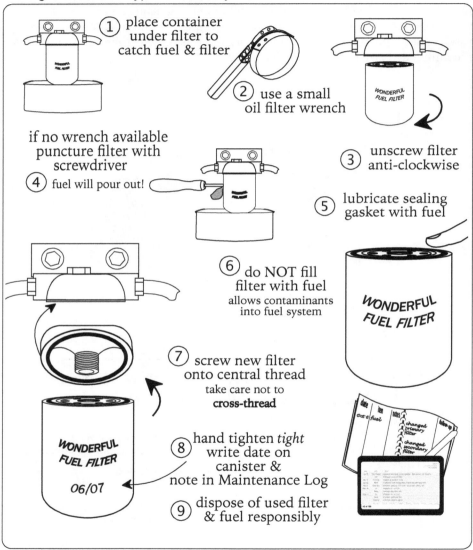

(1) place container under filter to catch fuel & filter

(2) use a small oil filter wrench

(3) unscrew filter anti-clockwise

if no wrench available puncture filter with screwdriver
(4) fuel will pour out!

(5) lubricate sealing gasket with fuel

(6) do NOT fill filter with fuel
allows contaminants into fuel system

WONDERFUL FUEL FILTER

(7) screw new filter onto central thread
take care not to **cross-thread**

WONDERFUL FUEL FILTER
06/07

(8) hand tighten *tight* write date on canister & note in Maintenance Log

(9) dispose of used filter & fuel responsibly

Change a Cup and Element Secondary Fuel Filter

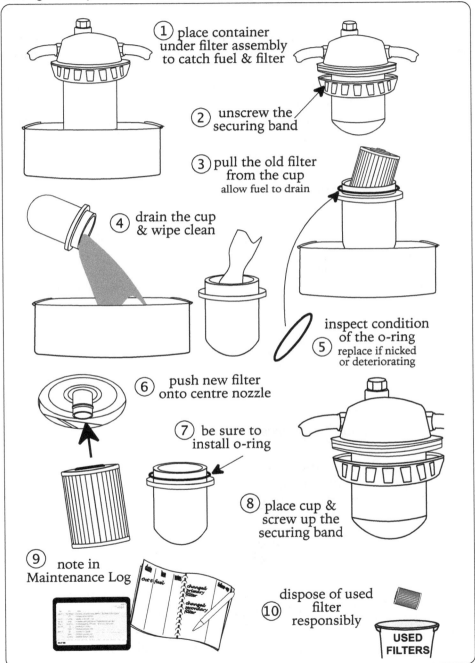

1. place container under filter assembly to catch fuel & filter
2. unscrew the securing band
3. pull the old filter from the cup
   allow fuel to drain
4. drain the cup & wipe clean
5. inspect condition of the o-ring
   replace if nicked or deteriorating
6. push new filter onto centre nozzle
7. be sure to install o-ring
8. place cup & screw up the securing band
9. note in Maintenance Log
10. dispose of used filter responsibly

USED FILTERS

5 Bleed the Diesel System

Air must be bled (purged) from the system any time work is done on the fuel system because the engine will not run with air in the fuel line. Today, some engines are designed to be self-purging (self-bleeding); however, this may not always work, so it's important to know how to complete this task manually:

• best practice is to manually bleed air from the system by pumping the lever on the lift pump. Fuel or air can be felt moving through the pump (air feels "spongy")

• activate an **electric fuel pump** by turning the key but not cranking the engine. The pump will run until pressure builds up, then switch off automatically

• always clean up spilled diesel as it can degrade wiring and hose materials

• precautions must be taken if attempting to bleed air by cranking the engine:

1. use the stop solenoid (or stop cable) to prevent the engine starting

2. do not crank the starter for more than 15 seconds before allowing to cool

3. if the boat is out of the water, remove the raw water impeller as running the pump dry can weaken and damage the vanes of the impeller

4. if in the water, be aware raw water is being pumped into the water-lift muffler but not expelled; water can back flood the engine, causing hydro-lock

5. drain the water-lift muffler or disconnect the raw water hose from the exhaust outlet, allowing the water to drain into the bilge while the engine is being cranked. Remember to reconnect the hose before running the engine.

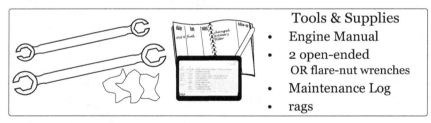

Tools & Supplies

• Engine Manual

• 2 open-ended OR flare-nut wrenches

• Maintenance Log

• rags

Release a Locked-up Mechanical Fuel Pump

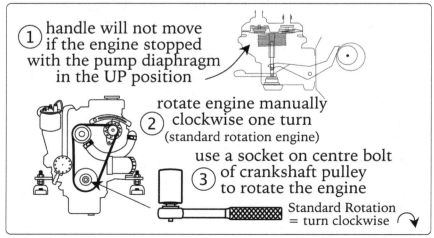

1. handle will not move if the engine stopped with the pump diaphragm in the UP position

2. rotate engine manually clockwise one turn (standard rotation engine)

3. use a socket on centre bolt of crankshaft pulley to rotate the engine

Standard Rotation = turn clockwise

Three Sections of the Fuel Supply Circuit

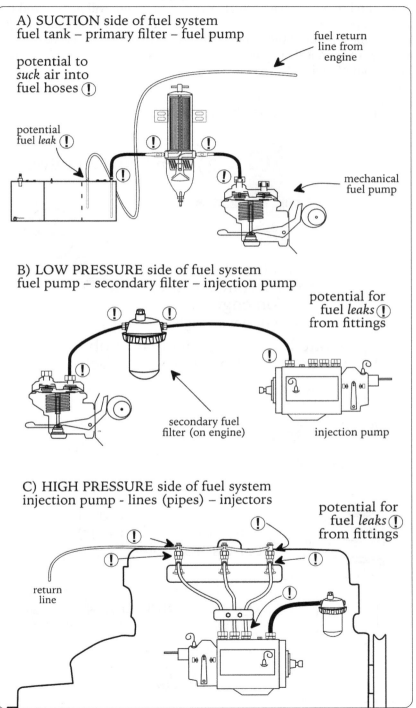

A) SUCTION side of fuel system
fuel tank – primary filter – fuel pump

fuel return
line from
engine

potential to
suck air into
fuel hoses ⓘ

potential
fuel *leak* ⓘ

mechanical
fuel pump

B) LOW PRESSURE side of fuel system
fuel pump – secondary filter – injection pump

potential for
fuel *leaks* ⓘ
from fittings

secondary fuel
filter (on engine)

injection pump

C) HIGH PRESSURE side of fuel system
injection pump - lines (pipes) – injectors

potential for
fuel *leaks* ⓘ
from fittings

return
line

Bleed the Suction & Low Pressure Fuel Lines

If only the fuel filter(s) have been changed, likely there will be no need to bleed the injection pump or injectors because the bleed nut on the secondary filter will be at the highest point of the system; the fuel between the filter, injection pump and injectors was not disturbed. (However, this would have to be done if the engine ran out of fuel).

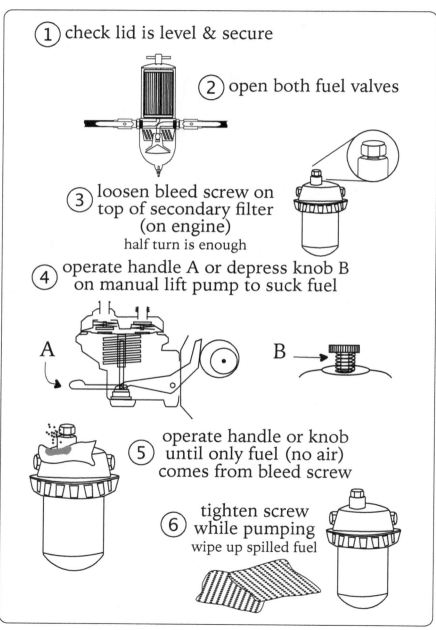

① check lid is level & secure

② open both fuel valves

③ loosen bleed screw on top of secondary filter (on engine)
half turn is enough

④ operate handle A or depress knob B on manual lift pump to suck fuel

A

B

⑤ operate handle or knob until only fuel (no air) comes from bleed screw

⑥ tighten screw while pumping
wipe up spilled fuel

Bleed the High Pressure Fuel Lines (Injection Pump and Injectors)

Bleed air from the injection pump and injectors if:

- engine was run out of fuel
- work was done on injection pump
- work was done on fuel lines or injectors

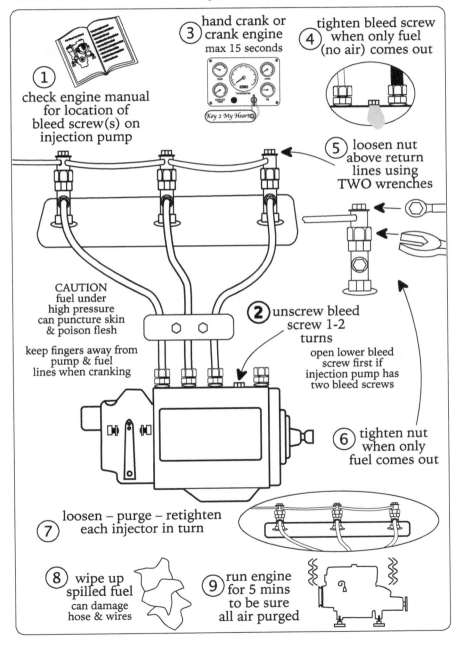

1 check engine manual for location of bleed screw(s) on injection pump

3 hand crank or crank engine
max 15 seconds

4 tighten bleed screw when only fuel (no air) comes out

5 loosen nut above return lines using TWO wrenches

CAUTION
fuel under high pressure can puncture skin & poison flesh

keep fingers away from pump & fuel lines when cranking

2 unscrew bleed screw 1-2 turns
open lower bleed screw first if injection pump has two bleed screws

6 tighten nut when only fuel comes out

7 loosen – purge – retighten each injector in turn

8 wipe up spilled fuel
can damage hose & wires

9 run engine for 5 mins to be sure all air purged

6 Check Diesel Tank(s) for Contamination

If possible, drain a sample of fuel from the bottom of the fuel tank to check for water, sediments and HUM. Drain as much contamination as possible.

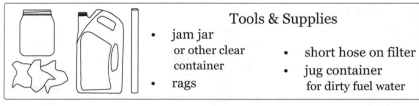

Tools & Supplies

- jam jar
  or other clear
  container
- rags

- short hose on filter
- jug container
  for dirty fuel water

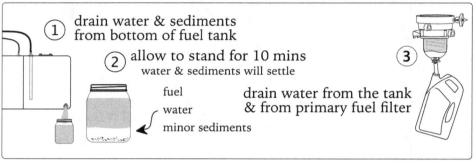

① drain water & sediments from bottom of fuel tank

② allow to stand for 10 mins
water & sediments will settle

fuel
water
minor sediments

③ drain water from the tank & from primary fuel filter

Fuel Tank in the Keel / Tank with no Drain

A fuel tank in the keel of a sailboat or one with no drain can be checked by using water finding paste smeared on a long stick. This is the same method – using ullage paste – which filling stations and ships use to check the fuel levels in tanks.

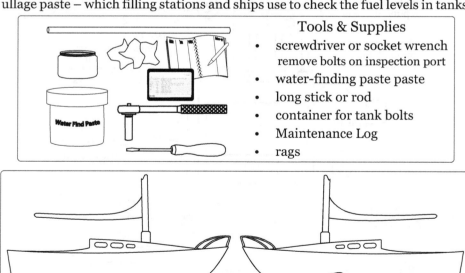

Tools & Supplies

- screwdriver or socket wrench
  remove bolts on inspection port
- water-finding paste paste
- long stick or rod
- container for tank bolts
- Maintenance Log
- rags

diesel fuel
tank in keel

tank may have
inspection port
under cabin sole

Check for Water in a Keel Fuel Tank or Tank with No Drain

If a tank is found to be badly contaminated with water or sediments, the tank may have to be pumped out and cleaned before being refilled with fresh diesel or diesel that has been passed through one or more filters (polished). Water Finding Paste is available from hardware stores as well as through major retailers online.

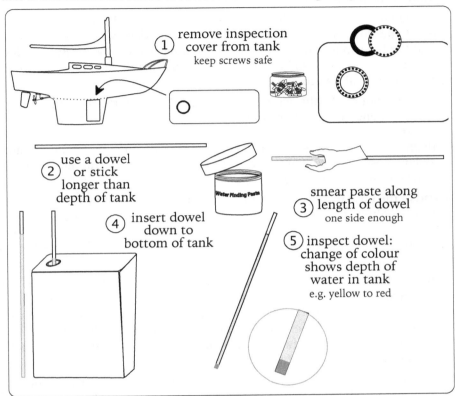

(1) remove inspection cover from tank
keep screws safe

(2) use a dowel or stick longer than depth of tank

(3) smear paste along length of dowel
one side enough

(4) insert dowel down to bottom of tank

(5) inspect dowel: change of colour shows depth of water in tank
e.g. yellow to red

7   Inspect Injection Pump and Injectors

Injection pumps require minimal maintenance. Keep clean and avoid "tinkering". Any adjustment should made by a professional injection pump shop:

- check if injection pump has its own oil dipstick – check level monthly & top up
- check if the governor has its own dipstick – check oil level monthly & top up
- keep area around pump, pipes and injectors clear of dirt. Wipe off any oil or fuel
- before & after engine start-up, check for any signs of a diesel or oil drip or leak
- identify the STOP lever (in case stop cable or solenoid fails). Verify in engine manual
- every 500 hours (see engine manual) verify injector pressure and spray pattern – this should be done in a professional shop

A vessel going to more isolated areas might want to carry a spare set of pipes, a spare injector (and copper seats (washers) if required).

Cautionary Tale

The skipper had spent the past week preparing for this outing with his wife and friends – cleansing the head, making a sign about not clogging the toilet, removing a lot of junk from the forepeak and washing down the bilge to remove any whiff of "boat smell".

In the engine compartment, he'd changed the oil, topped up the coolant and peered at the bowl of the primary fuel filter. The glass was clear, he hadn't changed the filter in a year; it didn't look like it needed changing. But he didn't want to take any chances, so he changed the filter, bled the fuel line and ran the engine to be sure all was good to go.

Just over an hour into the passage to an island, the starboard engine alarm sounded – the engine was overheating. The skipper immediately shut down both engines. He reassured his guests that they could still continue on one engine, and told them the problem was probably easily fixed. Sure enough, he found one of the coolant hoses had disconnected from its barb, spraying the header tank's scorching coolant into the bilge.

The end of the hose was badly mangled where it had been cut by the hose clamp being over-tightened and cutting into the rubber. This will not take long, the skipper reassured his guests again. The skipper cut the end off the hose, pushed it back on the barb and tightened the hose clamp – tight, but this time not too tight.

Meanwhile, the boat had turned beam on to the wind and the waves, and was rolling heavily – enough to be uncomfortable. Refilling the header tank with coolant was the hardest part. At last, the header tank and overflow bottle were full and coolant wiped off the engine. Not enough had gone into the bilge to set off the bilge pump, but he switched it to manual to avoid any risk of pumping the highly toxic ethylene glycol into the lake.

They'd almost reached the islands when more trouble began. Engine rpm fell, picked up, then fell again. The skipper was sure the problem, affecting both engines, must be fuel, so he shut down one engine to slow fuel consumption. He wondered what could be happening when he'd just changed both filters the day before.

The boat was still half a mile from shore when the engine petered out. He re-started the other engine, hoping at least to reach water shallow enough to anchor. The second engine died within 100 metres of the rocky shoreline, in 15 metres of water. The skipper quickly anchored and went to investigate.

The problem was indeed fuel – the new primary filter was brown and filled with a gunk. Two hours later, he'd changed the filter and bled both engines and was able to motor to the sandy bay on the other side of the largest island. The skipper was dismayed to find more gunk in the filter after the short run, but he determined to enjoy the weekend with his wife and friends and to leave worrying about getting home until Monday.

In the event, the weather lived up to the forecast, the wind dropped, the skies cleared and the crud in the fuel settled to the bottom of the fuel tank. On the Monday, he was able to motor back to his marina, to the great relief of everyone aboard. On the Tuesday, he called a cleaning service and paid hundreds of dollars to have his tank pumped out, cleaned and filled with fresh fuel treated with biocide, happy and greatly relieved not to have lost his boat.

3 Maintenance – Lubrication

Main Concerns

- no oil or a very low oil level will rapidly destroy or severely age an engine
- failure to change oil and oil filter regularly compromises engine protection, causing greatly accelerated engine wear

Task List

	Description	Frequency	Page
1	check engine oil level	daily	38
2	dipstick diagnostics - engine oil	weekly	38
3	check transmission fluid level	weekly	41
4	dipstick diagnostics - transmission	weekly	41
5	change engine oil & filter	100 hours	45
6	change transmission fluid	seasonal	52
7	grease control cable ends & engine mount threads	seasonal	54
8	lubricate ignition key slot	yearly	55
9	check injection pump & governor dipstick (if fitted)	3 monthly	55

The frequency of tasks generally depends on engine hours, though tasks should not be ignored just because the engine is not being used, unless the vessel has been laid-up. Engine oil & filter should be changed at least once a year and before lay-up. Best practice is to change the oil and filter at least as often as the engine manufacturer recommends. See page 187 for all the Task Lists.

Oil Is An Engine's Life Blood

Any compromise in the quality of oil or oil circulation will have serious consequences for the operation and life of the engine; oil works harder in a diesel because of the higher compression pressures. Checking the oil level and its colour and consistency before every engine start-up, and changing oil and filter regularly, are the best ways to ensure good performance and long life.

Engine oil has five essential functions:

1. lubrication – pistons and piston rings moving up and down the cylinders 40 times per second (@2500 rpm), would instantly destroy themselves without lubrication

2. heat transfer – circulating oil through the engine block transfers heat away from the hottest parts (pistons & cylinders) and helps keep all components at the same temperature to avoid warping of the cylinder head

3. cleaning – microscopic metal and carbon particles that could damage bearings are carried out of the engine and trapped in the oil filter. Changing the oil filter regularly is essential to keeping oil and the oil passages clean

4. corrosion protection – inhibitors help protect parts from pitting from sulphuric acid (formed when water vapour combines with sulphur in the fuel) and minimize rust (oxidation)

5. sealing – oil helps seal several moving parts of an engine, eg. between piston rings and cylinder walls

In order to fulfill these functions, oil must be able to flow instantly on engine start-up, even at low temperatures, through all the small passages (galleries) to reach all parts; it must not become so thin when hot that lubrication is lost; contaminants must be removed; and the additives in the oil must be renewed regularly to prevent impaired performance. If the wrong oil is used, if the filter is of low quality or if the oil & filter are not changed regularly, the engine oil cannot do its work, the life of the engine will be shortened, repairs likely increased and potentially catastrophic damage can occur.

Keeping the Lubrication System Happy

There are no secrets to keeping the lubrication system at peak efficiency:

- use an oil recommended by the engine manufacturer for the local (ambient) conditions
- buy good quality oil filters
- check the oil level and condition before every start-up. Top up as needed
- change the oil and the filter at least as often as recommended by the manufacturer
- make changing the oil & filter as easy and convenient as possible (more likely to be done regularly!)
- keep good notes in Maintenance Logbook, to spot changes and trends

1   Check Engine Oil Level

Check the level and condition of the engine oil before every engine start-up.
See page 4, Maintenance - Engine Essentials

2   Dipstick Diagnostics – Engine Oil
The simple dipstick is a valuable diagnostic tool that should be used regularly to assess the health of the engine and to identify trends (such as increasing carbon) – in addition to checking the oil level before every engine start-up. Ideal times to perform dipstick diagnostics include at least:

- before changing the oil (run the engine to warm and circulate the oil)
- mid-cycle between oil changes

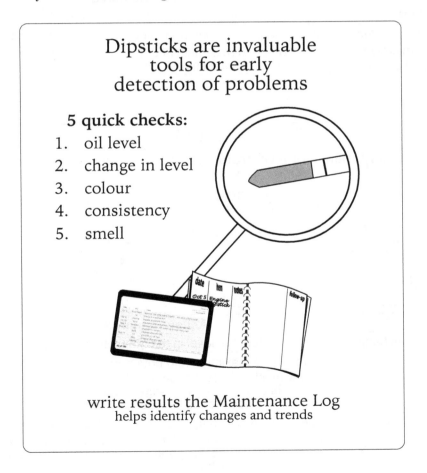

Dipsticks are invaluable
tools for early
detection of problems

5 quick checks:
1.   oil level
2.   change in level
3.   colour
4.   consistency
5.   smell

write results the Maintenance Log
helps identify changes and trends

Dipstick Diagnostics - Oil Level and Change in Oil Level

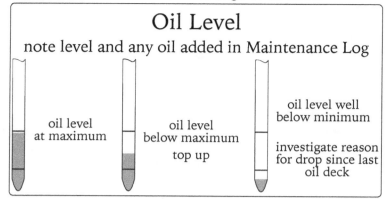

	Action Required
at maximum mark	Note the level in the Maintenance Log
below maximum mark	Top-up to maximum and note amount added in Log
at minimum mark (or tip of dipstick)	Top-up to maximum and note amount added in Log Has level dropped quickly since last oil level entry in Log?

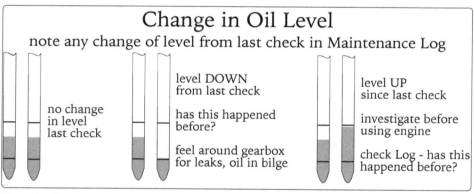

	Action Required
level unchanged	Note the level in the Maintenance Log
level much lower	Top-up to maximum and note amount added in Log. How much has level changed since last entry in Log? Is this normal? Investigate reason for drop – check around & under engine for leaks
level much higher	Where is the extra fluid coming from? Note rise in Log. Investigate reason - is oil thinner or emulsified (fuel leaking or coolant/water leaking and mixing with crankcase oil). Check *Oil Consistency*

Dipstick Diagnostics - Colour of Oil & Consistency of Oil

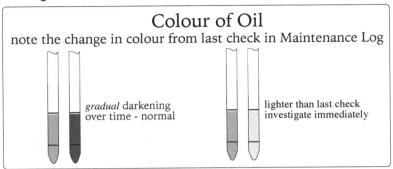

Colour of Oil
note the change in colour from last check in Maintenance Log

gradual darkening over time - normal

lighter than last check investigate immediately

	Action Required
darkening over time	Normal. Note the level in the Maintenance Log
lighter than before	Diesel fuel, water or coolant mixing with oil Needs immediate investigation and change of oil & filter
at minimum mark (or tip of dipstick)	Top-up to maximum and note amount added in Log. Has level dropped quickly since last oil level entry in Log?

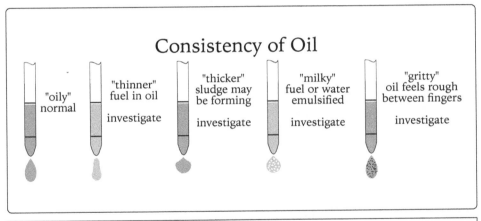

Consistency of Oil

"oily" normal

"thinner" fuel in oil

investigate

"thicker" sludge may be forming

investigate

"milky" fuel or water emulsified

investigate

"gritty" oil feels rough between fingers

investigate

	Action Required
"oily"	normal
thinner	Diesel fuel may be leaking and mixing into the oil Has oil level risen since last check?
thicker	Carbon sludge is likely forming Change oil & filter immediately and monitor
"milky"	Water or coolant is leaking and mixing into the oil Change oil & filter immediately Has coolant level dropped? Is heat exchanger leaking?
"gritty"	Any metal particles in the oil need to be investigated Send oil for laboratory analysis Change oil & filter immediately and monitor closely

Dipstick Diagnostics - Smell of the Oil

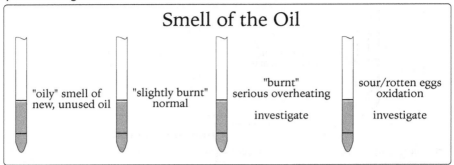

	Action Required
oil	Smell of new, unused oil
slightly burnt	Normal smell of used oil
burnt	Serious overheating has occurred – investigate why
sour/rotten eggs	Evidence of oxidation – oil acidic Change oil & filter and monitor

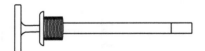

3   Check Transmission Fluid Level

Check the level of the transmission fluid regularly. Feel around transmission casing for any leak if the level has dropped.

See page 7, *Maintenance – Engine Essentials*

4   Dipstick Diagnostics – Transmission Fluid

The transmission dipstick is a valuable diagnostic tool which should be used regularly to assess the health of the transmission and especially to identify whether the transmission has overheated – eg. with plastic bag, line or netting around the propeller that slipped off. Ideal times to perform dipstick diagnostics on the transmission include at least:

• before changing the ATF (or engine oil) after running the engine and transmission to warm and circulate the fluid

• mid-cycle between oil changes

Gearbox Dipstick Diagnostics - ATF Level & Change in Level

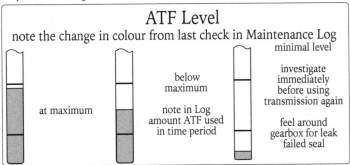

	Action Required
Check level when cold or bring transmission to normal operating temperature – see Operator's Manual	
at or close to maximum	Record level in Maintenance Logbook
below maximum	Top up to maximum & note amount added in the Log
at minimum or tip of dipstick	Has level dropped suddenly since last top up? If yes, check for leaks Top up and note amount added in Logbook

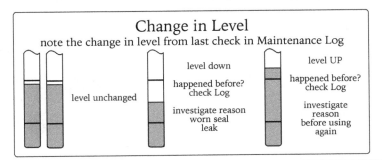

Change since last check	Action Required
same level	record level in Maintenance Log
below maximum	Top up to maximum & note amount added in the Log
lower level	Is level much lower? Check around gearbox for leak, leaking ATF cooler? Top up to fill maximum mark and record amount in the Logbook
higher level	Where is the extra fluid coming from? Overfilled? Check ATC consistency - look for evidence of water
at minimum or tip of dipstick	Has level dropped suddenly since last top up? If yes, check for leaks Top up and note amount added in Logbook

Transmission Dipstick Diagnostics – Colour and Consistency

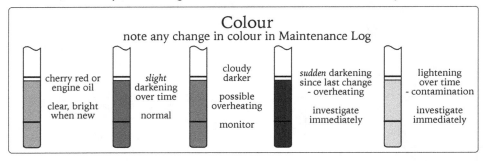

Colour	Action Required
cherry red or bright green or honey-coloured oil (depends on brand)	Clear and bright colour when new
slight darkening over time	Normal. Note colour change in Logbook
cloudy – darkening since last check	Transmission may be overheating. monitor & record in the Maintenance Log

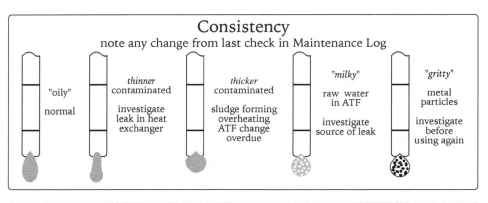

Consistency	Action Required
"corn oil" or "cherry syrup"	Normal
thinner	Diesel fuel may be mixing with the oil Has oil level risen since last entry in Logbook?
thicker	Formation of sludge or dirt inside transmission Replace ATF and check for cause. Record in the Log
"milkshake" or foaming "mayonnaise"	Water is mixing (emulsifying) with the ATF (oil) Is ATF heat exchanger leaking Flush and replace ATF (oil)
grainy	Any particles large enough to see or feel need to be investigated. Flush and replace ATF. Monitor closely. Record in the Logbook

Transmission Dipstick Diagnostics – Smell

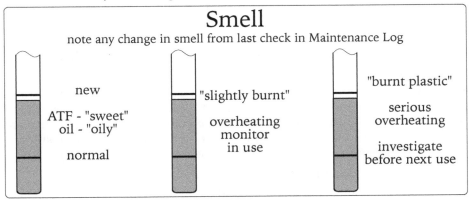

Smell	Action Required
slight sweet smell (ATF) "oily" (engine oil)	Normal
slightly burnt	Gearbox has overheated. Record in the Log re-check ATF after next use
"burnt plastic"	ATF is burnt and should be replaced

Turbocharger Best Practices

bearing rides on cushion of oil

Turbocharger bearings run on a thin layer of pressurized oil which lubricates and conducts heat away from the bearings. This flow of oil stops when the engine is stopped. If the turbo has not been allowed to cool down before shutdown, the residual heat can bake oil onto the bearings and the shaft creating an insulating layer which *reduces* heat transfer (cooling). This increases carbon build up (carbon loading), further insulating the bearings, causing overheating. Exhaust gases through the turbo can be as hot as 600 - 700°C (1112 - 1292°F).

- *always* allow an engine with a turbocharger to idle for 2 - 3 minutes before shutting down to allow the turbocharger to cool down. If not, the excessive heat can damage both the turbine and the shaft bearings
- turbos are more sensitive to dirty oil. Change the oil & filter at least as frequently as recommended by the engine manufacturer and any time the engine overheats. Overheating can cause oil to break down ("crack"), producing acids and sludge which attack bearings and block oil passages
- pre-fill a new oil filter with clean oil before installing. Any delay in oil supply or pressure when the engine restarts can leave bearings without oil
- keep the engine/turbocharger oil level topped up
- supply the engine room and turbo with abundant clean, cool and dry air
- keep the engine compartment, and the turbo clean and tidy (no loose rags)
- clean the air filter monthly or replace the paper filter as per schedule

5   Change the Engine Oil & Filter

Used engine oil contains moisture and sulphur compounds which will corrode internal engine parts and pit bearings if left in the engine for a prolonged period. Used oil may also carry sludge that will settle out and can harden and block small oil passages. It's therefore very important to change the oil and filter regularly and before lay-up to safeguard the engine from premature aging.

All oil filters are not born equal. There are important differences between "value" and quality filters. Saving money in the short term can mean more repairs and bigger bills later as bearings wear more, the engine has to work harder and contamination goes unchecked until the next oil & filter change. One study by General Motors showed that improved filtering decreased engine wear by 50%.

Oil filters must perform three key functions simultaneously:

1.   remove contaminants such as soot and metal particles (a filter's <u>efficiency</u>). Most engine wear is done by particles measuring 5 - 20μ (micron) – ie. specks too small to see. Oil filters cannot remove water, coolant, diesel fuel or salt in solution

2.   hold contaminants in the filter without clogging or collapsing (a filter's <u>capacity</u>)

3.   allow oil flow that does not lower the oil pressure (a filter's <u>cold flow rating</u>)

Efficiency must be balanced with capacity to retain contaminants and still allow oil to flow. There are over 50 grades of media used in filtration elements. Most use one or a combination of these media:

•   paper (cellulose) – cheapest medium and can capture 15 - 20μ particles

•   synthetic materials (eg. polyethylene-covered polypropylene)

•   fibreglass (micro-glass) – the most costly. Captures particles as small as 2 - 5μ.

Oil Filter Buyer's Guide

Unfortunately there is no straightforward way to identify top quality oil filters –

no standards or ratings printed on the side of the filter or available on a website. Paying more does not automatically guarantee the best value. Brand claims are just that – with no objective measurements to go along with the marketing. Beware of hype. Almost all oil filters globally are made by a handful of companies which label them for retail companies. These companies often change manufacturer and their manufacturing specifications without changing their brand labelling:

•   use the same brands selected by local trucking companies

•   avoid cheap brands (minimal paper elements & often inferior by-pass valves)

•   cut open a filter and inspect the element and by-pass valve

Oil Change Procedure - *follow these simple steps*

1. run the engine to warm warm the oil & stir any sludge and particles
2. pump out (or drain) used oil
3. replace filter
4. add new oil
5. run engine
6. add oil to maximum on the dipstick
7. dispose of used oil and filter responsibly
8. record in Maintenance Logbook

Warm Oil Flows More Easily

Warm oil has more particles in suspension and flows much more easily, so it's best to change the oil when the vessel is in the water and the engine can be operated (and cooled) in the normal way.

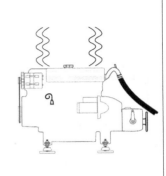

(1) **start engine and run in gear**
making sure vessel is **properly secured**
"in gear" warms engine quicker and
allows transmission ATF
to be changed at the same time

(2) **run until normal operating
temperature is reached,
then shut down**
running the engine mixes
particles & sludge
and makes pumping easier & quicker

Pump Used Oil Out of the Engine

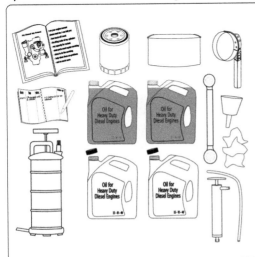

Tools & Supplies
- Engine Manual
- Maintenance Log & pen
- new oil filter
- permanent marker
- new oil
- container
- funnel - to add new oil
- oil filter wrench
- jugs for used oil
- manual oil change pump
  OR plastic bag
  last resort to catch oil
- rags - for clean up

Pump Used Oil Out of the Engine

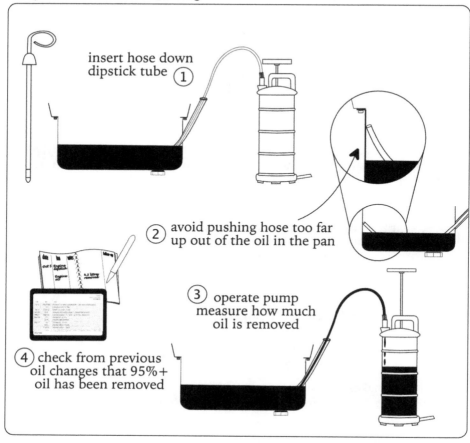

insert hose down
dipstick tube (1)

(2) avoid pushing hose too far
up out of the oil in the pan

(3) operate pump
measure how much
oil is removed

(4) check from previous
oil changes that 95%+
oil has been removed

Drain Oil from the Engine Sump

If no pump is available, oil can be drained from the sump. The challenge with most engines in confined spaces is to be able to insert and remove a large enough container under the engine to collect the oil without spilling.

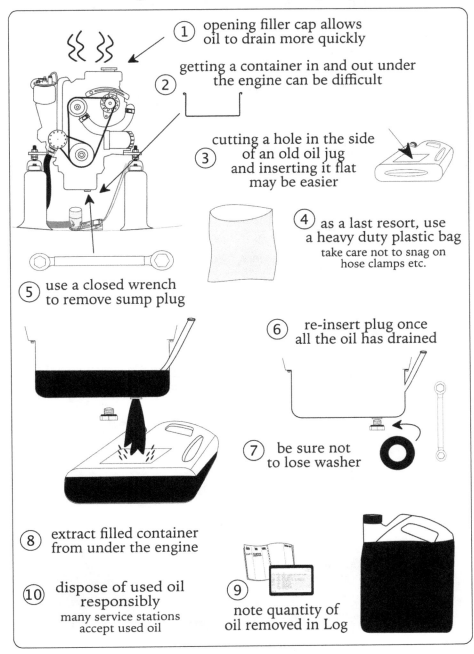

① opening filler cap allows oil to drain more quickly

② getting a container in and out under the engine can be difficult

③ cutting a hole in the side of an old oil jug and inserting it flat may be easier

④ as a last resort, use a heavy duty plastic bag
take care not to snag on hose clamps etc.

⑤ use a closed wrench to remove sump plug

⑥ re-insert plug once all the oil has drained

⑦ be sure not to lose washer

⑧ extract filled container from under the engine

⑩ dispose of used oil responsibly
many service stations accept used oil

⑨ note quantity of oil removed in Log

Remove the Oil Filter

Removing a horizontal oil filter that is full of oil risks spilling oil on wires, mounts etc. This can be minimized by cutting a shallow U-shape in the side of an empty oil jug or small container. Hold this against the engine as the oil filter is being unscrewed so that the used oil spills into the container – not the bilge. See drawing on the next page.

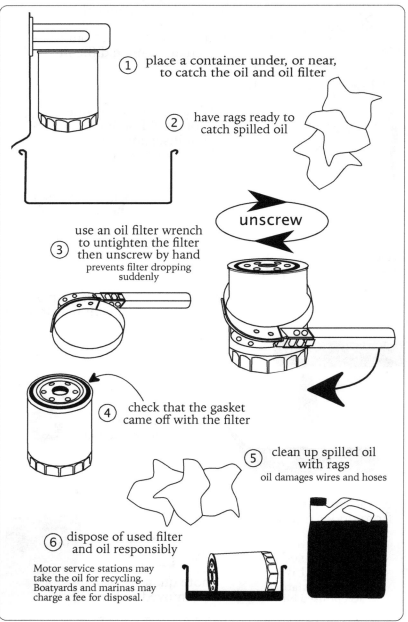

① place a container under, or near, to catch the oil and oil filter

② have rags ready to catch spilled oil

unscrew

③ use an oil filter wrench to untighten the filter then unscrew by hand
prevents filter dropping suddenly

④ check that the gasket came off with the filter

⑤ clean up spilled oil with rags
oil damages wires and hoses

⑥ dispose of used filter and oil responsibly
Motor service stations may take the oil for recycling. Boatyards and marinas may charge a fee for disposal.

Minimize Oil Spillage - Changing an Oil Filter on its Side

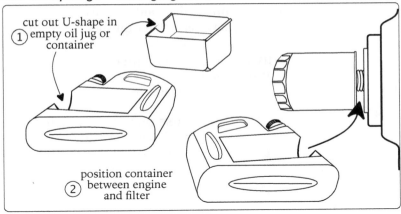

① cut out U-shape in empty oil jug or container

② position container between engine and filter

Install a New Oil Filter

① be careful to remove foil after opening
can block passages inside engine

② smear new oil around the rubber gasket
prevents dry binding when tightening

Oil for
Heavy Duty
Diesel Engines

covering the centre hole
prevents wrapper or dirt
entering engine

③ pre-fill filter with new oil (if filter is installed vertically)
shortens delay in lubricating engine

④ spin on new filter clockwise by hand
be careful not to **cross thread**

⑤ tighten firmly by hand or 1/4 turn with wrench

overtightening can made
filter impossible to remove

undertightening may allow
filter to vibrate loose and spray
oil under pressure

⑥ write date installed on the oil filter
mark direction to untighten

Add New Oil

Do not overfill – this can put pressure on the crankcase seals. Best practice is to add oil in small amounts, checking the level with the dipstick before adding more.

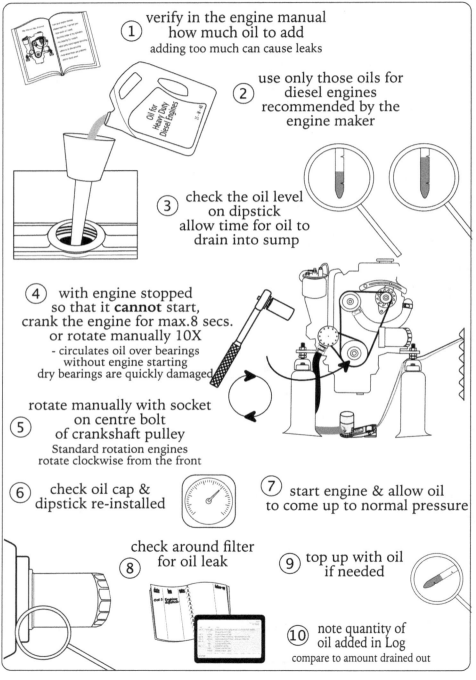

1. verify in the engine manual how much oil to add
   adding too much can cause leaks

2. use only those oils for diesel engines recommended by the engine maker

3. check the oil level on dipstick allow time for oil to drain into sump

4. with engine stopped so that it **cannot** start, crank the engine for max.8 secs. or rotate manually 10X
   - circulates oil over bearings without engine starting
   dry bearings are quickly damaged

5. rotate manually with socket on centre bolt of crankshaft pulley
   Standard rotation engines rotate clockwise from the front

6. check oil cap & dipstick re-installed

7. start engine & allow oil to come up to normal pressure

8. check around filter for oil leak

9. top up with oil if needed

10. note quantity of oil added in Log
    compare to amount drained out

Turbocharger

Most smaller marine diesel engines draw in air without any mechanical blower (naturally aspirated). However, turbochargers are becoming more common as manufacturers seek to boost engine performance without increasing engine size.

Turbochargers on smaller engines use the same oil and filter as the engine. However, always look in the engine manual to be sure the turbocharger does not have its own oil and filter circuit. Clean oil is *crucial* to the cooling and lubrication of turbocharger bearings. If the turbocharger has its own circuit, the oil & filter should be changed at least as often as the main engine oil.

(See *Turbocharger Best Practices* on page 44.)

6 Change the Transmission Fluid (Engine Oil)

Transmission fluid works almost as hard as engine oil and should be changed at least once per season (check transmission manual). The fluid lubricates the metal-to-metal surfaces, transfers heat away from the gears and inhibits rust and corrosion. To do this the transmission fluid contains many additives, such as detergents, surfactants, and antifoaming agents. These break down over time, or if the gearbox overheats. Most transmission manufacturers specify to use automatic transmission fluid (ATF), cherry red or green; others a specific grade of engine oil or hydraulic oil.

Regular inspection of the ATF or oil is important to monitor the transmission. Overheating, often caused by plastic or a rope around the prop, can do serious damage to a transmission. Change transmission fluid any time there is evidence of overheating.

Two methods are available to drain fluid from a marine transmission:

1. remove the drain plug from under the gearbox - this will ensure all the fluid and most of any sediment are removed. However, it can be difficult to get a container under the transmission. Use this method if damage is suspected.

2. remove the fill plug (dipstick) and use a pump. This is convenient. Lower the pump hose to the bottom of the casing with care. Not all the fluid (nor sediments) will be removed. Use this method for routine maintenance.

Tools & Supplies

- Automatic Transmission Fluid (ATF) or engine oil
- Transmission Manual
- funnel
- Maintenance Log
- rags
- manual oil change pump large or small

Change the Transmission Fluid (engine oil)

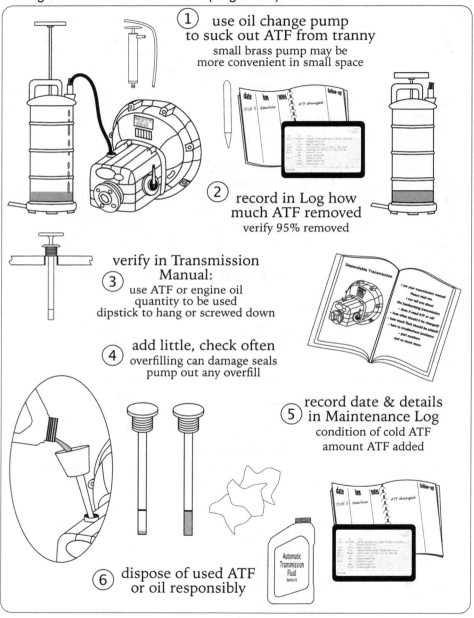

① use oil change pump
to suck out ATF from tranny
small brass pump may be
more convenient in small space

② record in Log how
much ATF removed
verify 95% removed

verify in Transmission
Manual:
③ use ATF or engine oil
quantity to be used
dipstick to hang or screwed down

④ add little, check often
overfilling can damage seals
pump out any overfill

⑤ record date & details
in Maintenance Log
condition of cold ATF
amount ATF added

⑥ dispose of used ATF
or oil responsibly

7 Grease the Control Cable Ends and Engine Mount Threads

Transmission, throttle, stop cables and the threads of engine mounts are often ignored when thinking of lubrication. However, a touch of grease on each can prevent rusting and keep them moving smoothly. In addition, getting in close to do this can reveal a loosening connection, water spray or a build-up of dirt.

Oil, grease and diesel fuel can all damage the rubber part of an engine mount, so care should be taken to keep petroleum products away from the soft parts of mounts. Hydrocarbon products can also damage cables and hoses.

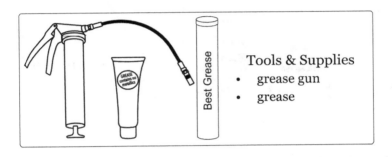

Tools & Supplies
- grease gun
- grease

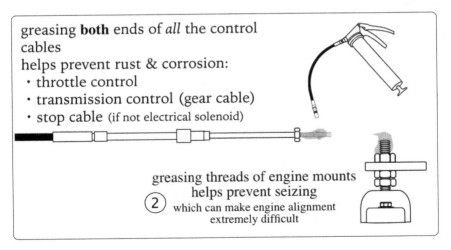

greasing **both** ends of *all* the control cables
helps prevent rust & corrosion:
- throttle control
- transmission control (gear cable)
- stop cable (if not electrical solenoid)

greasing threads of engine mounts
helps prevent seizing
which can make engine alignment
extremely difficult

8   Lubricate Ignition Key Slot

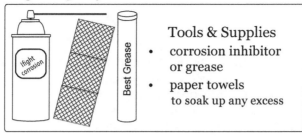

Tools & Supplies
- corrosion inhibitor
  or grease
- paper towels
  to soak up any excess

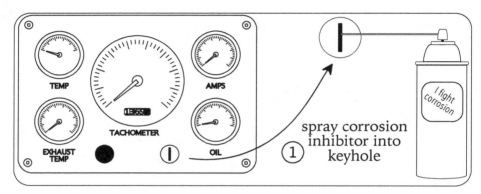

spray corrosion
inhibitor into
keyhole

9   Check Injection Pump & Governor Dipsticks

Some models of diesel injection pumps and governors have dipsticks which
should be checked. Inspect the pump housing for their location or look up in the
Engine Manual.

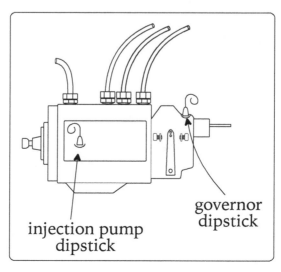

injection pump
dipstick

governor
dipstick

Cautionary Tale

Every time before the captain fired up the fishing boat's diesel engine, he sent one of the crew down to the engine room to pull the dipstick and check the oil level. "Good to go," the crew members reported all spring. Then one day in early summer, while out in the North Atlantic, the engine bogged down and finally quit. The boat had to be towed to port. An investigation revealed the engine had seized and would have to be replaced – at a total cost of $500,000 in replacement engine, installation and lost fishing revenue for the remainder of the season.

What went wrong? A worn rubber diaphragm in the engine's fuel lift pump had allowed diesel fuel to leak into the engine's crankcase. Over several weeks, the diesel had diluted the engine oil so much that it was too thin to lubricate the cylinders and bearings. So the engine had seized.

This expensive episode could have been avoided if the level of oil each day had been recorded in a Maintenance Log, even if there was not one crew member designated to be engineer. If the daily oil level had been accurately recorded in the Maintenance Logbook, almost certainly, someone would have noticed that the oil level was going *up*. Instead, no-one paid any more attention than a quick glance at the maximum mark on the dipstick – with expensive consequences.

4 Maintenance – Raw Water Cooling

Main Concerns

- vessel sinks because raw water floods through broken seacock
- vessel sinks because raw water hose fails and/or seacock is seized open
- engine overheats (and potentially seizes) because raw water pump fails

Task List

	Description	Frequency	Page
1	clean raw water intake thruhull	yearly	61
2	check emergency plug tied to seacock	yearly	61
3	check seacock open/closes smoothly	yearly	62
4	service raw water strainer	yearly	62
5	service raw water pump & impeller	yearly	63
6	check and change heat exchanger anode(s)	6 months	68
7	flush syphon break in fresh water	1 month	69

The frequency of tasks generally depends on engine hours, though tasks should not be ignored just because the engine is not being used, unless the vessel has been laid-up. See page 187 for all the Task Lists.

Heat of Combustion

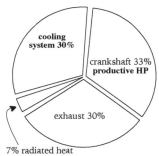

Only one-third of the heat generated by combustion is used for productive work - to propel the vessel. Another third is expelled in the exhaust gases. Another third must be removed by the engine's cooling circuits. If this heat is not removed, the engine will seriously overheat and the pistons seize.

The amount of heat removed by the cooling system is adjusted by the engine's thermostat. Its purpose is to keep the engine within an optimal temperature range. This maximizes fuel economy and engine performance, and minimizes carbon build-up and excess wear. If an engine runs too cold it can suffer reduced performance and carbon build-up, causing long-term damage and shorter engine life. (This can happen if the thermostat sticks open or is removed.)

Almost all vessels use one of three designs of cooling:

- indirect
- direct
- keel cooling

Water Words

raw water – water floating a vessel, water drawn into a boat for engine cooling

fresh water cooled – engine using mix of *ethylene glycol* coolant/antifreeze & fresh water in a closed circuit

fresh water – rivers, lakes

salt/sea water – seas, oceans

brackish (mix fresh & salt) – river estuaries, tidal swamps

potable – drinking water, marina dock supply

sweet water – good to drink

Indirect Cooling (Fresh Water Cooled)

Indirect-cooled engines have *two* circuits:

1. raw water, drawn into the vessel by a raw water pump, circulates through one side of a heat exchanger and is blown out of the vessel with the engine's exhaust gases.

2. a mixture of *ethylene glycol* coolant/antifreeze and fresh water circulates in a closed loop through the engine and through the other side of the heat exchanger. Heat from the engine is thus conducted by the coolant mix to the raw water, then mixed with exhaust gases and expelled from the boat.

Confusingly, these engines are sometimes called "fresh-water cooled" - referring to the mixture of fresh water and coolant/antifreeze circulating within the closed loop between the block and the heat exchanger, and NOT to the water drawn into the vessel by the raw water (impeller) pump.

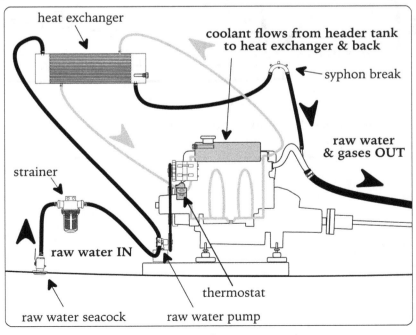

Direct Cooling

Raw water circulates directly through the engine block and is expelled from the water-lift muffler by the exhaust gases. These engines do not use coolant/antifreeze, and do not have a coolant/raw water heat exchanger. Direct cooling is almost always only used on vessels operating in fresh water, because hot salt water is highly corrosive to the engine block. The system is simpler than indirect cooling, but not as efficient, because the water flowing through the engine block cannot be pressurized, which means the engine cannot be run at its optimal temperature.

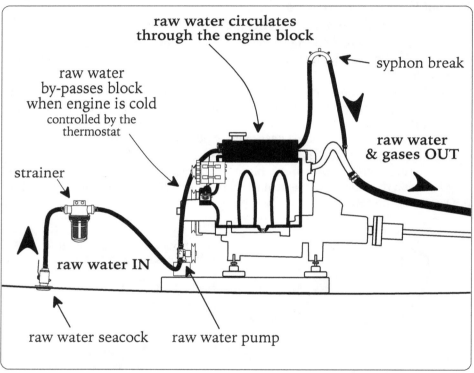

Keel Cooling

Most canal boats and some larger boats (especially fishing boats) circulate the engine's *ethylene glycol* coolant/antifreeze through a closed loop in the keel exposed to the raw water in which the vessel is floating (eg. canal or sea water).

Coolant/antifreeze flows either through a "skin tank" welded to the inside of the vessel's hull below the waterline (canal boats) or through pipes exposed to the seawater outside the hull (fishing boats). Coolant/antifreeze flows directly from the engine block to the skin tank or pipes in the keel and back to the engine.

In both designs, the skin tank or pipes in the keel act as the heat exchanger. The system is simple, not prone to clogging with weeds or silt, and allows a dry engine engine exhaust to be used.

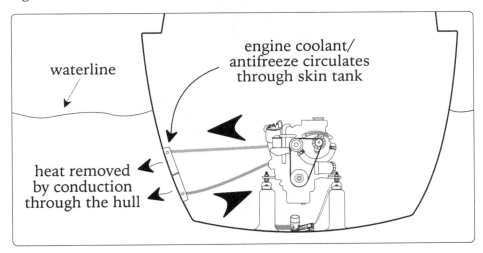

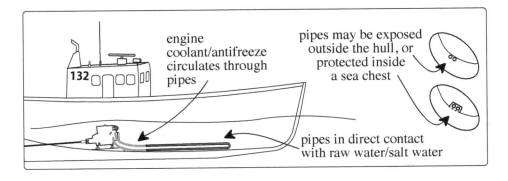

1   Clean Thruhull of Anti-Foul Paint and Marine Growth

Layers of anti-foul paint can build up on the face of grille-type thruhulls, partially blocking the engine's raw water intake, potentially causing the engine to overheat. Likewise, if there is no anti-foul paint on the grille or inside the thruhull, marine growth is likely to grow and to have the same effect.

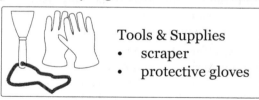

Tools & Supplies
* scraper
* protective gloves

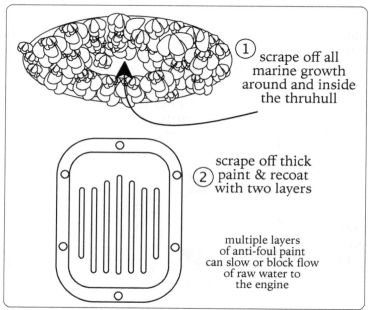

① scrape off all marine growth around and inside the thruhull

② scrape off thick paint & recoat with two layers

multiple layers of anti-foul paint can slow or block flow of raw water to the engine

2   Check Emergency Plug Tied to Every Seacock

Often overlooked, a tapered plug provides the last means to stop a potentially catastrophic flood of water into the boat if the hose fails and the seacock is seized or breaks. Best practice is to size the plug to fit the inside diameter of the hose barb and to tie it to the seacock on a lanyard, long enough for the plug to be used without untying. A soft-wood plug can also be prepared to be inserted into the thruhull from the *outside* of the hull.

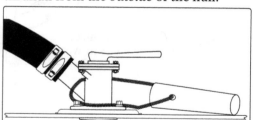

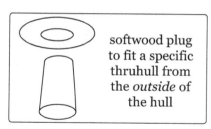

softwood plug to fit a specific thruhull from the *outside* of the hull

3   Check Seacock Opens/Closes Smoothly

Seacocks serve a vital purpose and should be tested regularly.

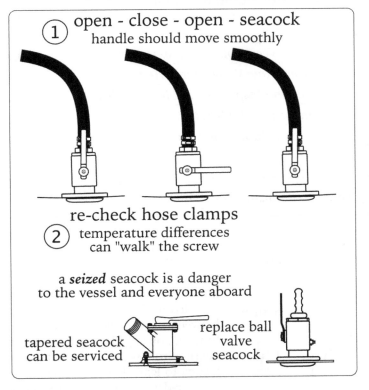

(1) open - close - open - seacock
handle should move smoothly

(2) re-check hose clamps
temperature differences
can "walk" the screw

a *seized* seacock is a danger
to the vessel and everyone aboard

tapered seacock
can be serviced

replace ball
valve
seacock

4   Inspect Raw Water Strainer

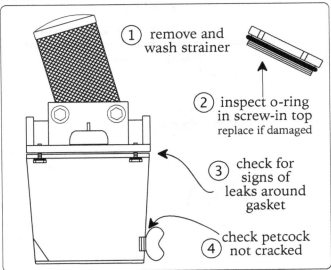

(1) remove and
wash strainer

(2) inspect o-ring
in screw-in top
replace if damaged

(3) check for
signs of
leaks around
gasket

(4) check petcock
not cracked

5   Service Raw Water Pump & Impeller

Servicing a raw water pump and inspecting the rubber/Nitrile impeller can be broken down into five tasks:

A)	*Inspect Weep Hole on Pump Housing*	page **63**
B)	*Service Raw Water Pump Housing*	page **63**
C)	*Remove and Inspect the Rubber Impeller*	page **65**
D)	*Damage to a Rubber/Nitrile Impeller*	page **65**
E)	*Find Missing Impeller Pieces*	page **67**

See page 165 to *Re-install Raw Water Pump Impeller & Face Plate*

A)   Inspect Weep Hole on Pump Housing

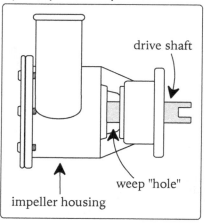

drive shaft

weep "hole"

impeller housing

Many raw water pumps, whether gear or belt driven, have a small weep hole or gap between the impeller housing and the shaft bearing housing. This is to protect the shaft bearing from water damage if the pump seal begins to leak. This is especially important on gear-driven pumps where a failure of the seals could allow raw water to enter the engine block.

Check for signs of water leaks from the weep hole - pump will need to be rebuild if seals are failing.

B)   Service Raw Water Pump Housing

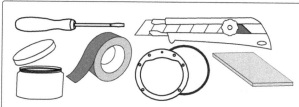

Tools & Supplies
- slot screwdriver
- container for screws
- emery cloth
- utility knife blade
- new gasket or o-ring

B) *Service Raw Water Pump Housing*

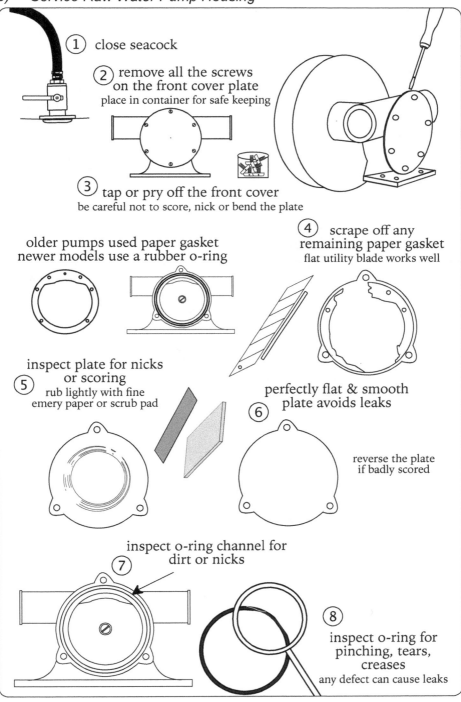

① close seacock

② remove all the screws
on the front cover plate
place in container for safe keeping

③ tap or pry off the front cover
be careful not to score, nick or bend the plate

older pumps used paper gasket
newer models use a rubber o-ring

④ scrape off any
remaining paper gasket
flat utility blade works well

inspect plate for nicks
or scoring
⑤ rub lightly with fine
emery paper or scrub pad

perfectly flat & smooth
plate avoids leaks
⑥

reverse the plate
if badly scored

inspect o-ring channel for
dirt or nicks
⑦

⑧
inspect o-ring for
pinching, tears,
creases
any defect can cause leaks

C) Remove and Inspect the Rubber/Nitrile Impeller

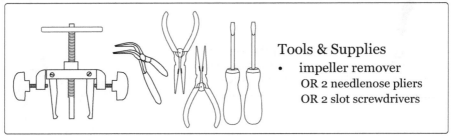

Tools & Supplies
- impeller remover
  OR 2 needlenose pliers
  OR 2 slot screwdrivers

See page 165 to *Re-install Raw Water Pump Impeller & Face Plate*

C) Inspect a Rubber/Nitrile Impeller

An impeller cannot be properly checked while it is compressed inside the pump housing. Best practice is to remove the impeller and inspect carefully in a good light. Any damage, such as tears or a piece missing, will be obvious:

- damaged vanes are more likely to break apart if the pump is run dry, even for a short time
- permanently bent vanes (taking a set) can greatly reduce the output, even though the pump continues to pump some water
- cavitation pitting occurs when water in the pump boils due to low pressure caused by partial lack of water. Pitting weakens the vanes

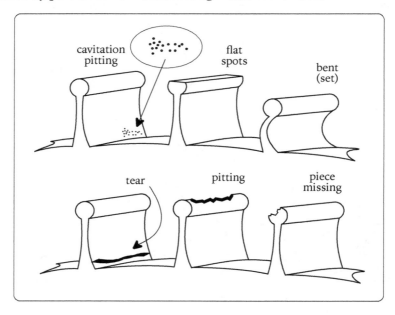

Remove and Inspect the Rubber/Nitrile Impeller

poor access is often the main
challenge to removing an impeller
try an assortment of tools to find
what works for a specific installation

inspect how impeller is secured
to the shaft of the pump
① may be a setscrew in the
side of the impeller

some impellers are secured
② with a key in a keyway

③ special puller works by
gripping & squeezing the
impeller's rubber hub,
while a long bolt screws down
pushing against the pump's shaft
& extracting the impeller

legs squeeze
the impeller

extraction bolt

most impellers can be pulled off their shaft
④ with **slow, steady, even** pulling using any
tool that does not tear or damage the vanes

needlenose or channel lock pliers
grip vanes with minimum pressure
(avoid scoring or cutting the vanes)
pull steadily & evenly on both sides
- tugging risks tearing a vane

slot screwdrivers
use one on each side
pry from the back of the impeller
be very careful not to score back plate
or to cut or damage vanes

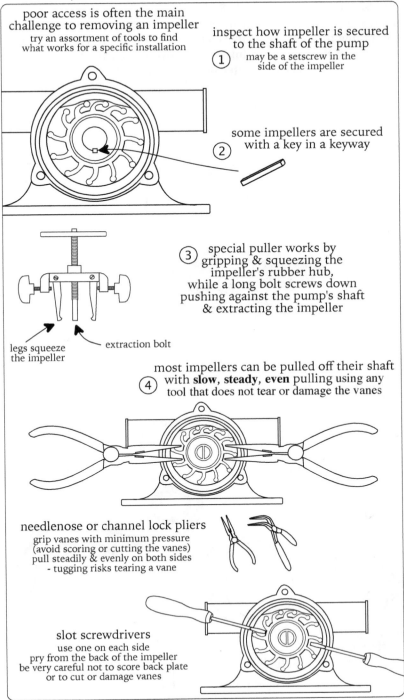

D) Find Missing Impeller Pieces

Best practice is to search for any missing pieces of the impeller – they could be blocking cooling tubes in the heat exchanger or may be trapped in the tight bend or small holes of the raw water injection elbow in the exhaust riser. A damaged impeller will likely reduce raw water flow and can cause engine overheating.

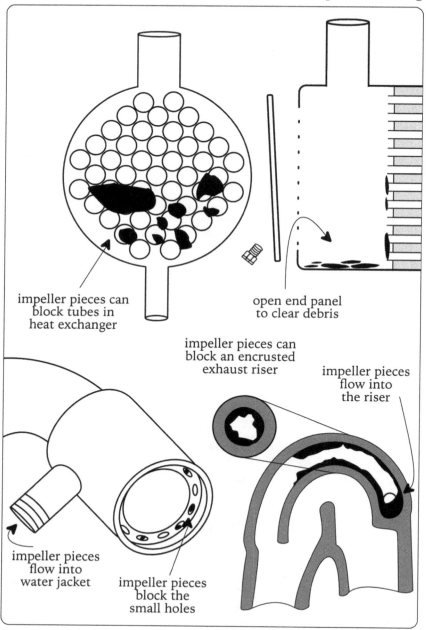

impeller pieces can block tubes in heat exchanger

open end panel to clear debris

impeller pieces can block an encrusted exhaust riser

impeller pieces flow into the riser

impeller pieces flow into water jacket

impeller pieces block the small holes

Anode(s)

Engines and heat exchangers are often made of different metals (eg. brass casing, copper tubes & tin solder, even steel bolts). These different metals must be protected from galvanic corrosion by an anode; if not, the raw water, acting as an electrolyte, conducts electricity to eat away at the least noble metal (galvanic corrosion is the most common source of heat exchanger leaks). This can be prevented by:

• using the correct anode for the type of raw water
• checking the anode at least seasonally and replacing when 50% consumed

Types of anodes:

• <u>aluminum</u> - can be used in all types of water - salt water, brackish, polluted and fresh water
• <u>zinc</u> - use in sea water or brackish water. Do not use in fresh water because they are prone to developing a whitish calcareous coating which prevents them from working.
• <u>magnesium</u> - use in fresh water. Do not use in salt or brackish water as these are electrically very active and will be consumed too quickly.

CAUTION: Do not mix different types of anodes on the same vessel.

Not all heat exchangers have anodes - look in the engine manual if no anodes can be found and verify that, indeed, the engine does not require anodes.

6   Check and Change Heat Exchanger Anode(s)

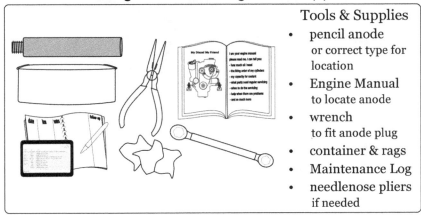

Tools & Supplies

• pencil anode
  or correct type for
  location

• Engine Manual
  to locate anode

• wrench
  to fit anode plug

• container & rags

• Maintenance Log

• needlenose pliers
  if needed

Check and Change Heat Exchanger Anode(s)

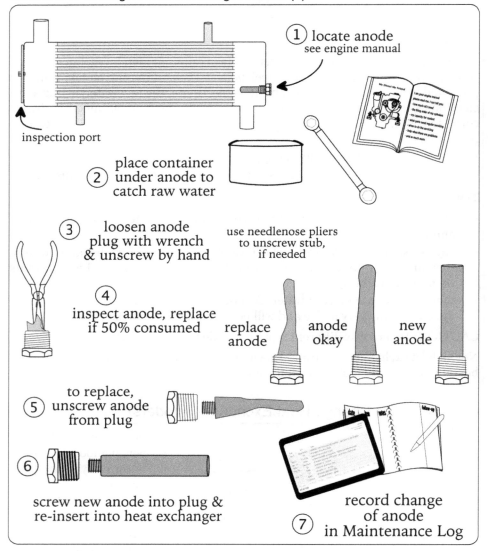

1. locate anode
   see engine manual

inspection port

2. place container under anode to catch raw water

3. loosen anode plug with wrench & unscrew by hand
   use needlenose pliers to unscrew stub, if needed

4. inspect anode, replace if 50% consumed

   replace anode

   anode okay

   new anode

5. to replace, unscrew anode from plug

6. screw new anode into plug & re-insert into heat exchanger

7. record change of anode in Maintenance Log

7   Flush and Clean the Syphon Break
Indirect and Direct cooling – all conditions

The purpose of the syphon break is to prevent raw water syphoning back into the engine after the motor has stopped. If the air vent, in the top of the syphon breaks, becomes encrusted with salt crystals or blocked (eg. impeller fragment) the wet muffler exhaust hose can slowly backfill with water, eventually flooding the engine cylinders with raw water. Water should not be able to pass by the impeller but may do if the impeller is damaged, has vanes missing or bent, which will allow water to seep by. This is an easy way to drown a marine diesel engine.

Flush and Clean the Syphon Break

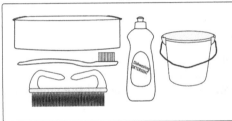

Tools & Supplies

- old toothbrush
  OR scrubbing brush
- wash basin
- (bucket of) fresh water
- detergent

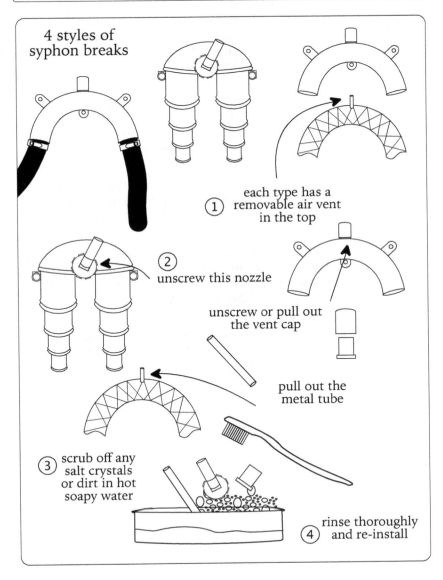

4 styles of
syphon breaks

(1) each type has a
removable air vent
in the top

(2) unscrew this nozzle

unscrew or pull out
the vent cap

pull out the
metal tube

(3) scrub off any
salt crystals
or dirt in hot
soapy water

(4) rinse thoroughly
and re-install

Cautionary Tale

The club's committee boat was out at least two or three evenings every week from May to October for the club's sailboat races. A roster of members, who took turns running the racing, as part of their work hours, also checked the engine oil and coolant before every outing.

Oil changes were done by another volunteer who was not a racer. He twice noted in the Logbook that the used oil appeared very slightly "milky" but the effect seemed to disappear each time the oil was changed. No-one paid much attention to this as the engine was old and well used. The engine was also using oil; not a lot, but the oil needed topping up before every outing, even though there was no oil in the bilge nor blue smoke.

One spring, a new member took over maintenance and used a checklist to be sure she did not miss anything that needed to be checked. She was surprised to find that the anode in the oil cooler/heat exchanger was non-existent – in fact, she was not sure the brass plug was for an anode, except for the screw threads on the inside of the plug.

The engine continued to use oil. One evening, with the setting sun shining on the water, the committee boat was followed in to the marina by another vessel. Her observant crew reported a sheen of oil on the water in the wake of the committee boat.

The mystery of the disappearing oil was solved. A mechanic came to detach the oil cooler and send it for testing. Sure enough the exchanger failed to hold pressure. The lack of an anode had allowed galvanic corrosion to attack the next least noble metal – the tin solder of the oil cooler/heat exchanger.

A substitute motor boat was chartered, at considerable expense, for the upcoming race weekend rather than cancel one of the highlights of the club's summer season. Two weeks passed before the replacement heat exchanger could be repaired, returned and re-installed – all because the anode was not checked regularly and replaced when 50% consumed.

5 Maintenance – Coolant/Antifreeze

Indirect Cooled Engines - all conditions

Main Concerns

- inadequate freezing protection
- internal corrosion due to loss of corrosion inhibitors in worn-out coolant/antifreeze

Task List

	Description	Frequency	Page
1	check coolant level in header tank or overflow bottle	weekly	**73**
2	inspect condition of coolant	weekly	**74**
3	drain and replace worn-out coolant/antifreeze	2 years	**74**

The frequency of tasks generally depends on engine hours, though tasks should not be ignored just because the engine is not being used, unless the vessel has been laid-up. See page 187 for all the Task Lists.

Ethylene Glycol Coolant/Antifreeze

Coolant is as important for the efficient operation and longevity of an indirect-cooled engine as fuel and oil. Engine coolant is often called "antifreeze", as if these terms were interchangeable; however this ignores all the other critical functions of coolant and can cause confusion with antifreeze used to winterize domestic water pumps (*propylene* glycol antifreeze). All coolants work as antifreeze; not all antifreeze is engine coolant.

Not renewing coolant when necessary or using the wrong type for the engine will not cause immediate engine failure, but removes important protections against rust, pitting, scale and aeration that can reduce engine performance and seriously shorten engine life. Failure to provide adequate freeze-protection against the lowest winter temperatures can cause the engine block to crack, effectively destroying the engine.

Colour and clarity are no guides to the type or condition of engine; "brown" coolant is most likely a mixture of two of more coolants. IAT and OAT coolants are not compatible. Chemicals in incompatible coolants combine to precipitate deposits and sludge, which inhibit cooling and reduce anti-corrosion effectiveness. The system should be drained, flushed and filled with fresh pre-mixed coolant/antifreeze:

- use coolant/antifreeze intended for diesel engines - it is specially formulated to reduce cavitation
- use "heavy duty" coolant - a boat's engine is always under load when the vessel is under way

Critical Functions of Coolant/Antifreeze

- keep engine within its optimal operating temperature range
- remove heat from the hottest areas (cylinder head and cylinder walls)
- equalize heat across all the parts of an engine to avoid hotspots and warping
- remove excessive heat from the engine by circulating coolant through a heat exchanger
- antifreeze – protect the engine and heat exchanger from ice expansion damage; freezing water expands 9% by volume and with up to 79,000 kPa (114,000 psi); more than enough to crack an engine block
- anti-boil – ethylene glycol boils at 197.3°C (387°F); mixing it with water raises the boiling point of the water, allowing an engine to run hotter without additional danger of aeration and cavitation. (Indirect cooling systems are pressurized by using a pressure cap on the header tank)
- be compatible with engine seals, hoses and metals (eg. copper, iron, aluminum)
- prevent the formation of sludge and scale. 1/16" scale has same insulation as 4" of cast iron and can reduce heat transfer by up to 40%
- protect against corrosion caused by aeration and oxidation. Air bubbles impede heat transfer, decrease circulation pump efficiency and promote cavitation and rusting
- protect against cavitation. Cavitation can occur where the speed of coolant flow increases and pressure drops, causing coolant to boil which forms air bubbles that can pit metal surfaces when the bubbles collapse with tremendous force

1 Check Coolant/Antifreeze Level in Header Tank or Overflow Bottle

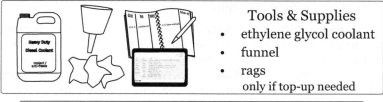

Tools & Supplies
- ethylene glycol coolant
- funnel
- rags
  only if top-up needed

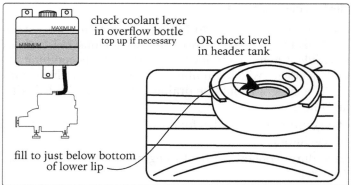

check coolant lever in overflow bottle
top up if necessary

OR check level in header tank

fill to just below bottom of lower lip

2   Inspect Condition of Coolant

Looking at the coolant, not just the coolant level in the header tank or overflow bottle, can give some basic indications of the condition of the coolant and health of the coolant system inside the engine. It can also give early warning of potential problems.

Clarity		Action Required
clear	normal	
cloudy	different coolants mixed together	drain, flush and use fresh coolant
Colour		
bright, clear	normal	
brown	different coolants mixed together	drain, flush and use fresh coolant
Contamination		
sediments "grit"	precipitation of additives, rust, scale	drain, flush and use fresh coolant
oil droplets	engine oil leaking into coolant	investigate oil cooler leaking cylinder heat gasket leaking

3   Drain and Replace Worn-out Coolant/Antifreeze

Using the same coolant/antifreeze too long without changing (approx. every two years), or using the wrong type for a diesel engine, will not cause engine failure in the short term, but removes important protections, reducing performance and shortening engine life.

Draining and refilling with new coolant also helps clear scale and sludge from the cooling passages inside the block. Avoid mixing different types of coolant/antifreeze – always record which type was used in the Maintenance Logbook.

The antifreeze property of coolant does not wear out; however topping up with water does dilute frost protection by raising the temperature at which the coolant freezes. Use a coolant hydrometer to check protection against freezing during winter lay-up. See page 147, *Lay-Up – Coolant/Antifreeze.*

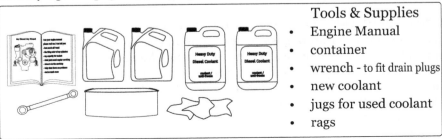

Tools & Supplies
- Engine Manual
- container
- wrench - to fit drain plugs
- new coolant
- jugs for used coolant
- rags

Drain and Replace Worn-out Coolant/Antifreeze

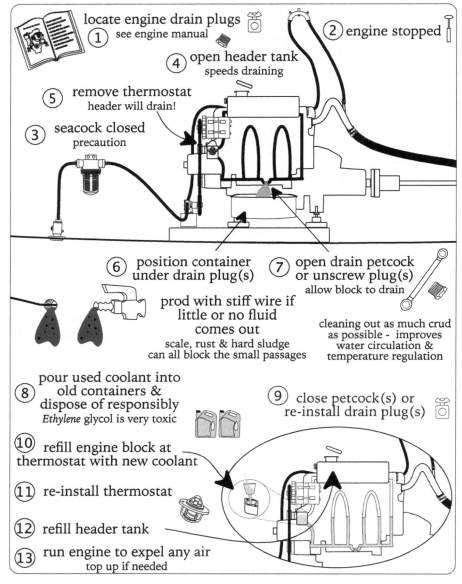

(1) locate engine drain plugs
see engine manual

(2) engine stopped

(4) open header tank
speeds draining

(5) remove thermostat
header will drain!

(3) seacock closed
precaution

(6) position container
under drain plug(s)

(7) open drain petcock
or unscrew plug(s)
allow block to drain

prod with stiff wire if
little or no fluid
comes out
scale, rust & hard sludge
can all block the small passages

cleaning out as much crud
as possible - improves
water circulation &
temperature regulation

(8) pour used coolant into
old containers &
dispose of responsibly
Ethylene glycol is very toxic

(9) close petcock(s) or
re-install drain plug(s)

(10) refill engine block at
thermostat with new coolant

(11) re-install thermostat

(12) refill header tank

(13) run engine to expel any air
top up if needed

Disposal of Ethylene Glycol Coolant/Antifreeze

Engine coolant is hazardous waste and should never be poured down a storm drain, into a sewer, into the sea or onto the ground. Most coolant is sweet-tasting and can attract and poison animals. *Ethylene* glycol is very toxic, can lead to kidney failure if ingested and kill marine and plant life even in small doses. One gallon (4L) of ethylene can poison 10,000 gallons of groundwater. Many marinas and motor repair shops have disposal containers and accept used coolant for recycling.

Cautionary Tale

Three boatowners were standing on the dock talking about engine coolant. One owned a trawler-type motorboat in which he and his wife cruised all summer. The second had taken over his father's 32-foot cruiser/racer sailboat after he'd declared himself too old for sailing; and the third was a new sailor with a new (to her) 42-foot blue water sailboat. This was her first boat and she was open to advice.

The trawler skipper said he and his wife had cruised over 5,000 miles in the last two years and never had an engine problem. "I check the level of coolant every day before starting the engine, just like checking the oil. And I always use the same brand and keep a supply on board. Before freeze-up in the fall, I test the coolant/antifreeze with a hydrometer to be sure she's good to -30°C just to be safe," he explained to the others.

"Dad used the Auto store's own brand and never had a problem. So I'm doing the same and the engine runs great," the racing sailor told the others. "Why pay more?"

The new sailor said the coolant/antifreeze in her 80-hp engine was orange, but she didn't know what it was and hadn't been able to find a coolant jug on board. "So what should I do?" she asked the two more experienced sailors.

Don't mix coolant types, the two sailors agreed. "You'll have to drain the coolant that's in the engine now and put in new coolant," the trawler owner told him. "Remember to buy coolant formulated for diesel engines, not gasoline engines," said the racer.

Three weekends later, the boatowners met up in the clubhouse. The two sailboat owners were surprised to be joined by the owners of the magnificent trawler who, when their boat was not in her slip, were usually gone cruising.

Their news was not good. "We've lost an engine," the skipper told them. "White smoke pouring out of the exhaust. Coolant tank bubbling. Engine oil looked like a milk shake. Blowing a head gasket would have been bad enough. Looks like we're going to have to rebuild the engine – a big hole in a wet liner, letting coolant into the cylinder. And all the liners are pot-marked like the moon. Cavitation damage, the mechanic's telling us."

"What causes that? You're so careful to keep the coolant topped up. I thought cavitation only happened on propellers," asked the lady sailor.

The skipper nodded. "Now we know it can happen inside an engine. "When the engine's running the wet liners vibrate. Pressure drops, making the coolant boil and form tiny air bubbles. When these collapse they cause pitting of the liner. Ours put a hole right through the liner into the cylinder."

"I thought the additives in diesel coolant prevented this?" asked the racing sailor.

"So did I. The mechanic thinks we had some electrical flow across the engine. He says this can cause the nitrites in the coolant, that are supposed to stop cavitation, to be used up. I was waiting to change the coolant and I guess I waited too long," said the trawler skipper.

6 Maintenance – Breathing

Main Concerns

- contamination of the air (oxygen) entering the engine with hair, dust etc.
- dirty air filter blocking or partially blocking air supply degrading engine performance and increasing fuel consumption
- inadequate ventilation in the engine room, making the engine work harder and raising the air temperature, which decreases the density of oxygen going into the engine cylinders

Task List

	Description	Frequency	Page
1	check and clean air filter	monthly	78
2	check the crankcase breather (and filter)	yearly	79
3	provide adequate air flow through engine room	3 monthly	80
4	inspect and repair sound insulation	yearly	81

See page 187 for all the Task Lists.

Five designs of air intake/air cleaner are in common use:

1. replaceable paper filter elements (similar to fuel filters)
2. reusable, cleanable rigid filter element
3. washable foam filter around a rigid air intake;
4. intake "silencer" – contains no air filter, but dampens air intake noise
5. air intake with no filter or housing – older diesel engines (eg. 1970s)

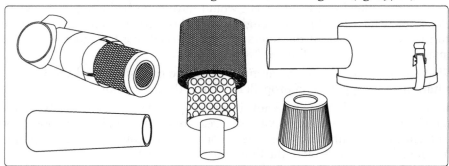

Why Clean the Air Filter?

Diesel engines consume huge volumes of air which must flow through the air intake and out through the exhaust. A typical naturally-aspirated 40hp engine draws approximately 136 cubic metres of air per hour (80 cfm), more than twice the volume of a regular shipping container. A turbocharged engine may draw twice this volume of air. Inevitably, even in a "clean" marine environment, dust, hair, belt dust, sand and insulation debris can be drawn into an engine's air intake

– and, hopefully, trapped in the air filter. Keeping the air filter clean and in good repair is important to:

- prevent contaminants getting inside the engine where they can stick with oil and cause abrasive damage
- allow air to flow as easily as possible into the engine with minimal drop in pressure

1 Clean the Air Filter

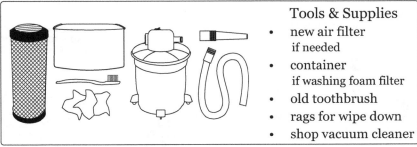

Tools & Supplies

- new air filter
  if needed
- container
  if washing foam filter
- old toothbrush
- rags for wipe down
- shop vacuum cleaner

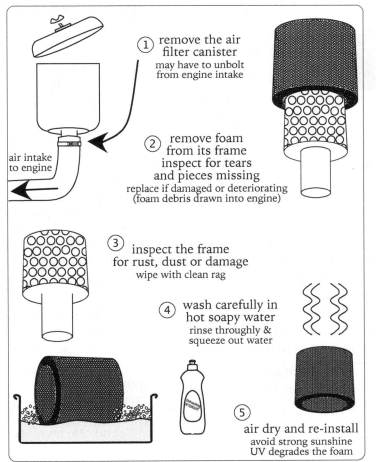

① remove the air
filter canister
may have to unbolt
from engine intake

air intake
to engine

② remove foam
from its frame
inspect for tears
and pieces missing
replace if damaged or deteriorating
(foam debris drawn into engine)

③ inspect the frame
for rust, dust or damage
wipe with clean rag

④ wash carefully in
hot soapy water
rinse throughly &
squeeze out water

⑤
air dry and re-install
avoid strong sunshine
UV degrades the foam

Service a Replaceable Filter Element

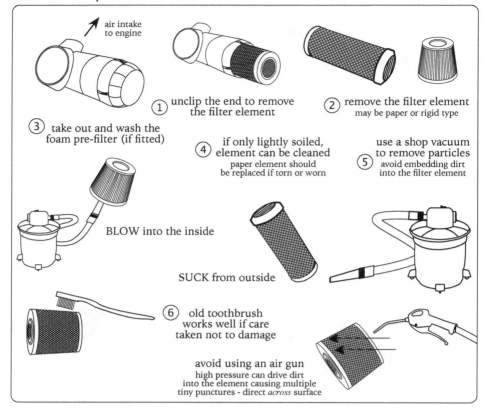

① unclip the end to remove the filter element

② remove the filter element
may be paper or rigid type

③ take out and wash the foam pre-filter (if fitted)

④ if only lightly soiled, element can be cleaned
paper element should be replaced if torn or worn

⑤ use a shop vacuum to remove particles
avoid embedding dirt into the filter element

BLOW into the inside

SUCK from outside

⑥ old toothbrush works well if care taken not to damage

avoid using an air gun
high pressure can drive dirt into the element causing multiple tiny punctures - direct *across* surface

2   Check the Crankcase Breather and Filter

If the engine is fitted with a crankcase breather filter, it should be checked yearly and changed according to manufacturer's recommendation (300 - 4000 hours). The purpose of the breather is to vent air pressure in the crankcase which can be caused mainly by gases escaping between piston rings and the cylinder wall (*blow-by*). Blow-by gases, carrying carbon particles, exhaust gases, unburnt fuel and water vapour, need to be removed before these become sludge.

This is done through the crankcase breather, which may be of 4 designs:

1.   gases are vented to the atmosphere (open hose down the side of the engine)
2.   gases pass through a filter before being vented to the atmosphere
3.   gases return directly through a hose to the air intake
4.   gases are filtered to remove oil and carbon before flowing to the air intake

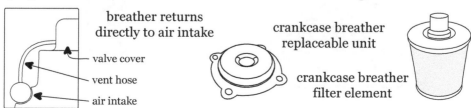

breather returns directly to air intake

valve cover

vent hose

air intake

crankcase breather replaceable unit

crankcase breather filter element

3 Check Adequate Air Flow Through Engine Room

Diesel engines require a lot of clean, cool air - typically 140 cubic metres (5000 feet[3]) per hour for a 40 hp engine. Any shortage will make a diesel engine work harder, can limit rpm, waste fuel, and increase carbon build-up and engine wear.

Cool air is denser, and therefore has more oxygen, so it's important to supply as much clean, cool, dry air as possible into the engine room. Air at 7°C (44°F) has 14% more oxygen than at 50°C (122°F). Lower temperatures also help engine cooling (through radiation) and the alternator(s) to run cooler and more efficiently.

Good Engine Room Ventilation

A good ventilation system should maintain the engine room temperature to no more than 16°C (30°F) above the ambient outside temperature (eg. maximum engine room temperature of 41°C (105°F) in 25°C (77°F) weather.

Passive ventilation relies on air finding its own way into the engine compartment, typically via a cowl vent or a scallop-shaped vent. Air flow can be restricted by insect screens, convoluted piping, fenders etc. piled high in a lazarette. Often, no allowance is made to vent the hot air *from* the hot engine room (or off-gassing batteries) when the engine is enclosed to suppress noise.

Active ventilation uses blowers to increase inflow and, in a well-designed system, outflow. Only fans rated for continuous duty should be installed for engine room ventilation; these are typically "squirrel cage" fans (axial fans). Inline bilge blowers, though often used for engine room ventilation, are designed to run for short periods to vent fumes and vapours (eg. gasoline, propane, hydrogen). They are not intended for continuous duty and typically have a service life of only 300 – 350 hours.

This table is a theoretical comparison of active and passive ventilation. Actual performance will depend on specific installation, (eg. length & bends in ducting).

inlet diameter	air flow cubic metres/hour (cubic feet per hour)	
	passive - cowl vent*	active - squirrel cage blower
7.6 cm (3")	88 cmh (3110 cfh)	277 cmh (9,780 cfh)
10 cm (4")	156 cmh (5520 cfh)	550 cmh (19,440 cfh)

*SOURCE: cui.com & calculations   * based on flow through a pipe at 4.8 kph (3 miles/hour)*

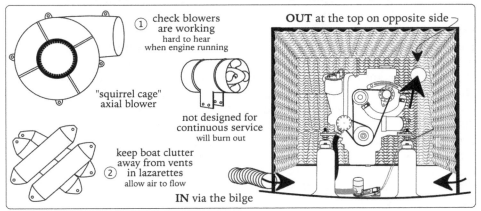

① check blowers are working
hard to hear when engine running

"squirrel cage" axial blower

not designed for continuous service
will burn out

keep boat clutter away from vents
② in lazarettes
allow air to flow

OUT at the top on opposite side

IN via the bilge

4 Inspect & Repair Sound Insulation

Cleaning and repairing engine room sound insulation is good preventative maintenance. Disintegrating or torn foam or foil can get sucked into the air intake, partially blocking the air cleaner or, worse, entering the engine (if no filter). Dirt, discarded rags, dropped washers, bolts and hose clamps trap water and dirt, aiding corrosion. A flashlight helps to make a thorough inspection.

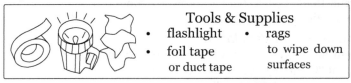

Tools & Supplies
- flashlight
- foil tape or duct tape
- rags to wipe down surfaces

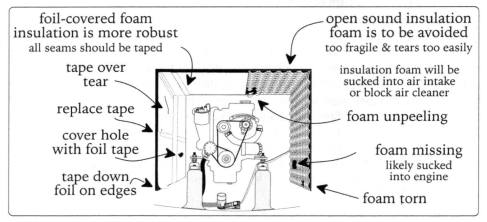

foil-covered foam insulation is more robust
all seams should be taped

tape over tear

replace tape

cover hole with foil tape

tape down, foil on edges

open sound insulation foam is to be avoided
too fragile & tears too easily

insulation foam will be sucked into air intake or block air cleaner

foam unpeeling

foam missing
likely sucked into engine

foam torn

Cautionary Tale

The repair was done. All that remained was to re-install the air filter on the engine and the tired mechanic could go home. He climbed up into the cockpit to start the engine, confident the engine would now run smoothly. He turned the key and the engine started almost immediately.

After checking the instruments, he was looking over the transom and was shocked to see hundreds of blue specks rising in a puff of black smoke. The engine did not stop, did not even slow down or "choke" on whatever it was that had apparently been sucked into the engine and blown out of the exhaust.

He shut down the engine, then climbed onto the swim platform to retrieve some of the blue confetti landing there. A quick examination of the specks left no doubt in his mind; he knew what they were – shreds of a mechanic's blue paper rags.

He went down to the engine room. Sure enough, the rags he'd left beside the engine were gone; sucked into the air intake more than two feet away. "No harm done," he thought with relief, then realized how close he'd come to disaster.

If the rags had been cotton, not paper, most likely they'd have got caught in the intake or exhaust valves or inside the cylinders. This would have necessitated removing the cylinder head to clean out the debris. "How lucky I was," he thought, as he re-installed the air filter and tightened its retaining band, vowing never to be so careless again.

7 Maintenance – Electrical

Main Concerns

- repeatedly discharging a wet-cell battery over 50% shortens battery life
- over-charging and chronic under-charging
- corrosion and voltage drop caused by dirty battery posts & terminals
- loose connections causing intermittent failures
- allowing electrolyte level to fall below plate level in an unsealed wet-cell battery

Task List

	Description	Frequency	Page
1	keep battery fully charged or trickle charge	daily	83
2	check battery open circuit voltage with multimeter	weekly	84
3	keep battery terminal connections tight	monthly	84
4	clean battery tops and terminals	monthly	85
5	check electrolyte levels in unsealed wet-cell batteries	monthly	87
6	add distilled water to wet-cell battery	monthly	89
7	check specific gravity of a wet-cell battery	3 months	90
8	test battery(s) with load tester	yearly	92

The frequency of tasks generally depends on engine hours, though tasks should not be ignored just because the engine is not being used, unless the vessel has been laid-up. See page 187 for all the Task Lists.

Sulphation

Soft lead sulphates form on lead acid battery plates every time a battery is discharged, and lift off the plates and are reabsorbed into the sulphuric acid mix (electrolyte) as the battery is recharged. However, if the battery is not *fully* recharged, the soft sulphates begin to harden effectively smothering that part of the plate and killing a percentage of the battery's capacity. A battery may still show 12.65V when tested with a multimeter but effectively be dead because it no longer has the capacity to produce current at 12v. The simplest way to check a battery is to perform a load test (See *Load Testing a 12 Volt Battery* on page 92).

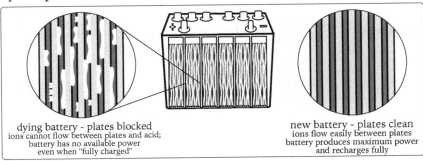

dying battery - plates blocked
ions cannot flow between plates and acid;
battery has no available power
even when "fully charged"

new battery - plates clean
ions flow easily between plates
battery produces maximum power
and recharges fully

1   Keep Lead Acid Battery(s) Charged

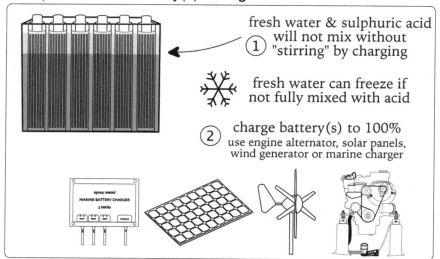

fresh water & sulphuric acid will not mix without "stirring" by charging ①

fresh water can freeze if not fully mixed with acid

② charge battery(s) to 100%
use engine alternator, solar panels, wind generator or marine charger

Lithium-iron batteries should not be kept at 100%, which may shorten battery life. LFP batteries are not damaged by being partially charged and prefer to be charged and discharged regularly. They absorb a charge much more quickly than lead acid batteries and have a slow rate of self-discharge. A LFP's battery management system (BMS) will disconnect the battery as it approaches 100% charge - potentially damaging a charging source such as an alternator. This is unlike a lead acid battery which will continue to accept a minimal *float* charge from the alternator even when it is nominally fully charged. The BMS will also protect the battery by disconnecting if it nears zero capacity (typically 5%).

Trickle Charging Lead Acid Batteries

Self-discharge, hardening sulphation and freezing can be prevented if the batteries are kept fully charged by trickle charging during any period when not being used. Do not leave even a properly installed, sealed marine battery charger unattended for long periods. Best practice is to check at least weekly.

NOTE: Charging times will vary according to the age and condition of the battery; times will be shorter for older batteries with less plate material and therefore lower storage capacity.

Time Required to Charge a 12-Volt Wet-Cell Battery in Storage

% of charge	open circuit voltage	hours to charge @ 5 amps	hours to charge @ 10 amps	hours to charge @ 20 amps
100%	12.73V	0	0	0
80%	12.50V	10	5	3
60%	12.24V	21	10	15
40%	11.96V	31	16	8
20%	11.66V	41	21	10

SOURCE: Trojan Battery Company & Battery Council International

2   Check Battery Open Circuit Voltage with a Multimeter

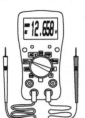

The simplest way to check the voltage of a battery is to use a multimeter across the posts (open circuit voltage). This measures the average voltage across all six cells (of a 12 volt battery), rather than the voltage of each specific cell. However, it does not measure a battery's *health* – voltage might be 12.65 (fully charged) but if the plates are sulphated, available energy can be much lower, or even nil. Allow a battery to stabilize for at least 30 minutes after charging before taking a reading. Voltage will be elevated during and immediately after charging, giving a false reading. See *Sulphation* on page 82.

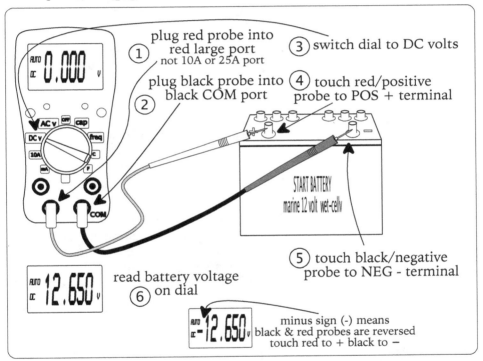

① plug red probe into red large port
not 10A or 25A port

② plug black probe into black COM port

③ switch dial to DC volts

④ touch red/positive probe to POS + terminal

⑤ touch black/negative probe to NEG - terminal

⑥ read battery voltage on dial

START BATTERY
marine 12 volt wet-cellv

minus sign (-) means black & red probes are reversed touch red to + black to −

3   Keep Battery Terminal Connections Tight

Battery connections that are not tight are responsible for a lot of intermittent electrical problems – one of the most difficult types of trouble to identify. Hand tight wing nuts are not tight *enough* and will likely work loose. Use hex or lock nuts and tighten *just tight* using a short wrench. Do not overtighten.

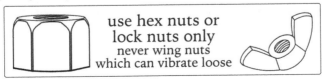

use hex nuts or lock nuts only
never wing nuts which can vibrate loose

4   Clean Battery Tops & Terminals

Dirt and dried acid crystals on top of batteries accelerate corrosion and can fall inside battery cells. Dirty terminals are a common source of voltage drop (especially to the starter motor) and intermediate failures in the negative circuit. Best practice is always clean the top and terminals before servicing the batteries.

White powder which can form is anhydrous sulphuric acid (ie. without water) which forms when electrolyte spills, or fumes condense, and dries out.

Tools & Supplies

- disposable gloves
- safety glasses
- baking soda
  neutralizes acid
- flashlight
- battery cleaner tool
- scrub brush
- old toothbrush
  OR steel brush
- rags
- plastic bag
  for safe disposal acid rags
- bucket fresh water
  for emergency

Maintaining Lithium-Iron (LiFePo4, LFP) Batteries

Almost all 12-volt lithium batteries for marine use are LiFePo4 (lithium iron phosphate, LFP) using lithium iron phosphate for the positive electrode (cathode), graphite for the negative electrode (anode), and lithium salts in a non-water solvent as the electrolyte. These batteries are sealed.

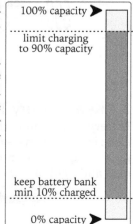

All lithium-iron batteries require a Battery Management System (BMS) which controls the battery, preventing over charge, balancing cells and protecting the battery (by disconnecting) if the voltage falls too low. The BMS may be internal (most common) or external. LFP batteries do not need to be kept fully charged and prefer a state of charge that goes up and down.

- keep batteries clean and cool
- limit battery *charging to maximum of ± 90% capacity*
- *keep battery at least 10% charged*
- follow manufacturer's instructions for the specific batteries

See also *Lithium-Iron Batteries* on page 83.

Clean the Battery Case A

(1) wear safety glasses & gloves
    remove jewellery
    be aware of your route to safety
    & have fresh water close-by

(2) loosen any restraining straps &
    remove the battery box lid

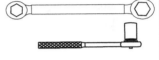

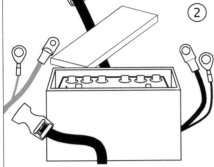

(3) disconnect wires to
    access the posts
    disconnect NEGATIVE *first*
    be mindful with metal tools
    near the battery posts

(4) look down the battery sides
    for any evidence of
    leaked electrolyte
    flashlight can help to see more easily
    treat any liquid as ACID *not* water
    use baking soda to neutralize
    mop up with rags & discard safely

    electrolyte leak can be caused by:
    vent caps not fully secured before vessel heeled
    overcharging causing boiling
    not acid but rain or sea water
    case cracked (usually caused by freezing)

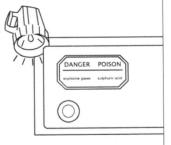

DANGER   POISON
explosive gases   sulphuric acid

(5) scatter baking soda on
    any powder (corrosion)
    which has formed
    neutralizes the acid
    corrosion causes resistance
    and can prevent electrical flow

    white powder is
    anhydrous sulphuric acid
    (ie. without water) which forms
    when electrolyte spills or
    fumes & dries out

(6) use a wire brush or old toothbrush
    to scrub away any stubborn corrosion

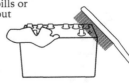

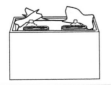

(7) use damp rags to wipe up powder
    wear gloves: this is corrosive!
    do NOT pour water as this will flow
    down the sides into the battery box

Cleaning Battery Case B

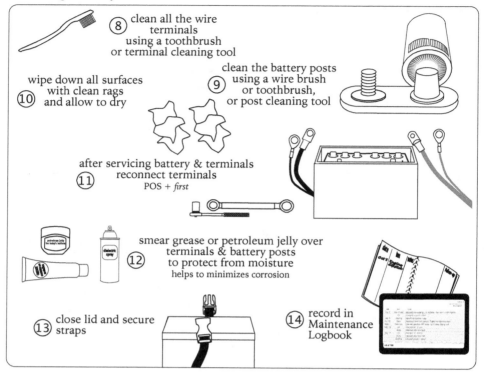

8 clean all the wire terminals using a toothbrush or terminal cleaning tool

10 wipe down all surfaces with clean rags and allow to dry

9 clean the battery posts using a wire brush or toothbrush, or post cleaning tool

11 after servicing battery & terminals reconnect terminals
POS + *first*

12 smear grease or petroleum jelly over terminals & battery posts to protect from moisture
helps to minimizes corrosion

13 close lid and secure straps

14 record in Maintenance Logbook

5   Check the Electrolyte Levels of Wet-Cell Batteries

The level of electrolyte will go down in unsealed wet-cell batteries during charging and discharging. Levels should not change in sealed batteries (such as AGM, "maintenance-free"). The level of electrolyte needs to be kept at the correct level in each battery cell:

• **too low** - plates will be exposed (especially if the vessel heels) causing early failure of the exposed part, partially destroying the storage capacity of the battery

• **too high** - acid may likely leak out, causing corrosion around battery terminals

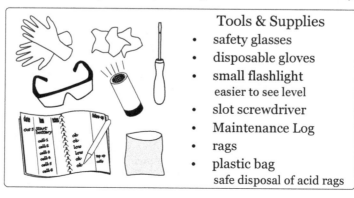

Tools & Supplies
• safety glasses
• disposable gloves
• small flashlight
  easier to see level
• slot screwdriver
• Maintenance Log
• rags
• plastic bag
  safe disposal of acid rags

Check the Electrolyte Levels of Wet-Cell Batteries

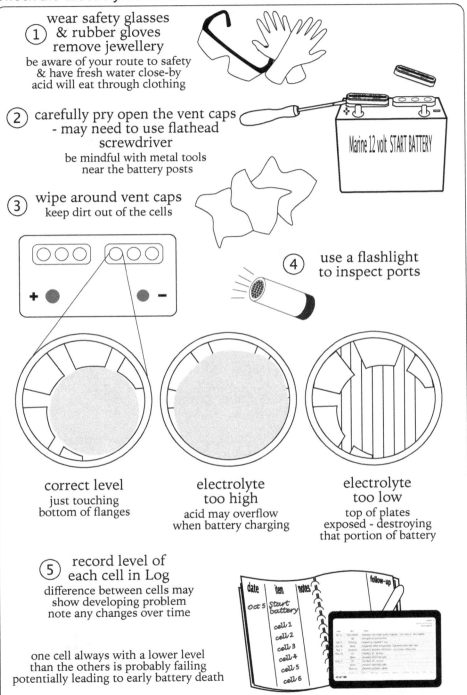

(1) wear safety glasses
& rubber gloves
remove jewellery
be aware of your route to safety
& have fresh water close-by
acid will eat through clothing

(2) carefully pry open the vent caps
- may need to use flathead
screwdriver
be mindful with metal tools
near the battery posts

Marine 12 volt START BATTERY

(3) wipe around vent caps
keep dirt out of the cells

(4) use a flashlight
to inspect ports

correct level
just touching
bottom of flanges

electrolyte
too high
acid may overflow
when battery charging

electrolyte
too low
top of plates
exposed - destroying
that portion of battery

(5) record level of
each cell in Log
difference between cells may
show developing problem
note any changes over time

date | item | notes
Oct 5 | Start battery
| cell 1
| cell 2
| cell 3
| cell 4
| cell 5
| cell 6

follow-up

one cell always with a lower level
than the others is probably failing
potentially leading to early battery death

6   Add Water to Unsealed Wet-Cell Battery

An unsealed wet-cell battery that is being trickle-charged will lose water through evaporation (the electrolyte heats up during charging). This water needs to be replaced, to ensure the plates are not exposed - which would effectively kill that part of the battery. Use distilled or low-mineral, boiled water.

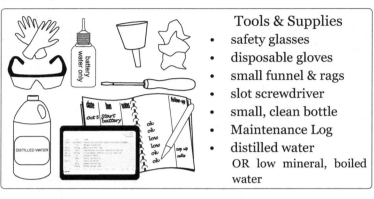

Tools & Supplies

- safety glasses
- disposable gloves
- small funnel & rags
- slot screwdriver
- small, clean bottle
- Maintenance Log
- distilled water
  OR low mineral, boiled water

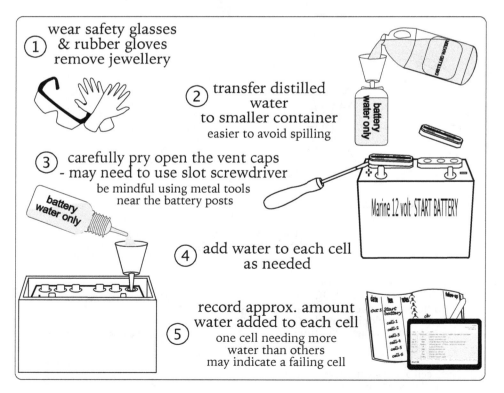

1. wear safety glasses & rubber gloves remove jewellery

2. transfer distilled water to smaller container
   easier to avoid spilling

3. carefully pry open the vent caps - may need to use slot screwdriver
   be mindful using metal tools near the battery posts

4. add water to each cell as needed

5. record approx. amount water added to each cell
   one cell needing more water than others may indicate a failing cell

7 Check Specific Gravity of a Wet-Cell Battery

Checking the specific gravity is an accurate way to verify the state of electrical charge of each cell of a battery and to identify any cell that may be failing. Unfortunately this cannot be done with sealed, "maintenance-free" batteries which can still be checked with a multimeter (open voltage test on page 84), or by load testing (page 92) or by viewing its colour indicator (if fitted).

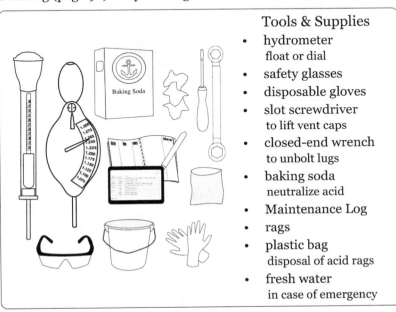

Tools & Supplies

- hydrometer
  float or dial
- safety glasses
- disposable gloves
- slot screwdriver
  to lift vent caps
- closed-end wrench
  to unbolt lugs
- baking soda
  neutralize acid
- Maintenance Log
- rags
- plastic bag
  disposal of acid rags
- fresh water
  in case of emergency

Sight glass colours of a sealed battery

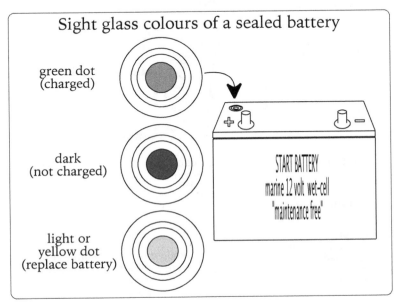

green dot
(charged)

dark
(not charged)

light or
yellow dot
(replace battery)

START BATTERY
marine 12 volt wet-cell
"maintenance free"

Check Specific Gravity of a Wet-Cell Battery

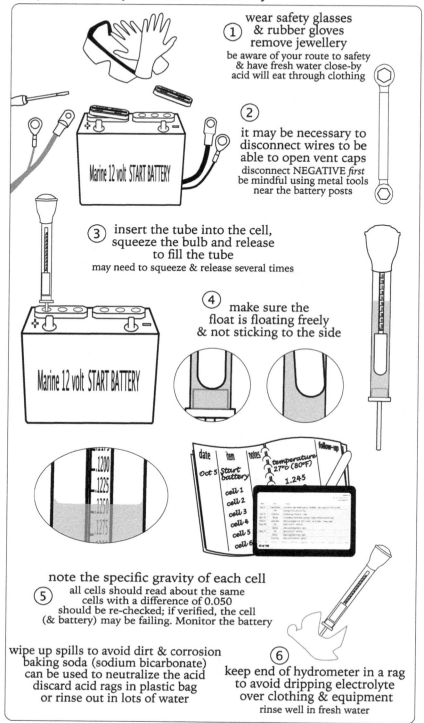

(1) wear safety glasses
& rubber gloves
remove jewellery
be aware of your route to safety
& have fresh water close-by
acid will eat through clothing

(2) it may be necessary to
disconnect wires to be
able to open vent caps
disconnect NEGATIVE *first*
be mindful using metal tools
near the battery posts

Marine 12 volt START BATTERY

(3) insert the tube into the cell,
squeeze the bulb and release
to fill the tube
may need to squeeze & release several times

(4) make sure the
float is floating freely
& not sticking to the side

Marine 12 volt START BATTERY

.1200
.1225
.1250
.1275

date | item | notes
Oct 5 | start battery | temperature 27°C (80°F)
1.245
cell 1
cell 2
cell 3
cell 4
cell 5
cell 6

follow-up

(5) note the specific gravity of each cell
all cells should read about the same
cells with a difference of 0.050
should be re-checked; if verified, the cell
(& battery) may be failing. Monitor the battery

wipe up spills to avoid dirt & corrosion
baking soda (sodium bicarbonate)
can be used to neutralize the acid
discard acid rags in plastic bag
or rinse out in lots of water

(6) keep end of hydrometer in a rag
to avoid dripping electrolyte
over clothing & equipment
rinse well in fresh water

Adjust Specific Gravity Readings for Temperature

A change in the temperature of electrolyte changes its specific gravity; however, readings only need to be corrected for temperature if the battery acid is significantly hotter or colder than 26°C (80°F) or greatly different than the last check-up recorded in the Maintenance Log (eg. early spring to mid summer).

	voltage V	4°C 40°F	10°C 50°F	15°C 60°F	21°C 70°F	27°C 80°F	32°C 90°F	38°C 100°F
100%	12.7	1.249	1.253	1.257	1.261	1.265	1.269	1.273
75%	12.4	1.209	1.213	1.217	1.221	1.225	1.229	1.233
50%	12.2	1.174	1.178	1.182	1.186	1.190	1.194	1.198
25%	12	1.139	1.143	1.147	1.151	1.155	1.159	1.163
0%	11.9	1.104	1.108	1.12	1.116	1.120	1.124	1.28

SOURCE: Trojan Batteries and calculations

8   Load Testing a 12 Volt Battery

A "fully charged" battery (open voltage testing 12.65 volts) may still lack the power to crank an engine if the battery is badly sulphated, (ie. much of the plates are covered by hardened lead sulphate crystals stopping the flow of sulphites from the lead antimony plates into the electrolyte). The simplest way to check the work capacity of a battery is to perform a load test - does the voltage remain stable when the work load is applied? See *Sulphation* on page 82.

A load test can also be done by attaching multimeter leads to the Start battery, then cranking the engine starter and watching the battery voltage on a multimeter – does the voltage decline slowly or quickly?

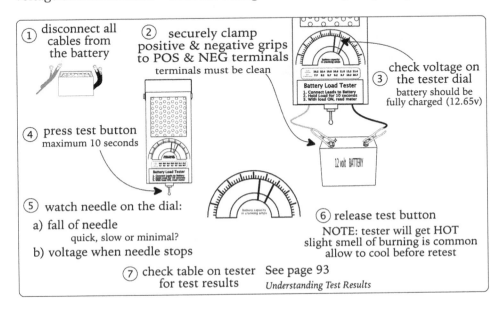

① disconnect all cables from the battery

② securely clamp positive & negative grips to POS & NEG terminals
terminals must be clean

③ check voltage on the tester dial
battery should be fully charged (12.65v)

Battery Load Tester

④ press test button
maximum 10 seconds

12 volt BATTERY

⑤ watch needle on the dial:
a) fall of needle
quick, slow or minimal?
b) voltage when needle stops

⑥ release test button
NOTE: tester will get HOT
slight smell of burning is common
allow to cool before retest

⑦ check table on tester for test results   See page 93
Understanding Test Results

Understanding Battery Load Test Results

voltage before test	above 12.50v	80 – 100 % charged
	12.10 – 12.50v	marginal – recharge
	below 12.10v	too low to test
fall of needle	fast	failing or undercharged
	slow	normal
	minimal	excellent condition
voltage where the needle stops	green zone	battery good
	weak zone	recharge & retest
	red zone	undercharged or failing

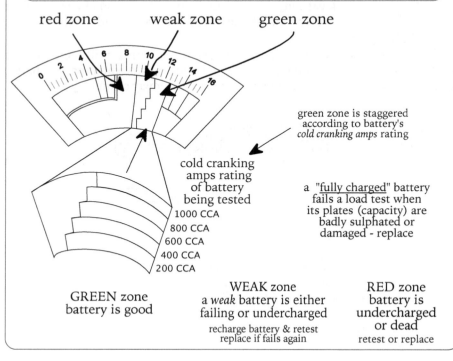

red zone   weak zone   green zone

green zone is staggered
according to battery's
cold cranking amps rating

cold cranking
amps rating
of battery
being tested

1000 CCA
800 CCA
600 CCA
400 CCA
200 CCA

a "fully charged" battery
fails a load test when
its plates (capacity) are
badly sulphated or
damaged - replace

GREEN zone
battery is good

WEAK zone
a *weak* battery is either
failing or undercharged
recharge battery & retest
replace if fails again

RED zone
battery is
undercharged
or dead
retest or replace

Cables or Wires, Cabling or Wiring?

The words *cable* and *wire* are often used interchangeably for electrical circuits on boats (and elsewhere); however, there are clear differences:

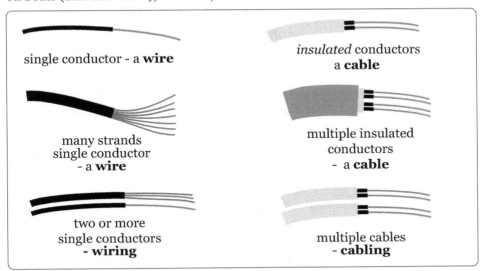

single conductor - a **wire**

insulated conductors
a **cable**

many strands
single conductor
- a **wire**

multiple insulated
conductors
- a **cable**

two or more
single conductors
- **wiring**

multiple cables
- **cabling**

Cautionary Tale

"Click" was the only sound when the ignition key was turned. A quick investigation with a multimeter showed, 1) terminals on the battery posts were tight, 2) battery was fully charged (12.6 volts), and 3) the positive cable at the Starter was also showing 12.58 volts. The engine cranked when the solenoid was by-passed. Initial diagnosis was a fault with the solenoid.

Next day the engine started as soon as the ignition key was turned; this seemed to confirm the diagnosis of an intermittent fault in the solenoid (most likely a corroded connection). A week later the same problem happened again but this time the Starter failed to turn even when the solenoid was by-passed. Second diagnosis was a "faulty Starter". A new Starter was ordered and installed.

No problems for a month, then exactly the same symptoms appeared again. In desperation in an isolated anchorage, the original Starter was re-installed and worked perfectly. When the lonely "click" happened yet again, the skipper decided not to leave harbour until the fault was identified and remedied for sure.

Working systematically, the intermittent fault was traced to a build-up of "varnish" on the inside of the terminal bolted to the negative post of the battery. Why was this intermittent break in the circuit not found on day one? Because when the voltage at the Starter was tested with the multimeter, the engine block was used as the ground, not the negative terminal on the battery, so there was no break in the circuit. All the terminal post connectors on all the boat's battery were replaced and the engine cranked reliably after that.

8   Maintenance – Drive Train
coupling - prop shaft - stern gland
stern-tube - cutlass bearing - propeller

Main Concerns

- vibration problems caused by neglect of the drive train & correct alignment
- boat floods due to lack of maintenance of hard-to-reach components

Task List

	Description	Frequency	Page
1	check coupling transmission/prop shaft	3 months	95
2	inspect propeller shaft	yearly	97
3	inspect stern gland (stuffing box)	3 months	98
4	inspect the strut	yearly	101
5	inspect cutlass bearing	yearly	102
6	inspect propeller shaft anode	6 months	103
7	scrape the propeller, strut & shaft	as needed	103
8	inspect the propeller	yearly	104
9	inspect propeller nuts are tight & cotter pin	yearly	104
10	inspect a folding propeller	yearly	105
11	inspect the anode on a feathering propeller	6 months	105
12	grease a feathering propeller	1 - 2 years	105

The frequency of tasks generally depends on engine hours, though tasks should not be ignored just because the engine is not being used, unless the vessel has been laid-up. See page 187 for all the Task Lists.

1   Check Coupling Between Transmission & Prop Shaft

The coupling connects the transmission's output flange to the propeller shaft, transferring the full torque (rotational energy) of the engine and taking the full thrust of the propeller moving the vessel through the water. Only strengthened bolts should be used to connect the coupling; ordinary bolts will stretch or break (shear).

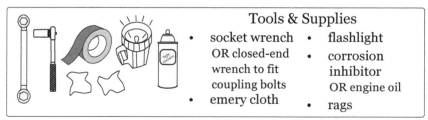

Tools & Supplies
- socket wrench OR closed-end wrench to fit coupling bolts
- emery cloth
- flashlight
- corrosion inhibitor OR engine oil
- rags

Inspect the Shaft Coupling and Bolts

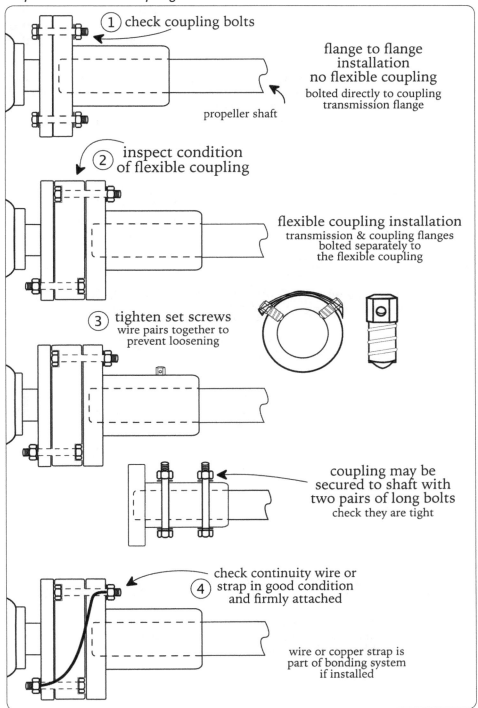

① check coupling bolts

**flange to flange
installation
no flexible coupling**
bolted directly to coupling
transmission flange

propeller shaft

② inspect condition
of flexible coupling

flexible coupling installation
transmission & coupling flanges
bolted separately to
the flexible coupling

③ **tighten set screws**
wire pairs together to
prevent loosening

**coupling may be
secured to shaft with
two pairs of long bolts**
check they are tight

④ check continuity wire or
strap in good condition
and firmly attached

wire or copper strap is
part of bonding system
if installed

2 Inspect the Propeller Shaft

A propeller shaft – of stainless steel or bronze – should give many years of trouble-free service, but is best not ignored. Inspect the shaft for any signs of wear – which are typically indications of other trouble, such as mis-alignment or that a worn-out stuffing box needs servicing.

Crevice corrosion can weaken a stainless steel shaft and often goes unnoticed unless specifically looked for. If crevice corrosion is suspected, unscrew and pull back the gland, packing, or stern gland bellows to get a good look at the condition of the shaft underneath. If there is evidence of corrosion under the coupling, the coupling will need to be removed for closer inspection.

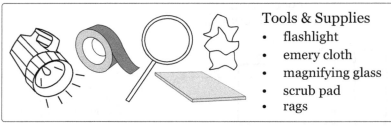

Tools & Supplies
- flashlight
- emery cloth
- magnifying glass
- scrub pad
- rags

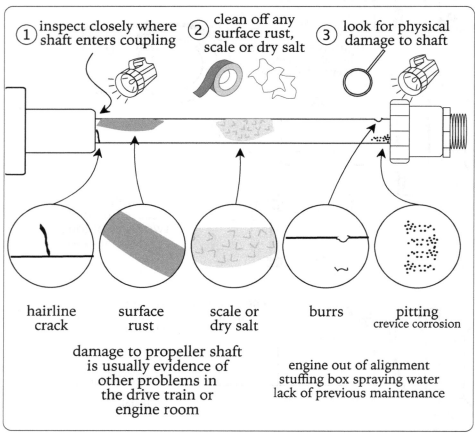

① inspect closely where shaft enters coupling

② clean off any surface rust, scale or dry salt

③ look for physical damage to shaft

hairline crack

surface rust

scale or dry salt

burrs

pitting
crevice corrosion

damage to propeller shaft is usually evidence of other problems in the drive train or engine room

engine out of alignment
stuffing box spraying water
lack of previous maintenance

3   Inspect the Stern Gland (Stuffing Box)

Failure of the shaft seal can allow *a lot* of water to flood into what, in many vessels, is one of the most difficult places to reach. Regular inspection and proper maintenance are important. No shaft seal – whether traditional stuffing box or dripless seal – can work trouble-free if the engine is out of alignment with the propeller shaft. Engine alignment is beyond the scope of this book; alignment is best done by an experienced marine mechanic.

A) traditional stuffing box   B) dripless shaft seal

A)   Inspect a Traditional Stuffing Box

A traditional stuffing box keeps out water by compressing square-shaped packing (often impregnated with teflon) between the packing gland and the propeller shaft. Over time, as the packing is worn down, the gland needs to be tightened to remain watertight. Any time the vessel is out of the water, the threads on the packing gland should be checked and packing replaced especially if only a few threads remain to allow the gland to be tightened.

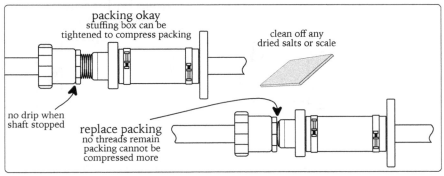

Importance of the Stuffing Box Hose

The hose holding the stuffing box to the stern tube is the most vulnerable part of the installation because it must withstand the twisting motion (torque) caused by friction between the propeller shaft and the packing. The best designs of traditional stuffing boxes incorporate "dogs" to reduce this force. Without them, a worn or low-quality hose is liable to eventually tear, allowing water to flood into the boat. Only use thick-walled hose.

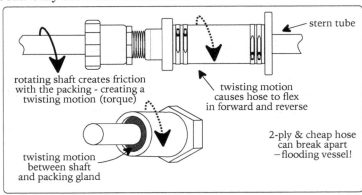

Inspect the Stuffing Box Hose and Hose Clamps

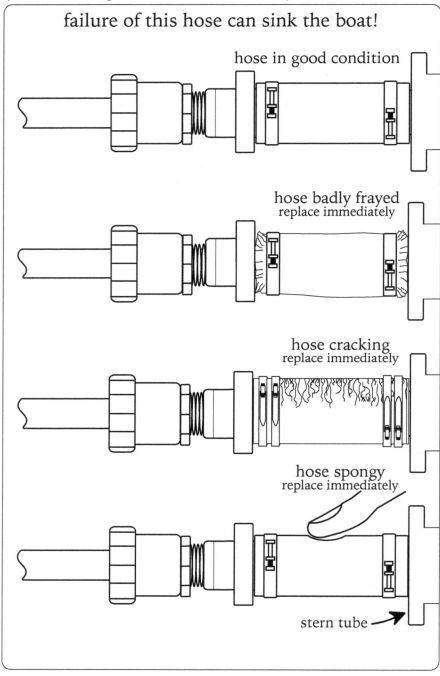

failure of this hose can sink the boat!

hose in good condition

hose badly frayed
replace immediately

hose cracking
replace immediately

hose spongy
replace immediately

stern tube

B) Inspect a Dripless Shaft Seal

The seal (face or lip), bellow and hose clamps should all be inspected closely at least twice per season. Failure of the bellows or hose clamps can sink the vessel!

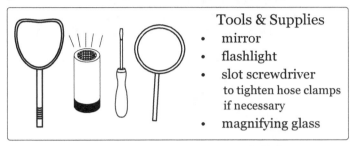

Tools & Supplies
- mirror
- flashlight
- slot screwdriver
  to tighten hose clamps
  if necessary
- magnifying glass

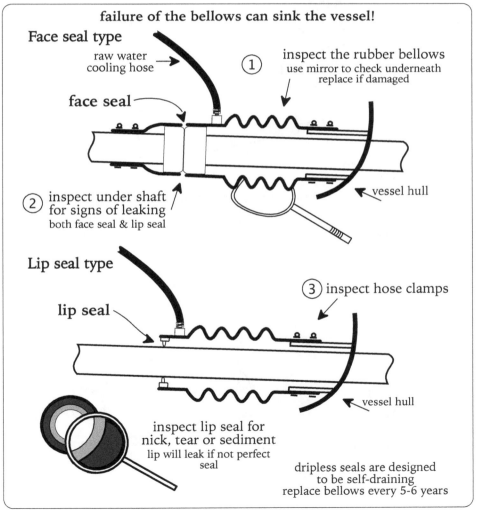

failure of the bellows can sink the vessel!

Face seal type

raw water cooling hose →

① inspect the rubber bellows
use mirror to check underneath
replace if damaged

face seal

② inspect under shaft for signs of leaking
both face seal & lip seal

vessel hull

Lip seal type

lip seal

③ inspect hose clamps

vessel hull

inspect lip seal for nick, tear or sediment
lip will leak if not perfect seal

dripless seals are designed to be self-draining
replace bellows every 5-6 years

4   Inspect the Strut

Damage, out of straightness or twisting in the strut can put the engine out of alignment, cause vibration, noises and rapid wear of the cutlass bearing. The strut should be inspected every time the vessel comes out of the water. Damage is unlikely, unless a rope or netting got wrapped around the propeller or the vessel collided with a rock or underwater object, but a simple check on the strut should not be neglected.

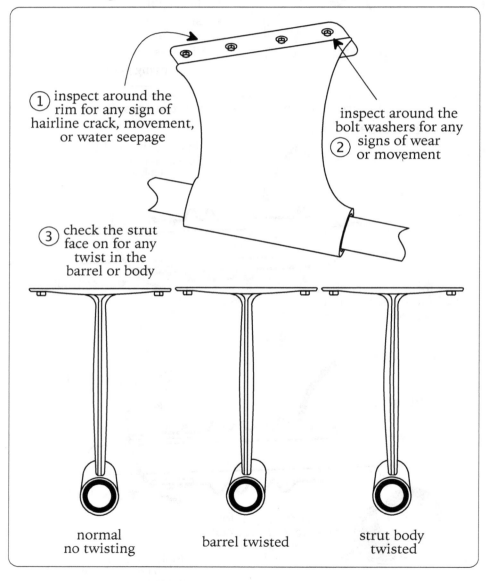

① inspect around the rim for any sign of hairline crack, movement, or water seepage

② inspect around the bolt washers for any signs of wear or movement

③ check the strut face on for any twist in the barrel or body

normal
no twisting

barrel twisted

strut body
twisted

5   Inspect the Cutlass Bearing

Some wear to the rubber in a cutlass bearing, over several years, is normal; however, noticeable deterioration from the previous inspection (as noted in the Maintenance Logbook!) should be investigated and the root cause identified and rectified before the cutlass bearing is replaced. Damage to a cutlass bearing is always a symptom - find the cause! If the cause is not found, vibration is only likely to increase, causing more damage to the drive train.

Cutless or Cutlass?

"Cutless" is a brand name trademarked by Duramax Marine. This rubber/Nitrile bearing "cut less" than previous designs of this type of bearing, which used lignum vitae, a type of wood. "Cutlass bearing" is now generally used a generic term to cover all makes of this type of bearing with a rubber/Nitrile insert.

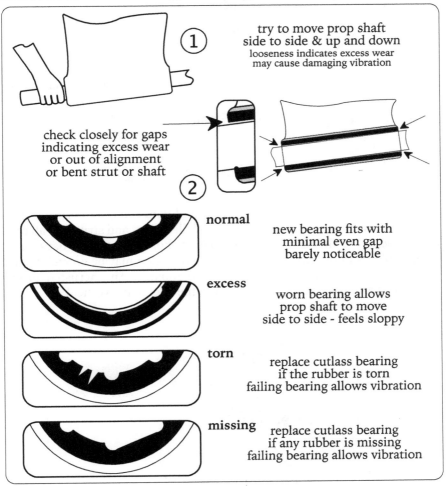

① try to move prop shaft side to side & up and down
looseness indicates excess wear may cause damaging vibration

check closely for gaps indicating excess wear or out of alignment or bent strut or shaft

②

normal
new bearing fits with minimal even gap barely noticeable

excess
worn bearing allows prop shaft to move side to side - feels sloppy

torn
replace cutlass bearing if the rubber is torn failing bearing allows vibration

missing
replace cutlass bearing if any rubber is missing failing bearing allows vibration

NOTE: Replacing the cutlass bearing is beyond the scope of this book, as it is best done with a specialist tool (if accessible) or the cutlass bearing may have to be cut out with a hacksaw if it is inaccessible inside the stern tube.

6 Inspect the Propeller Anode

Steel coupling bolts on a stainless shaft with a bronze propeller will be subject to galvanic corrosion if they are not protected by an active anode on the propeller shaft. To be effective, the anode must be electrically connected to the metals it is protecting - this can be verified using the continuity test on a multimeter.

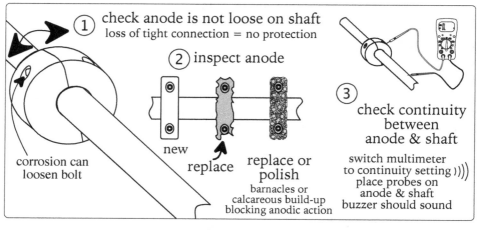

1. check anode is not loose on shaft
   loss of tight connection = no protection

2. inspect anode

new

replace

replace or polish

corrosion can loosen bolt

barnacles or calcareous build-up blocking anodic action

3. check continuity between anode & shaft

switch multimeter to continuity setting)))
place probes on anode & shaft
buzzer should sound

7 Clean the Propeller, Strut & Shaft

Tools & Supplies
- face mask
- metal scraper with lanyard

Barnacles, mussels and other marine fauna and flora can grow surprisingly fast, especially in warm sea water. Propeller, shaft and strut may all require scraping after a vessel has been at anchor for just 3 or 4 days. In some places in the tropics, two weeks' immersion may be enough to encase the propeller in a ball of marine zoology. An encrusted propeller looses almost all thrust and will likely cause the engine to overheat.

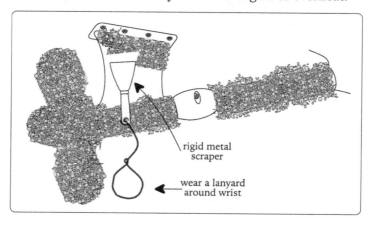

rigid metal scraper

wear a lanyard around wrist

8 Inspect the Propeller

Imperfections in the propeller create noise and vibration that can damage other parts of the drive train. The propeller should be looked at carefully every time the vessel comes out of the water. The blades should be smooth to the touch, and a uniform "bronze" colour (manganese bronze propellers). A change in the hue towards reddish "copper" may indicate the propeller is not being protected by an anode and has been losing zinc (dezincification). This structurally weakens the blades, which are likely to eventually break apart. A sound propeller hit with a rubber hammer will "ring"; compromised metal will give a short, dead "thud".

Dezincification is the loss of zinc from brass alloys. This is due to an electrochemical reaction between the zinc and surrounding water. Brass is an alloy of copper and zinc (proportions of each differ with different types of brass alloy). Pinkish colouring to the metal is a characteristic indication of loss of zinc. Loss of zinc leaves behind sponge-like copper which is easily broken. All brass in contact with water may be susceptible to dezincification, including the brass shell of a cutlass bearing, heat exchanger(s) (especially if the pencil anode is not renewed) and brass fittings used in place of bronze fittings in contact with water.

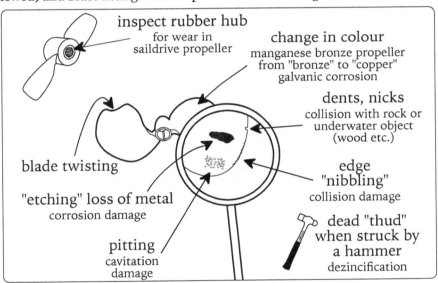

inspect rubber hub
for wear in
saildrive propeller

change in colour
manganese bronze propeller
from "bronze" to "copper"
galvanic corrosion

dents, nicks
collision with rock or
underwater object
(wood etc.)

blade twisting

edge
"nibbling"
collision damage

"etching" loss of metal
corrosion damage

dead "thud"
when struck by
a hammer
dezincification

pitting
cavitation
damage

9 Inspect the Propeller Nuts and Cotter Pin

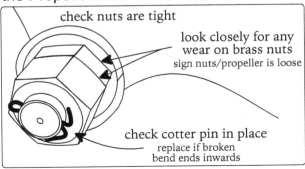

check nuts are tight

look closely for any
wear on brass nuts
sign nuts/propeller is loose

check cotter pin in place
replace if broken
bend ends inwards

10 Inspect a Folding Propeller

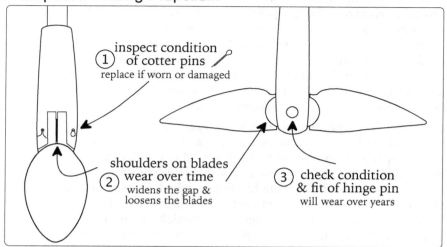

① inspect condition of cotter pins
replace if worn or damaged

② shoulders on blades wear over time
widens the gap & loosens the blades

③ check condition & fit of hinge pin
will wear over years

11 Inspect the Anode on a Feathering Propeller

A feathering prop consists of a several different metals and *must* be protected by its own anode.

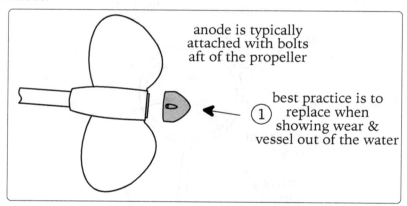

anode is typically attached with bolts aft of the propeller

① best practice is to replace when showing wear & vessel out of the water

12 Grease a Feathering Propeller

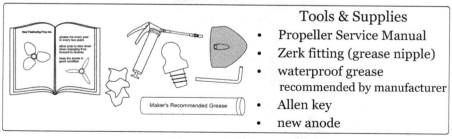

Maker's Recommended Grease

Tools & Supplies

- Propeller Service Manual
- Zerk fitting (grease nipple)
- waterproof grease
  recommended by manufacturer
- Allen key
- new anode

Grease a Feathering Propeller

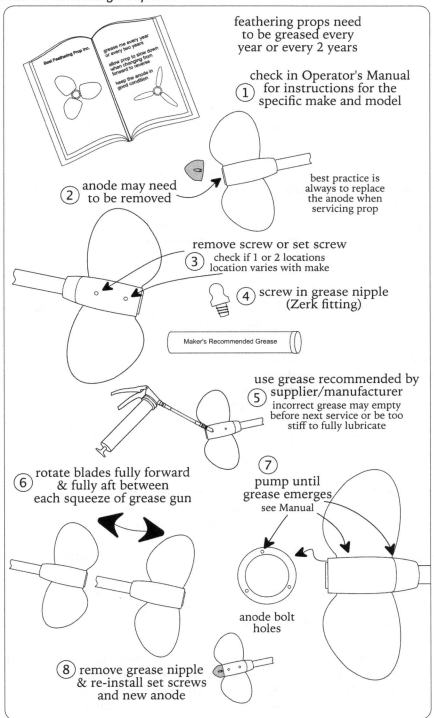

feathering props need
to be greased every
year or every 2 years

(1) check in Operator's Manual
for instructions for the
specific make and model

(2) anode may need
to be removed

best practice is
always to replace
the anode when
servicing prop

remove screw or set screw
(3) check if 1 or 2 locations
location varies with make

(4) screw in grease nipple
(Zerk fitting)

Maker's Recommended Grease

(5) use grease recommended by
supplier/manufacturer
incorrect grease may empty
before next service or be too
stiff to fully lubricate

(6) rotate blades fully forward
& fully aft between
each squeeze of grease gun

(7)
pump until
grease emerges
see Manual

anode bolt
holes

(8) remove grease nipple
& re-install set screws
and new anode

Cautionary Tale

Fall was arriving and the skipper knew that if he didn't leave now, he'd be delayed for another year before being able to sail down the river to the ocean, a 1000 miles away.

The diesel engine had never given any trouble in the two years the skipper had owned the boat but, as a precaution, he had a mechanic take a look. He made a thorough check of hoses, belts, wires, oil, coolant and ATF and after running the engine, gave two thumbs up. One problem he did find was a cracked engine mount bracket, but he took the piece away with him, welded the crack and re-installed the mount in the morning.

Passage down the river was steady but slow. The winds were fickle so he motored for more than 12 hours each day, eager to reach salt water before hauling out for the winter.

When the sailboat reached the top of the tidal reach, the skipper began to feel both ebb tide, speeding him downstream, and the flood tide slowing his progress to a crawl. One morning at anchor, the engine started straight away but when he put the vessel in gear nothing happened. He looked over the side and saw the propeller was not turning.

Quickly, he re-anchored and then went down below. What he found shocked him. The coupling and propeller shaft had fallen off the back of the transmission, three engine mounts had cracked and the engine was leaning on one side.

Next day, he sailed down on the end of the ebb tide to the town where mechanics at a yacht club he'd phoned were waiting for him. The tide was still running too fast to make the narrow entrance into the club's marina before being swept past, but as he approached, a large motor boat came out to tow the boat safely inside.

Repairs to the engine mounts took only two days and she was good to leave again. All went well as he steered for the upstream side of the exit. He could see the tide rushing ahead of him and increased rpm to control the boat as she emerged into the swirling water.

As he pushed the throttle forward, suddenly a tremendous banging noise started under his feet. He'd no idea what it could be. Already the boat was being carried sideways downstream by the tide. He had to get back into the marina, so he turned in the tightest loop the boat's full keel was capable of. All the time, the banging was continuing. He was sure he was going to lose propulsion at any moment.

As soon as the boat was inside the marina, he took the engine out of gear, letting the boat's speed and weight carry him towards the closest dock. Unfortunately, the boat did not turn fast enough and crashed into the dock, gouging a grove in the port topside.

Later that morning, the skipper offered to dive into the frigid water to check the cutlass bearing, but the mechanics said that was not necessary; they were sure the bearing was the source of the banging. As there was no travel-lift, he decided – after a gut-wrenching discussion – to attempt a traditional, but little-used, technique. He would take his boat into the bay next to the club at high tide, careen the boat on her full keel, supported with her beaching legs, then wait for the bay to dry out at low tide.

After careful preparations that took the remainder of the day, the manoeuvre was not difficult; though until the boat settled, the skipper was nervous his boat might settle on a rock and fall over.

The two mechanics arrived next morning as promised. The skipper did not have a spare cutlass bearing but the mechanics found one in their workshop that was the same size as the shaft but smaller than the stern tube. With careful hammering on a wooden block, they forced the new bearing inside the brass sleeve of the old bearing.

All the work was all done by lunchtime, and then only to wait for high tide to refloat the boat, celebrate a job well done and continue the passage to the ocean.

9 Saildrives – Maintenance, Lay-Up & Recommission

Main Concerns

* failure of a seal allowing water into the lower-unit damaging the gears
* failure of the rubber boot allowing water to flood the vessel
* scratches and paint damage on the lower-unit, leading to premature consumption of the anode, allowing corrosion damage to the saildrive unit and propeller

Task List

	Description	Frequency	Page
1	check saildrive gear oil level & top up	daily	109
2	change gear oil in lower unit	100 - 250 hrs*	109
3	burp air from gear oil dipstick		112
4	inspect exterior rubber fairing flange	yearly	113
5	inspect interior rubber sealing ring & water sensor alarm	yearly	114
6	inspect saildrive anodes	6 months	115
7	inspect and repair paint protection	monthly	116
8	clean raw water intake	monthly	116
9	inspect the propeller	yearly	104
10	grease a feathering propeller	yearly	105

*Saildrive gear oil should be changed more often than inline transmission fluid – generally 100 to 250 hours. Follow manufacturer's recommendation for the model. See page 187 for all the Task Lists.

Regular maintenance is essential as saildrives are less forgiving than in-line transmissions for any lack of attention. Best practice is to check the oil level before every engine start-up (along with the engine oil). This is more important with saildrives because, 1) gear oil can leak unseen from the lower saildrive unit. (An in-line gearbox can be checked for leaks by feeling around the casing and by inspecting the bilge), 2) the lower unit is immersed in water under pressure which can contaminate and damage a saildrive. Check in the manual whether engine oil or ATF should be used for lubrication (some specifications have changed).

Saildrive Oil Seals

If seals fail, corrosive raw water (salt or fresh) can enter under pressure into the lower unit, mix with the gear oil and cause extensive damage. Seals can only be checked with the vessel out of the water, so the saildrive's oil dipstick should be checked for signs of emulsification (oil mixing with water) regularly. Water mixed with oil looks "milky" or like "mayonnaise". Seals last 5 – 10 years depending on maintenance and service intensity. Changing seals is typically a dealer-only procedure.

1   Check Gear Oil Level & Top Up

Regularly checking the saildrive dipstick is very important for two reasons:

1.   keeping gear oil topped up as necessary
2.   early detection of any water infiltration and failure of the lower-unit seals

See *Dipstick Diagnostics Transmission Fluid* on page 41

2   Change the Saildrive Gear Oil

Changing the gear oil regularly is especially important because of the risk of water leaking into the lower unit and damaging the gears:

- change the oil at least every year (follow manufacturer's recommendation)
- follow the correct procedure for the specific make & model of saildrive
- check to use ATF or 15W-20 (some specifications have changed)
- inspect dipstick for signs of emulsification (oil mixing with water). See page 43
- saildrive oil is formulated to give some protection if water enters the gearcase
- seals will likely need replacing if water is mixed with oil (emulsified)

Follow the appropriate drawings:

A)   Vessel IN the water – Pump Out the Used Oil   page **110**
B)   Vessel IN the water – Pump In New Gear Oil   page **110**
C)   Vessel OUT of the water – Drain Old Used Oil   page **111**
D)   Vessel OUT of the water – Add New Gear Oil   page **112**

Record all work done and fluids changed in the Maintenance Logbook

A) *Vessel IN the water – Pump Out the Used Oil*

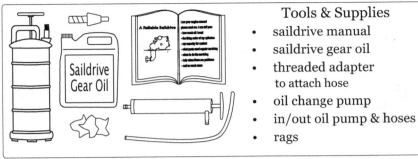

Tools & Supplies

- saildrive manual
- saildrive gear oil
- threaded adapter
  to attach hose
- oil change pump
- in/out oil pump & hoses
- rags

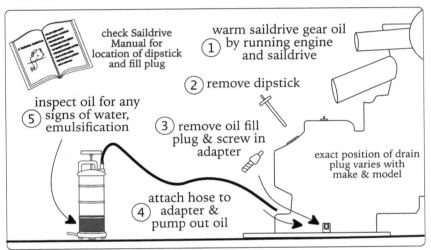

check Saildrive Manual for location of dipstick and fill plug

1. warm saildrive gear oil by running engine and saildrive

2. remove dipstick

5. inspect oil for any signs of water, emulsification

3. remove oil fill plug & screw in adapter

exact position of drain plug varies with make & model

4. attach hose to adapter & pump out oil

B) *Vessel IN the water – Pump In New Gear Oil*

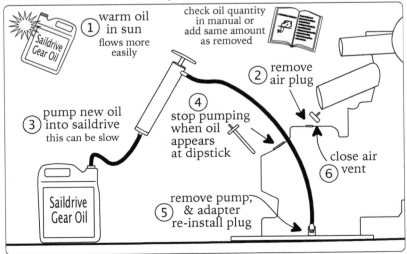

1. warm oil in sun
   flows more easily

check oil quantity in manual or add same amount as removed

2. remove air plug

3. pump new oil into saildrive
   this can be slow

4. stop pumping when oil appears at dipstick

5. remove pump, & adapter re-install plug

6. close air vent

C Vessel OUT of the water - Drain Old Used Oil

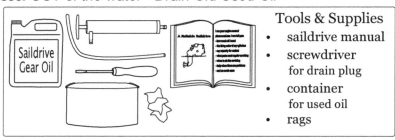

Tools & Supplies

- saildrive manual
- screwdriver
  for drain plug
- container
  for used oil
- rags

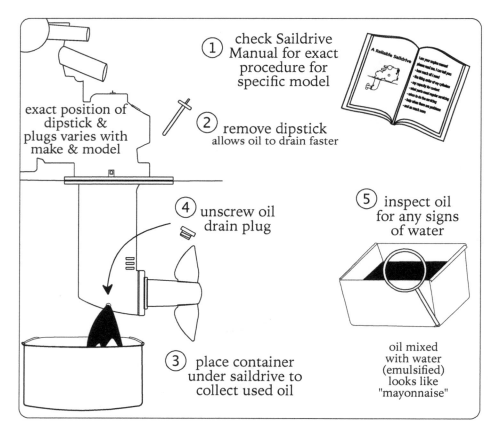

① check Saildrive Manual for exact procedure for specific model

exact position of dipstick & plugs varies with make & model

② remove dipstick
allows oil to drain faster

④ unscrew oil drain plug

⑤ inspect oil for any signs of water

③ place container under saildrive to collect used oil

oil mixed with water (emulsified) looks like "mayonnaise"

See *Dipstick Diagnostics - Transmission Fluid* on page 41

D) *Vessel OUT of the water – Add New Gear Oil*

Best practice is to pump fresh oil into the drain port at the bottom of the saildrive because this helps eliminate air pockets that can prevent lubrication.

If oil is poured into the saildrive from the top, wait 10 minutes with dipstick *out* to allow air to rise through the oil. "Burp" the air the first time the saildrive is run.

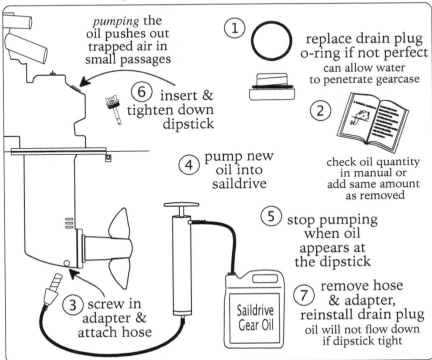

pumping the oil pushes out trapped air in small passages

① replace drain plug o-ring if not perfect
can allow water to penetrate gearcase

② check oil quantity in manual or add same amount as removed

⑥ insert & tighten down dipstick

④ pump new oil into saildrive

⑤ stop pumping when oil appears at the dipstick

③ screw in adapter & attach hose

Saildrive Gear Oil

⑦ remove hose & adapter, reinstall drain plug
oil will not flow down if dipstick tight

3   *Burp Air from Saildrive Gear Oil Dipstick*

With the vessel in the water - remove the dipstick the first time the saildrive is operated after a gear oil change to allow any trapped air to escape. Air can be trapped in the small passages of the lower unit (gear case). After engine shut down, check the level of gear oil and top up to maximum on the dipstick.

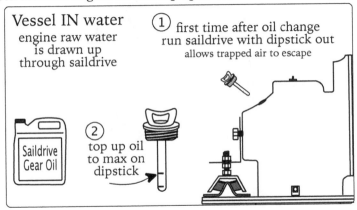

Vessel IN water
engine raw water is drawn up through saildrive

① first time after oil change run saildrive with dipstick out
allows trapped air to escape

② top up oil to max on dipstick

Saildrive Gear Oil

Watertight Seal (boot, bladder, foot sealing membrane)

A rubber double membrane (boot), between the upper and lower parts of a saildrive, prevents water entering the boat; however, failure can sink the vessel. Some models offer a built-in sensor & alarm (which requires a reliable electrical system). The boot should be replaced every 7 – 10 years. This is typically a dealer-only procedure. Failure to replace the boot may void a vessel's insurance.

In addition, a rectangular rubber fairing flange may be "glued" to the hull around the saildrive to reduce turbulence around the opening in the hull

- flange does not affect watertight seal (which is inside the hull of the boat)
- use removable adhesive (NOT permanent) to reattach flange if it detaches

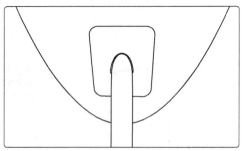

4   Inspect Exterior Rubber Fairing Flange

Though often referred to as a "seal", the primary purpose of the flange is to reduce turbulence. Turbulence will tend to tug and eventually pull the flange off the hull if a loose corner is not repaired.

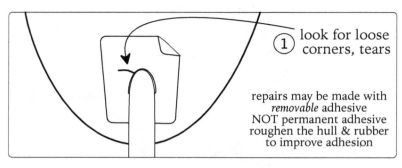

① look for loose corners, tears

repairs may be made with *removable* adhesive
NOT permanent adhesive
roughen the hull & rubber
to improve adhesion

5   Inspect Interior Rubber Sealing Ring & Water Sensor Alarm

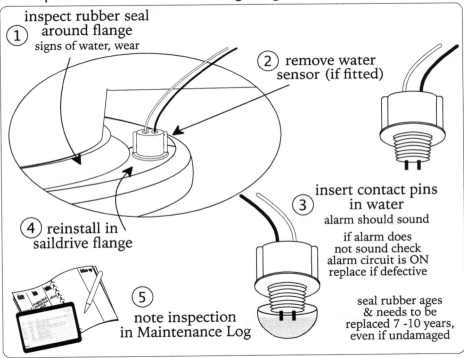

1 inspect rubber seal around flange
signs of water, wear

2 remove water sensor (if fitted)

3 insert contact pins in water
alarm should sound

if alarm does not sound check alarm circuit is ON replace if defective

4 reinstall in saildrive flange

5 note inspection in Maintenance Log

seal rubber ages & needs to be replaced 7 -10 years, even if undamaged

6   Inspect Saildrive Anodes

Saildrives can be quickly eaten away by corrosion because their aluminum casing is galvanically very active, much more active than a bronze thruhull or exposed steel keel. Aluminum has only a slightly greater electrical potential than materials typically used as anodes (including aluminum!) so protection is minimal. Any compromise in protection is likely to allow corrosion:

•   use the correct anode(s) for the vessel's location (salt or fresh water). Replace when 50% consumed

•   a saildrive may have three anodes – on upper unit (inside boat), lower unit/leg and on the propeller cone

•   do not assume anodes installed by dealer or previous owner are correct for the vessel in the current location or the current propeller

•   saildrive anode(s) are sized to protect *only* the saildrive and the original propeller; installing a feathering prop (with greater surface area) can increase the cathodic load on the anode – protection will need to be increased

•   paint coverage is part of a saildrive's anti-corrosion regime. Any scratches increase the area of metal to be protected by an anode. The anode will be consumed faster.

For more on anodes, see page 68, *Check and Change Heat Exchanger Anode(s)*

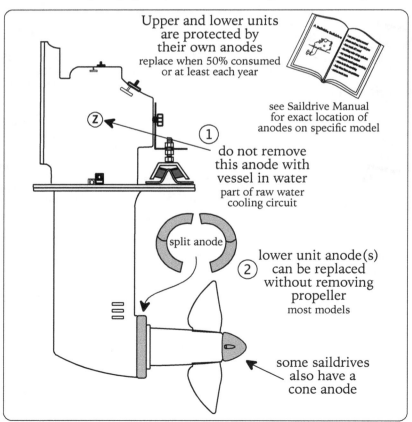

Upper and lower units
are protected by
their own anodes
replace when 50% consumed
or at least each year

see Saildrive Manual
for exact location of
anodes on specific model

Ⓩ

①

do not remove
this anode with
vessel in water
part of raw water
cooling circuit

split anode

② lower unit anode(s)
can be replaced
without removing
propeller
most models

some saildrives
also have a
cone anode

7   Inspect and Repair Paint Protection

Touch-up any damage or scratches immediately:

- use 2-part epoxy sealer/paint if original manufacturer's paint is not available
- underwater damage – touch up with two-part underwater epoxy paint
- use only an anti-foul paint formulated specifically for aluminum outboards, saildrives or sterndrives. Never use paint with (cuprous) copper oxide as this will promote galvanic corrosion
- keep the anode clean of marine growth and never paint an anode

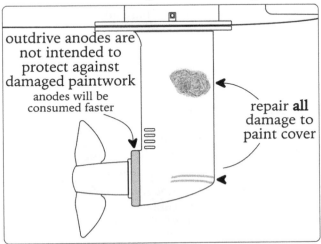

outdrive anodes are not intended to protect against damaged paintwork

anodes will be consumed faster

repair **all** damage to paint cover

8   Clean Raw Water Intakes

Engines with saildrives draw their raw water for engine cooling through intake ports in the saildrive's lower unit. Raw water is drawn up through a passage from the intake ports then should flow first to a sea strainer before reaching the raw water pump. Any marine growth or blockage of the inlet ports will decrease engine cooling capacity.

- regularly clean the inlet grilles on the lower unit

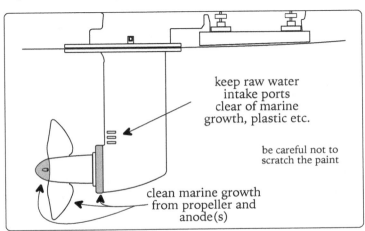

keep raw water intake ports clear of marine growth, plastic etc.

be careful not to scratch the paint

clean marine growth from propeller and anode(s)

9 Inspect the Propeller
See page 104, *Maintenance – Drive Train*

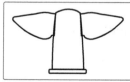

10 Grease a Feathering Propeller
See page 105, *Maintenance – Drive Train*

Saildrive Lay-up Task List

	Description	Page
1	change gear oil in lower unit	109
2	burp air from gear oil dipstick	112
3	inspect exterior rubber fairing flange	113
4	inspect interior rubber sealing ring & water sensor alarm	114
5	inspect saildrive anodes	115
6	inspect and repair paint protection	116
7	clean raw water intake	116
8	inspect the propeller	104
9	grease a feathering propeller	105
10	drain raw water from saildrive	117
11	protect lower unit from marine growth	118

1 – 9 Lay-up Tasks
Tasks 1 – 7 are fully explained on pages 109 – 116 of this chapter.
Tasks 8 & 9 are covered in the previous chapter, pages 104 and 105.

10 Drain Raw Water from Saildrive

In locations where there is a danger of cold weather, the raw water circuit must be either completely drained or protected against freezing by flushing with *propylene* glycol antifreeze. This includes the raw water passage in the saildrive.

When the vessel is out of the water, make sure all the raw water in the saildrive drains from the intake ports by opening the seacock in the saildrive's upper unit. To flush the raw water circuit in the engine, see page 129, *Lay-Up – Raw Water Cooling*.

Drain Raw Water from Saildrive (Out of Water)

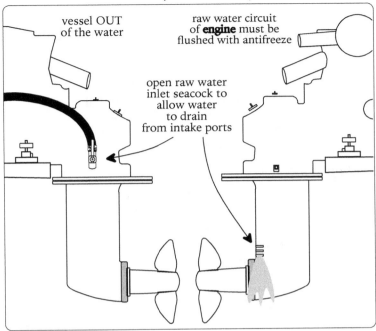

vessel OUT
of the water

raw water circuit
of **engine** must be
flushed with antifreeze

open raw water
inlet seacock to
allow water
to drain
from intake ports

11 (In Water) Protect Lower Unit from Marine Growth

Especially in tropical waters marine growth can quickly engulf an exposed surface not protected with anti-foul paint. The raw water intake and the seal forward of the propeller are particularly vulnerable to clogging.

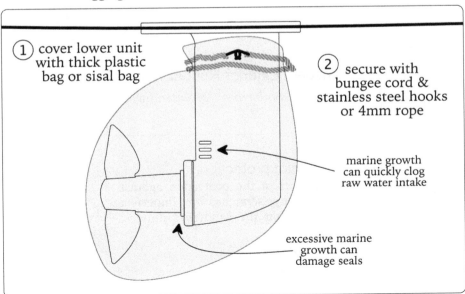

1 cover lower unit
with thick plastic
bag or sisal bag

2 secure with
bungee cord &
stainless steel hooks
or 4mm rope

marine growth
can quickly clog
raw water intake

excessive marine
growth can
damage seals

Saildrive Recommission Task List

	Description	Page
1	check level of gear oil	109
2	inspect interior rubber sealing ring & water sensor alarm	114
3	inspect exterior rubber fairing flange	113
4	inspect and repair paint protection	116

Vessel Laid-up in the Water

	Description	Page
5	remove covering from propeller & shaft	178
6	inspect saildrive anodes	115
7	inspect and repair paint protection	116
8	clean raw water intake	116

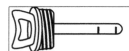

1   Check Level of Gear Oil

See page 109, *Saildrives – Maintenance*

2   Inspect Interior Rubber Sealing Ring & Water Sensor Alarm

See page 114, *Saildrives – Maintenance*

3   Inspect Exterior Rubber Fairing Flange

See page 113, *Saildrives – Maintenance*

4   Inspect and repair paint protection

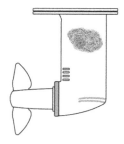

Paint is a very important part of the protection against corrosion on a saildrive. Any scratches or imperfect paintwork increases the load on the saildrive's anodes, which will be consumed faster.

See page 116, *Saildrives – Maintenance*

Vessel Laid-up in the Water

5   Remove Covering from Propeller and Shaft

If the vessel was laid up in the water, any plastic or sisal bag protecting the propeller and shaft from marine growth should be removed. It may be necessary to scrape off barnacles where the bag was tied.

Take care not to damage the paint.

See page 178, *Recommission – In Water*

6   Inspect Saildrive Anodes

If the vessel was laid-up in the water, the anodes should be checked and changed, if nearly 50% consumed. Saildrives are very susceptible to corrosion (because the lower unit is aluminum). Care should be taken to ensure the anodes are *always* in good order.

If the vessel is out of the water - anodes should have been checked before the lay-up. See page 115, *Saildrives – Maintenance*

7   Inspect and repair paint protection

Paint is an important part of the protection against corrosion on a saildrive. Any scratches or imperfect paintwork increases the load on a saildrive's anodes which will be consumed faster. Use 2-part underwater paint to repair damage, if the boat is in the water.

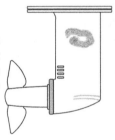

See page 116, *Saildrives – Maintenance*

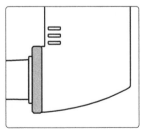

8   Clean Raw Water Intake

If the vessel was laid up in the water, the raw water intake ports should be cleaned as thoroughly as possible.

See page 116, *Saildrives – Maintenance*

Lay-Up – Winter Protection
& Tropical Storage

Main Concerns
- neglect in vessel lay-up leads to accelerated aging and future breakdowns
- small omissions or errors can have very expensive consequences
- thoroughness and good note-taking make recommissioning quicker and easier - saves time and money in the long run

Non-use of a marine diesel system can cause much more damage than regular hard use – damage ranging from thickened sludge plugging oil passages to complete destruction of the engine block and other system components.

The best way to avoid potentially serious and expensive damage is to properly de-commission all the systems in preparation for lay-up. This is essential where freezing is a possibility and in tropical conditions. Winter can destroy an unprotected engine by cracking the block. Humidity combined with heat will rust out unprotected steel. Time and effort invested in a comprehensive lay-up will protect the engine and components from damage and help slow aging.

NOTE: Lay-up and winterizing of potable water and sewage systems, safeguarding of electronics etc. are **not** covered in this book. This book covers only the diesel propulsion system. (However, some of the same considerations and precautions may be applied to laying-up other boat systems and equipment, eg. house batteries, windlass, pumps etc.).

10 Lay-Up – Engine Essentials

Main Concerns

- forgetting what was done or not done when laying up the vessel
- slowing processes of decay – rusting, deterioration of hoses and wires, growth of mildew, bad smells
- impregnation of bad odours etc. – hard to remove from upholstery etc.
- a slow leak can sink any boat

Task List

	Description	Page
1	change engine oil & filter	45
2	change transmission fluid	52
3	slacken tension on belts	123
4	clean the bilge	124
5	wipe down the engine	125
6	grease engine mounts	54
7	write up good notes in Maintenance Logbook	1

Most of the tasks to be done to lay-up a vessel should also be being completed as part of regular, ongoing maintenance to avoid future problems.
See page 187 for all the Lay-Up Task Lists.

1 Change Engine Oil & Filter

Cleaning out used oil contaminated with acids and carbon is essential before lay-up to protect internal metals from corrosion and the small passages from being blocked by sludge which will thicken during the lay-up period.

See page 45, *Maintenance – Lubrication*

2 Change Transmission Fluid

Additives in transmission fluid (or engine oil used in the transmission) wear out with use, especially if the gears have overheated perhaps with plastic or a rope caught, even temporally, around the propeller.

See page 52, *Maintenance – Lubrication*

3 Slacken Tension Off Belts

Tools & Supplies

- two pairs of wrenches to fit nuts and bolt heads OR socket wrenches

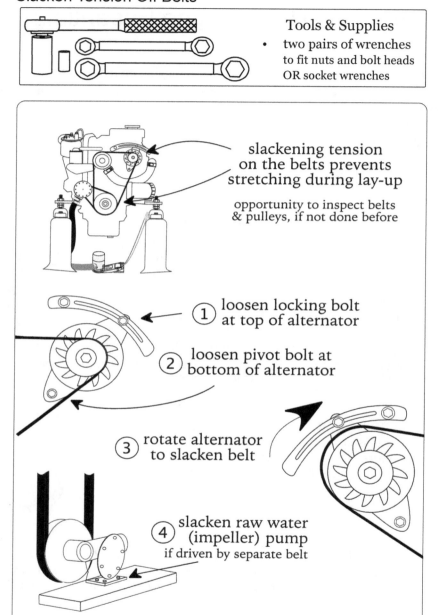

slackening tension on the belts prevents stretching during lay-up

opportunity to inspect belts & pulleys, if not done before

① loosen locking bolt at top of alternator

② loosen pivot bolt at bottom of alternator

③ rotate alternator to slacken belt

④ slacken raw water (impeller) pump if driven by separate belt

4   Clean the Bilge

Leaving water in the bilge raises the humidity in the engine compartment – accelerating rusting (oxidation), encouraging mildew, and providing a potential pathway for stray current if the bilge pump and float switch are left connected. Over time, oily, contaminated water creates a pungent "boat odour" which will permeate everything in the vessel – clothing, cushions, wood surfaces etc. and be very difficult to remove.

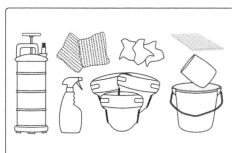

Tools & Supplies

- oil change pump
  or bucket and scoop
- degreaser
- diapers
- oil absorbent cloths
- rags
- scrub pad

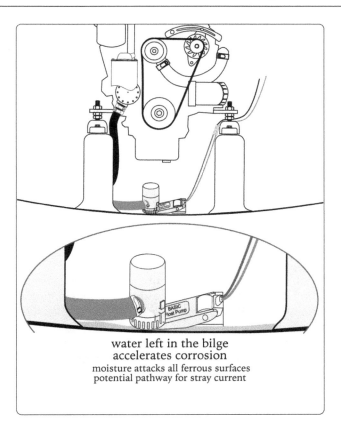

water left in the bilge
accelerates corrosion
moisture attacks all ferrous surfaces
potential pathway for stray current

5   Wipe Down the Engine

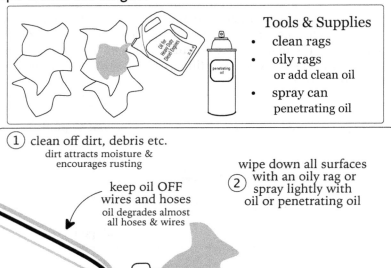

Tools & Supplies

- clean rags
- oily rags
  or add clean oil
- spray can
  penetrating oil

(1) clean off dirt, debris etc.
dirt attracts moisture &
encourages rusting

wipe down all surfaces
(2) with an oily rag or
spray lightly with
oil or penetrating oil

keep oil OFF
wires and hoses
oil degrades almost
all hoses & wires

no need to oil
non-ferrous components
eg. alternator, heat-exchanger

(3) oil threads of
engine mounts
if not greased

6   Grease Engine Mounts

Engine mounts are often overlooked and often fail to get the service that would
keep them in good condition. Rusted threads can make engine alignment very
difficult, if not impossible. Diesel, oil or grease on the rubber mounts will cause
hardening, decreasing their flexibility over time. Changing engine mounts can be
difficult, with the whole engine sometimes needing support; simple servicing can
avoid the time, cost and effort of premature replacement.

See page 54, *Maintenance – Lubrication*

7   Write Up Good Notes in Maintenance Logbook

See page 1, *Value of the Maintenance Log*

11 Lay-Up – Diesel Fuel

Main Concerns

- fuel leak inside the boat
- water infiltration into fuel tank(s)
- growth of HUM in the diesel. See page 20 for more information on HUM

Task List

	Description	Page
1	add biocide to last fuel fill	22
2	check the fuel deck cap is correctly and fully closed	21
3	change primary fuel filter	24
4	bleed engine	29
5	close all fuel valves	127
6	check fuel vent cannot back-flood water	127

Most of the tasks to lay-up a vessel should also be done as part of regular, ongoing maintenance to avoid future problems. See page 187 for all the Lay-Up Task Lists.

1 Add Biocide to Last Fuel Fill

See page 22, *Maintenance - Diesel Fuel*

Condensation and Filling the Fuel Tank(s)

The main reason to fill up the fuel tank(s) before laying-up a vessel is to ensure that the biocide and diesel are thoroughly mixed to prevent HUM growth. The amount of water that might condense from the air in a partially-filled diesel tank is minimal, except in very wet climates, such as the Pacific North-West and in monsoon rains, when humidity may be close to 100%. Do not plug an air vent, as a fuel tank must be able to breath as the temperature changes.

An alternative is to completely drain the fuel tank(s) and filters:

- no danger of a fuel leak
- no growth of HUM
- tank(s) can be refilled with fresh fuel when the vessel is recommissioned.

(Steel tanks are better kept full to avoid rusting (oxidation)

2 Check Deck Fill Fuel Cap is Closed

See page 21, *Maintenance – Diesel Fuel*

3 Change Primary Fuel Filter

See page 24, *Maintenance – Diesel Fuel*

4 Bleed Fuel System

See page 29, *Maintenance – Diesel Fuel*

5 Close All Fuel Valves – Supply & Return

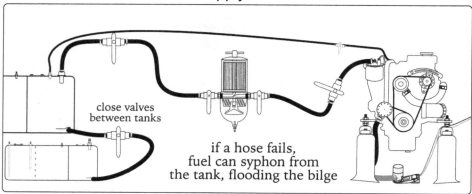

close valves
between tanks

if a hose fails,
fuel can syphon from
the tank, flooding the bilge

6 Check Fuel Vent Cannot Back Flood

Check that the fuel vent (often located on the
cabin trunk by the side deck) cannot back-flood
if the deck floods with rain water or when a
build-up of snow melts in sunshine. However,
do not plug the vent to prevent backflooding -
air in the tank needs to be able to expand and
contract with changes in temperature.

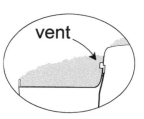

vent

12 Lay-Up – Lubrication

Main Concerns
- sludge and debris settling and hardening in small oil passages
- oil drains off bearing surfaces during lay-up, allowing metal surfaces to rust
- allowing acids in used oil to attack metal surfaces by failing to regularly change engine oil & filter

Task List

	Description	Page
1	change engine oil and filter	**45**
2	change transmission fluid	**52**
3	grease control cable ends & engine mount threads	**54**
4	lubricate ignition key slot	**55**
5	check injection pump & governor dipsticks (if fitted)	**55**
6	fill up transmission with ATF (or engine oil)	**128**

See page 187 for all the Lay-Up Task Lists.

1   Change Engine Oil & Filter
See page 45, *Maintenance – Lubrication*

2   Change Transmission Fluid
See page 52, *Maintenance – Lubrication*

3   Grease Control Cable Ends & Engine Mount Threads
See page 54, *Maintenance – Lubrication*

4   Lubricate Ignition Key Slot
See page 55, *Maintenance – Lubrication*

5   Check Injection Pump & Governor Dipsticks (if fitted)
See page 55, *Maintenance – Lubrication*

6   Fill the Transmission with ATF (or Engine Oil)
Some manufacturer's recommend filling the transmission/gearbox with ATF (or oil) during prolonged lay-up (more than 9 months). Check the Operator's Manual. If this is done, leave a clear note on the transmission and in the Maintenance Log to be certain the excess fluid is pump out before using the transmission again – overfilling can damage seals when the transmission heats up.

13 Lay-Up – Raw Water Cooling

Main Concerns

 water freezing and cracking engine block, destroying components and splitting hoses

 high humidity accelerating rusting (oxidation) of iron or steel components inside and outside the engine, coupling bolts, exhaust riser, engine mount studs and other components

Laying-up the Raw Water Cooling Circuit

Many of the tasks to lay-up the raw water circuit are the same whether for:

*   winter protection (winterizing)
*   tropical storage
*   lay-up in temperate climates
*   indirect cooled engine
*   direct cooled engine

Select one of the tables on next two pages (Indirect Cooled or Direct Cooled) and complete the tasks listed for either Winter Protection or Tropical Storage.

Vessels in temperate climates (with no risk of freezing, and without high temperatures or high humidity) are best laid-up for Tropical Storage. Damp, cold conditions can still accelerate rusting (oxidation).

Tasks, and the tools & supplies required, are set out in an easy-to-follow, logical work order. Not all tasks need to be done on all vessels – depends on the type of cooling system and the potential weather conditions throughout the period of lay-up. Be sure to protect the diesel system from more extreme weather than the "normal" conditions.

Most of the tasks to be done to lay-up a vessel should also be completed as part of a vessel's regular, ongoing maintenance to avoid future problems.

See page 187 for all the Lay-Up Task Lists.

Indirect Cooling Task List

These are the necessary tasks to lay-up a vessel using *indirect cooling* where there's a danger of freezing conditions or high heat and humidity. Follow the page references to tasks already detailed in earlier chapters.

For more about indirect cooling see page 58, *Maintenance – Raw Water Cooling*.

	Winter Protection	**Tropical Storage**	**Page**
1	check all hoses & replace if needed		7
2	--	--	
3	--	--	
4	--	--	
5	--	--	
6	--	--	
7	--	--	
8	add antifreeze to circuit	--	137
9	run engine & antifreeze through entire raw water circuit	--	137
10	drain antifreeze from hose to seacock (if not filled with antifreeze) vessel OUT of water - open seacock vessel IN water - close seacock	drain all raw water hoses vessel OUT of water - open seacock vessel IN water - close seacock	139
11	drain strainer (if not filled with antifreeze)	drain strainer	140
12	service raw water pump and impeller		63
13	--	drain heat exchanger	141
14	check heat exchanger anode		68
15	--	protect thruhull from marine growth	142
16	service exhaust riser		143
17	clean syphon break		69
18	drain water-lift (if not filled with antifreeze)	drain water-lift muffler	145

* #2 - #7 apply to Direct Cooled engines only, see next page *Direct Cooling Task List*

Direct Cooling Task List

Necessary tasks to lay-up a vessel using *direct cooling* where there's a danger of freezing conditions or high heat and humidity. Follow the number to the relevant task detailed on the pages listed below.

For more about direct cooling see page 59, *Maintenance – Raw Water Cooling*.

	Winter Protection	**Tropical Storage**	**Page**
1	inspect hoses & hose clamp		7
2	drain raw water from engine block	--	**132**
3	check & change engine anode		**133**
4	remove engine thermostat	--	
5	fill engine block with antifreeze	--	
6	re-install engine thermostat	--	
7	add antifreeze to header tank	--	
8	add antifreeze to circuit	--	
9	run engine to flush circuit	--	
10	drain raw water hoses (if not filled with antifreeze) vessel OUT of water - open seacock vessel IN water - close seacock	drain all raw water hoses vessel OUT of water - open seacock vessel IN water - close seacock	**139**
11	drain strainer (if not filled with antifreeze)	drain strainer	**140**
12	service raw water pump and impeller		**63**
13	--	--	
14	--	--	
15	--	protect thruhull from marine growth	**142**
16	service exhaust riser		**143**
17	clean syphon break		**69**
18	drain water-lift muffler (if not filled with antifreeze)	drain water-lift muffler	**145**

* #4- #9, #13, #14 Indirect Cooled engines only, see previous page *Indirect Cooling Task List*

1   Inspect Hoses and Hose Clamps
Indirect and Direct cooled engines – All Conditions

 No hose lasts for ever. Raw water and coolant hoses should be inspected now, if they have not been checked as part of regular, on-going maintenance.

See page 7, *Maintenance – Engine Essentials*

2 Drain Raw Water from the Engine Block

Direct Cooled Engines

Draining *all* the water from the engine block before running *propylene* glycol antifreeze through the cooling system is **essential** on direct cooled engines. Failure to do this will almost certainly lead to the engine block cracking in severe freezing conditions. This is because the thermostat will stay closed in the brief time the engine is running; antifreeze will not go inside the engine block.

Antifreeze (of whatever colour) being expelled from the exhaust does NOT show that antifreeze has circulated through the cooling passages *inside* the engine. The block must be drained of raw water, thermostat removed, and the block filled with propylene antifreeze.

Where there is no freezing, best practice is to drain the engine block and refill the with fresh water prior to lay-up. This is especially true in the tropics, where dissipation of engine heat is much less efficient than in colder climates. Draining and cleaning crud, scale and rust from cooling passages will promote more even cooling across the block during future engine use.

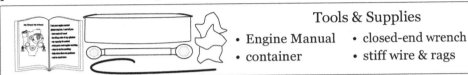

Tools & Supplies
- Engine Manual
- container
- closed-end wrench
- stiff wire & rags

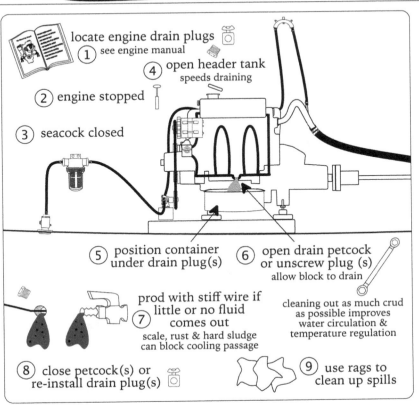

locate engine drain plugs
(1) see engine manual

(4) open header tank
speeds draining

(2) engine stopped

(3) seacock closed

(5) position container under drain plug(s)

(6) open drain petcock or unscrew plug (s)
allow block to drain

prod with stiff wire if little or no fluid comes out
(7)
scale, rust & hard sludge can block cooling passage

cleaning out as much crud as possible improves water circulation & temperature regulation

(8) close petcock(s) or re-install drain plug(s)

(9) use rags to clean up spills

3 Check and Change Engine Block Anode(s)
Indirect and Direct cooled engines - all conditions

The engine block of directly cooled motors are protected from galvanic corrosion by one or more anodes. Anodes are usually (but not always) located in the cylinder head or close to the top of the engine, allowing the anode to be changed without draining the whole engine block. Check the location of all anodes in the Engine Manual. Anode plugs may have been painted the same colour as the engine, though the plug is usually made of brass. It may be marked with a 'Z'.

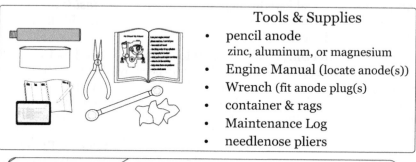

Tools & Supplies
- pencil anode
  zinc, aluminum, or magnesium
- Engine Manual (locate anode(s))
- Wrench (fit anode plug(s))
- container & rags
- Maintenance Log
- needlenose pliers

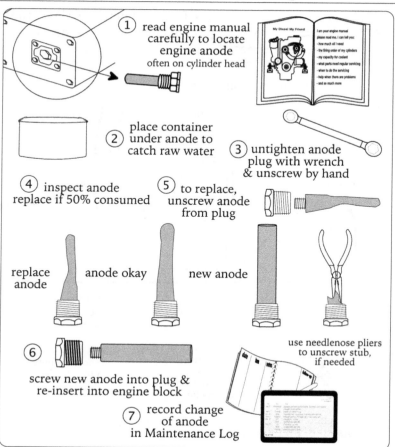

1. read engine manual carefully to locate engine anode
   often on cylinder head

2. place container under anode to catch raw water

3. untighten anode plug with wrench & unscrew by hand

4. inspect anode
   replace if 50% consumed

5. to replace, unscrew anode from plug

replace anode

anode okay

new anode

use needlenose pliers to unscrew stub, if needed

6. screw new anode into plug & re-insert into engine block

7. record change of anode in Maintenance Log

4   Remove the Engine Thermostat
Direct-cooled engines - Winter Protection

The engine thermostat needs to be removed in order to fill the lower part of the engine block with *propylene* glycol antifreeze; if the thermostat is not removed trapped raw water may freeze and damage the block. Merely pumping antifreeze through the raw water cooling hose is NOT enough to protect the engine block from freezing and cracking. This is because the raw water by-passes the block until the engine reaches its normal operating temperature and the thermostat opens. This can take several minutes, during which time it would be necessary to continue to supply many litres of antifreeze through the cooling system.

Have a new thermostat gasket available before removing the old gasket, as the old gasket may disintegrate when removed because of heat, compression and time.

Tools & Supplies

- thermostat gasket or o-ring if needed
- Engine Manual
- closed-end wrench
- rubber hammer
- utility knife
- Maintenance Log
- marker and rags

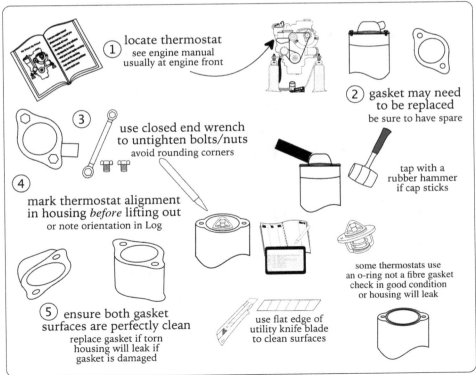

1 locate thermostat
   see engine manual
   usually at engine front

2 gasket may need to be replaced
   be sure to have spare

3 use closed end wrench to untighten bolts/nuts
   avoid rounding corners

   tap with a rubber hammer if cap sticks

4 mark thermostat alignment in housing *before* lifting out
   or note orientation in Log

   some thermostats use an o-ring not a fibre gasket check in good condition or housing will leak

5 ensure both gasket surfaces are perfectly clean
   replace gasket if torn housing will leak if gasket is damaged

   use flat edge of utility knife blade to clean surfaces

5 Fill the Block with Propylene Glycol Antifreeze
Direct-cooled engines

 If the raw water is drained from the block before lay-up for Tropical Storage (best practice to clean passages), the block should be refilled with clean fresh water to prevent rapid rusting (oxidation) inside the engine.

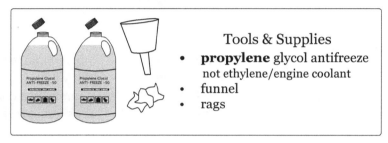

Tools & Supplies
- **propylene** glycol antifreeze
  not ethylene/engine coolant
- funnel
- rags

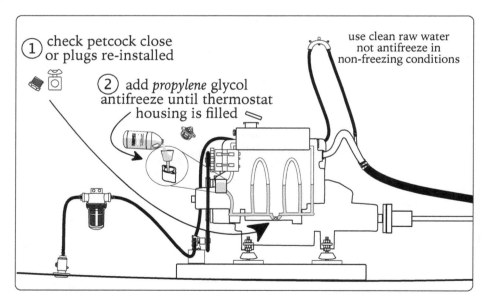

① check petcock close
or plugs re-installed

② add *propylene* glycol antifreeze until thermostat housing is filled

use clean raw water
not antifreeze in
non-freezing conditions

6 Re-install the Engine Thermostat
Direct Cooling - Winter Protection (& Tropical Storage)

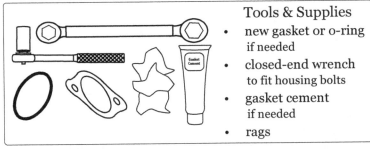

Tools & Supplies

- new gasket or o-ring
  if needed
- closed-end wrench
  to fit housing bolts
- gasket cement
  if needed
- rags

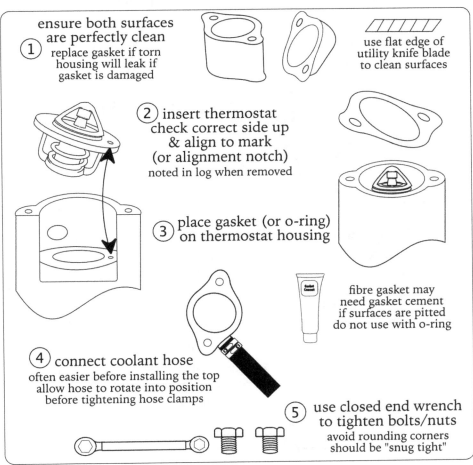

(1) ensure both surfaces
are perfectly clean
replace gasket if torn
housing will leak if
gasket is damaged

use flat edge of
utility knife blade
to clean surfaces

(2) insert thermostat
check correct side up
& align to mark
(or alignment notch)
noted in log when removed

(3) place gasket (or o-ring)
on thermostat housing

fibre gasket may
need gasket cement
if surfaces are pitted
do not use with o-ring

(4) connect coolant hose
often easier before installing the top
allow hose to rotate into position
before tightening hose clamps

(5) use closed end wrench
to tighten bolts/nuts
avoid rounding corners
should be "snug tight"

7   Add Propylene Glycol Antifreeze to Header Tank
Direct Cooling - Winter Protection

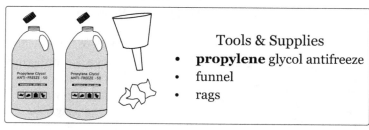

Tools & Supplies
* **propylene** glycol antifreeze
* funnel
* rags

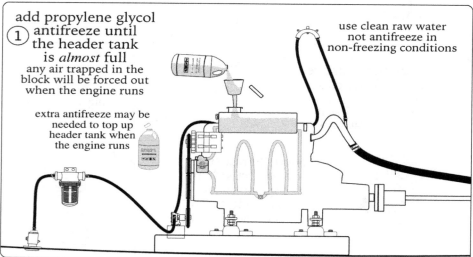

① add propylene glycol antifreeze until the header tank is *almost* full
any air trapped in the block will be forced out when the engine runs

extra antifreeze may be needed to top up header tank when the engine runs

use clean raw water not antifreeze in non-freezing conditions

8   Add Propylene Glycol Antifreeze to Raw Water Circuit
Indirect and Direct Cooling - Winter Protection

There are several ways to add propylene glycol to the raw water cooling circuit, depending on access and space in the engine compartment, access to the seacock etc. – use whichever method is easiest. On saildrives, disconnect the raw water intake hose on the upper unit. See page 117, *Saildrives – Lay-up.*

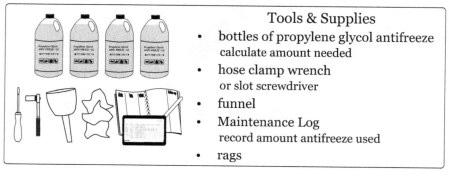

Tools & Supplies
* bottles of propylene glycol antifreeze
  calculate amount needed
* hose clamp wrench
  or slot screwdriver
* funnel
* Maintenance Log
  record amount antifreeze used
* rags

3 Ways to Add Propylene Glycol Antifreeze

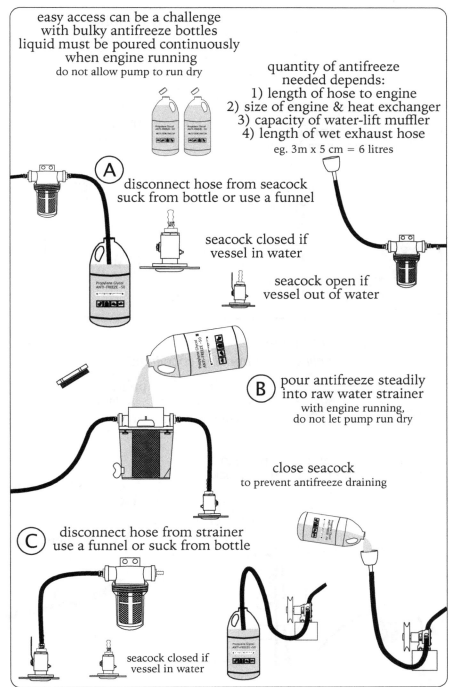

easy access can be a challenge
with bulky antifreeze bottles
liquid must be poured continuously
when engine running
do not allow pump to run dry

quantity of antifreeze
needed depends:
1) length of hose to engine
2) size of engine & heat exchanger
3) capacity of water-lift muffler
4) length of wet exhaust hose
eg. 3m x 5 cm = 6 litres

A disconnect hose from seacock
suck from bottle or use a funnel

seacock closed if
vessel in water

seacock open if
vessel out of water

B pour antifreeze steadily
into raw water strainer
with engine running,
do not let pump run dry

close seacock
to prevent antifreeze draining

C disconnect hose from strainer
use a funnel or suck from bottle

seacock closed if
vessel in water

9   Run Engine to Flush Raw Water Circuit
Indirect and Direct Cooling - Winter Protection

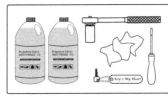

Tools & Supplies
- propylene glycol antifreeze
- hose clamp wrench or slot screwdriver
- ignition key (to start engine)
- rags

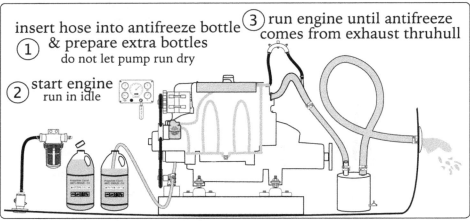

insert hose into antifreeze bottle & prepare extra bottles ③ run engine until antifreeze comes from exhaust thruhull
① do not let pump run dry

② start engine run in idle

10   Drain Raw Water Hoses
Direct and Indirect cooling - non-freezing conditions

Tools & Supplies
- bucket or container
- hose clamp wrench
- or slot screwdriver
- rags

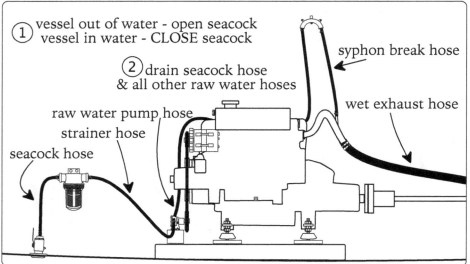

① vessel out of water - open seacock
vessel in water - CLOSE seacock

② drain seacock hose & all other raw water hoses

syphon break hose

wet exhaust hose

raw water pump hose
strainer hose
seacock hose

11 Drain the Raw Water Strainer

Indirect and Direct Cooling - Winter Protection

The strainer does not need to be drained **if** it is filled with propylene glycol antifreeze.

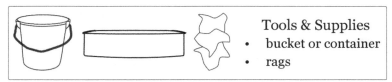

Tools & Supplies
- bucket or container
- rags

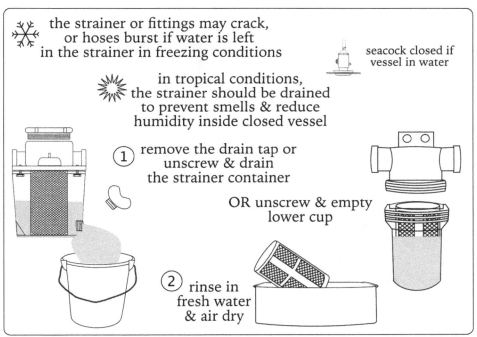

the strainer or fittings may crack, or hoses burst if water is left in the strainer in freezing conditions

seacock closed if vessel in water

in tropical conditions, the strainer should be drained to prevent smells & reduce humidity inside closed vessel

① remove the drain tap or unscrew & drain the strainer container

OR unscrew & empty lower cup

② rinse in fresh water & air dry

12 Service Raw Water Pump & Impeller

See page 63, *Maintenance – Raw Water Cooling*

A)	Inspect Weep Hole on Pump Housing	page **63**
B)	Service a Raw Water Pump Housing	page **64**
C)	Remove and Inspect a Rubber Impeller	page **65**
D)	Damage to a Rubber/Nitrile Impeller	page **65**
E)	Find Missing Impeller Pieces	page **67**

Seacock OPEN or CLOSED?

 In severe freezing conditions it is possible for the small amount of water inside a closed seacock to freeze and to crack the seacock. This risk has to be balanced against the risk of a failure of the hose etc. if the seacock is left open.

13   Drain the Heat Exchanger(s)
Indirect and Direct Cooling - all conditions

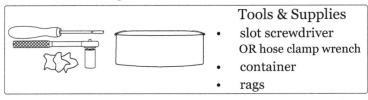

Tools & Supplies

• slot screwdriver
  OR hose clamp wrench
• container
• rags

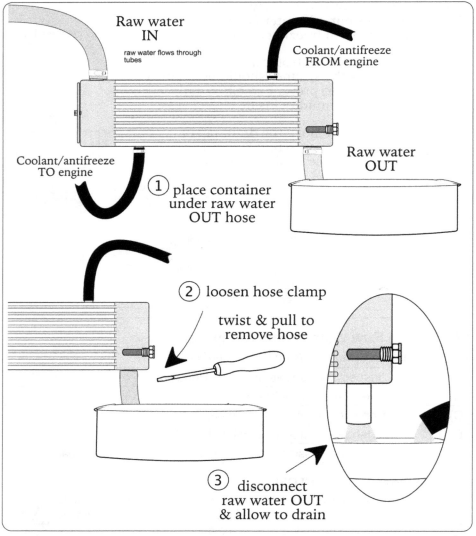

Raw water
IN

raw water flows through
tubes

Coolant/antifreeze
FROM engine

Coolant/antifreeze
TO engine

Raw water
OUT

① place container
under raw water
OUT hose

② loosen hose clamp

twist & pull to
remove hose

③ disconnect
raw water OUT
& allow to drain

14 Check Heat Exchanger Anode

See page 68, *Maintenance - Raw Water Cooling*

15 Protect Raw Water Thruhull from Marine Growth

Indirect and Direct cooling - Tropical Conditions

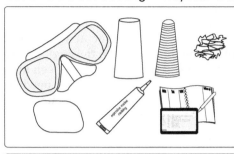

Tools & Supplies

- scuba goggles
- soft wood plug
  OR rubber cone
- tube of caulking
- thin plastic patch
  eg. cut from coolant bottle
- Maintenance Logbook

protecting the raw water inlet
from marine growth
barnacles, mussels, oysters
is important if the vessel
is to be laid-up in warm water

mussels, oysters can grow to full size
inside the thru-hull making extraction
difficult & time-consuming
especially under water

Two methods can be used
to protect the thru-hull

① insert soft wood plug or
rubber plug into thru-hull
a tightly crumbled plastic bag
can be used if necessary

do **not** force
could damage seacock
does not need to be watertight
aim is to fill the space

② cover the thru-hull
with a plastic patch

apply a narrow bead of underwater glue
or *non-permanent* marine sealant
this will be scrapped off when
the vessel is recommissioned

record action taken in the
Maintenance Logbook and leave
prominent notice on the chart table
or by engine ignition

16   Service the Exhaust Riser
Indirect and Direct cooling - all conditions

Even a partially blocked exhaust riser can make starting more difficult and cause an engine to overheat by slowing the flow of water. A rusted riser may fail at any time, releasing toxic gases inside the vessel. Best practice is to inspect and thoroughly clean the inside of the riser at least every two years. However, unbolting the riser from the engine's exhaust manifold can be a challenge if the riser has not been unbolted for a long time. A new exhaust gasket may be needed. If it cannot be unbolted fairly easily, the riser can still at least be partially inspected and cleaned by removing the raw water and wet exhaust hoses.

The exhaust riser is secured either by bolts threaded into the exhaust manifold, or with nuts on studs. Steel bolts and nuts on studs most usually can be removed with patience, careful work – use penetrating fluid, a closed-end wrench. A sharp blow to the wrench with a heavy hammer or by applying focused heat may also help free a frozen fastener. Just applying brute force on a frozen bolt or nut will likely cause the bolt or stud to twist and break off; the stud would then have to be drilled out!

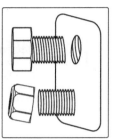

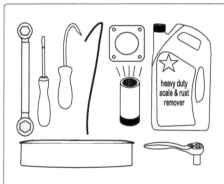

Tools & Supplies
- slot screwdriver
- pry tool
- container
- closed-end wrench
- hose clamp wrench
- stiff wire
- scraper blade
- exhaust gasket
  if riser unbolted

Service the Exhaust Riser

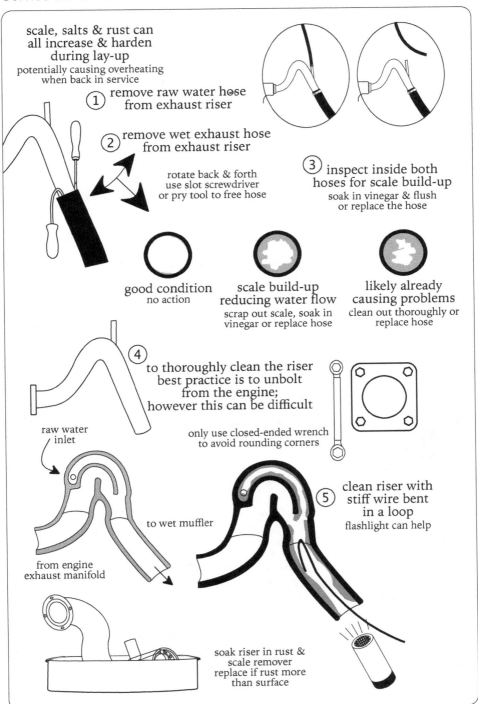

scale, salts & rust can
all increase & harden
during lay-up
potentially causing overheating
when back in service

(1) remove raw water hose
from exhaust riser

(2) remove wet exhaust hose
from exhaust riser

rotate back & forth
use slot screwdriver
or pry tool to free hose

(3) inspect inside both
hoses for scale build-up
soak in vinegar & flush
or replace the hose

good condition
no action

scale build-up
reducing water flow
scrap out scale, soak in
vinegar or replace hose

likely already
causing problems
clean out thoroughly or
replace hose

(4) to thoroughly clean the riser
best practice is to unbolt
from the engine;
however this can be difficult

only use closed-ended wrench
to avoid rounding corners

raw water
inlet

to wet muffler

from engine
exhaust manifold

(5) clean riser with
stiff wire bent
in a loop
flashlight can help

soak riser in rust &
scale remover
replace if rust more
than surface

17 Clean the Raw Water Syphon Break

See page 69, *Maintenance – Raw Water Cooling*

18 Drain the Water-Lift Muffler

Indirect and Direct cooling - all conditions

Especially in hot conditions, water left inside the water-lift muffler acts as a reservoir to accelerate rusting (oxidation) inside the engine's exhaust manifold. Best practice is always to drain the muffler. In freezing conditions, the muffler may crack if *any* water is left inside; drain and add a cup of antifreeze.

Tools & Supplies
- hose clamp wrench OR slot screwdriver
- rags

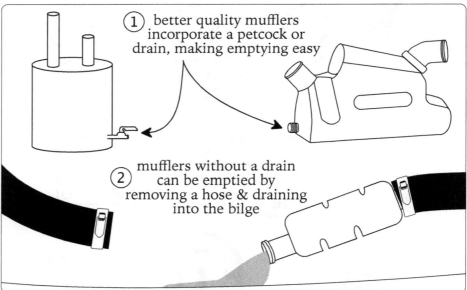

(1) better quality mufflers incorporate a petcock or drain, making emptying easy

(2) mufflers without a drain can be emptied by removing a hose & draining into the bilge

Cautionary Tale

The exhaust was unusual for a small sailboat. Instead of the engine's hot exhaust gases mixing with raw water inside a riser, then flowing down to a water-lift muffler before being expelled from the vessel, this boat was installed with a North Sea exhaust.

Hot exhaust went *up* into a large stainless steel canister suspended from the roof of the engine room. Raw water entered at the top, mixed and cooled the gases before flowing *down* into a stainless steel pipe draining on both sides of the vessel.

Advantages of the system were that the raw water drained from the canister and flooding the engine. And, because the exhaust pipe exited both sides of the vessel, there was less danger of a following sea pushing water up into the engine. The system worked so well the skipper rarely gave it any thought.

When the time came to lay up the boat for winter, he drained the raw water hoses, removed the impeller, changed the anode in the heat exchanger, poured a little antifreeze into the raw water strainer – and the raw water winterizing was done.

When he returned to the boat after the particularly cold winter, he re-installed the impeller, checked the engine oil, charged the battery, completed the other recommissioning tasks and thought that he was good to go.

The boat was launched; the engine fired up as soon as he turned the key and plenty of raw water spilled from the exhaust thruhulls on both sides of the vessel.

Not until he peered into the engine compartment later did he notice some water in the bilge. His body stiffened. Where was the salt water coming from? He quickly checked all the seacocks but they were dry. He stood still for a moment to listen. Not a sound, except the lapping of waves against the side of the boat.

He shone a flashlight into the bilge at the back of the engine, hoping to see if the stern gland was leaking without having to climb down into the confined space.

As light from the flashlight moved across the engine, he noticed drops of water on top of the engine. He had no idea how they could have gotten there, so he wiped down the engine, then turned on the bilge pump to clear the water from the bilge.

Two days later, he had to move the boat to the crane dock to take on the boat's mast. All went well, but he was puzzled to again find water in the bilge and water on the top of the engine. He started the engine at the dock and opened up the compartment to take a look.

Water was pouring from the big stainless exhaust canister down onto the top of the engine. No big deal, he thought, just a hose clamp needs tightening. He tightened all the hose clamps on the exhaust and wiped down the water. But when he ran the engine again, water still dripping down.

So he disconnected the canister and carried it out of the boat onto the dock. He poured in water at the top. Sure enough, some of it leaked around the rim at the bottom.

Nothing to do, he thought, but send it to be re-welded. But how did that happen? The most likely explanation, he decided, was that a little water, left in the canister when it had drained the last time before winter lay-up, had filled small dips in the bead of welding around the bottom of the inside. And that when the water which had frozen over the winter the pressure had been enough to crack the canister!

The canister was repaired and re-installed, leaving the skipper with a $125 welder's bill – the real cost of the splash of antifreeze he'd failed to put in the canister before winter.

14 Lay-Up – Coolant/Antifreeze

Main Concerns

- coolant/antifreeze too weak or too strong to provide adequate frost protection
- mixing different types of coolant causing deposits to precipitate and sludge to form, inhibiting cooling and reducing anti-corrosion effectiveness

Task List

	Description	Page
1	check coolant level in header tank or overflow bottle	6
2	drain and replace coolant/antifreeze	74
3	test frost protection of coolant/antifreeze	147

Most of the tasks to be done to lay-up a vessel should also be being completed as part of regular, ongoing maintenance to avoid future problems.

See page 187 for all the Lay-Up Task Lists.

1 Check Coolant Level in Header Tank or Overflow Bottle

See page 6, *Maintenance – Coolant/Antifreeze*

2 Drain and Replace Coolant/Antifreeze

See page 74, *Maintenance – Coolant/Antifreeze*

3 Test Frost Protection of Coolant/Antifreeze

The lowest winter temperatures are often unpredictable, even in regions where cold winters are the norm; so it's prudent to verify that the engine is properly protected against the lowest possible freezing conditions. This can be done easily using an *ethylene glycol* coolant hydrometer. Coolant/antifreeze that freezes can crack the block and destroy the engine.

CAUTION: Stronger is not necessarily better when it comes to ethylene glycol coolant/antifreeze. Using 100% coolant provides significantly less protection than a mix of 50/50 or 70 coolant/30 water). See graph on the next page.

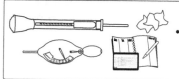

Tools & Supplies

- coolant hydrometer not same as battery hydrometer
- Maintenance Log
- Rags

Freezing Point of Ethylene Glycol Coolant/Antifreeze

Stronger is not necessarily better when it comes to mixing coolant/antifreeze with water. Above a 60/40 mix, the antifreeze freezes at a higher temperature – at just -10°C (14°F) with 100% coolant concentration. Always premix water and coolant/antifreeze before adding to the header tank to ensure complete mixing.

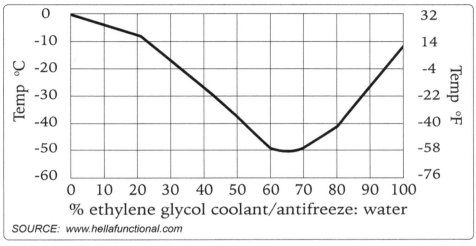

SOURCE: www.hellafunctional.com

Testing Coolant/Antifreeze with Hydrometer

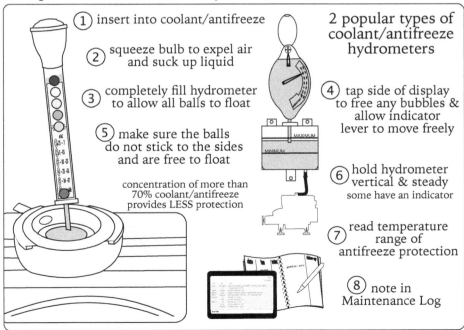

1. insert into coolant/antifreeze

2. squeeze bulb to expel air and suck up liquid

3. completely fill hydrometer to allow all balls to float

5. make sure the balls do not stick to the sides and are free to float

concentration of more than 70% coolant/antifreeze provides LESS protection

2 popular types of coolant/antifreeze hydrometers

4. tap side of display to free any bubbles & allow indicator lever to move freely

6. hold hydrometer vertical & steady
   some have an indicator

7. read temperature range of antifreeze protection

8. note in Maintenance Log

15 Lay-Up – Breathing

Main Concerns

- high humidity accelerating rusting (oxidation) inside the engine
- high humidity accelerating rusting and mildew growth inside engine room
- rain water (or snow melt water) flooding engine room during lay-up
- animals entering engine room via ventilation routes to hibernate or eat wiring insulation

Task List

	Description	Page
1	clean air filter/air intake	78
2	seal air intake with plastic	149
3	disconnect exhaust hose from exhaust manifold	144
4	drain water-lift muffler	145
6	prevent rodents entering exhaust thruhull	151

Most of the tasks to be done to lay-up a vessel should also be being completed as part of regular, ongoing maintenance to avoid future problems.
See page 187 for all the Lay-Up Task Lists.

1   Clean Air Filter/Air Intake

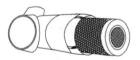

See page 78, *Maintenance – Breathing*

2   Seal Air Intake with Plastic

 Keeping humidity out of the engine is especially important in hot or hot and humid climates in order to keep rusting (oxidation) of the cast iron components and steel block to the minimum.

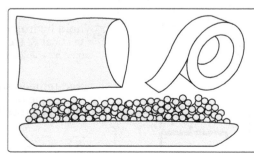

Tools & Supplies
- large plastic bag
  garbage bag
- sticking tape
- silica gel beads
  OR cat litter

Keep Humidity Out of the Air Intake

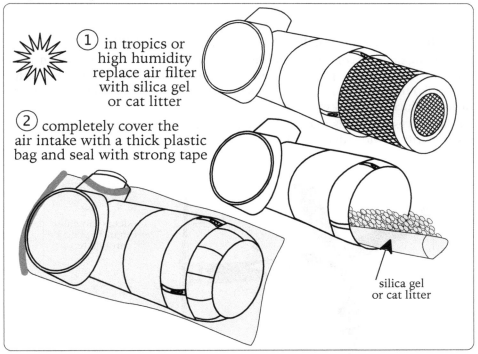

(1) in tropics or
high humidity
replace air filter
with silica gel
or cat litter

(2) completely cover the
air intake with a thick plastic
bag and seal with strong tape

silica gel
or cat litter

3   Disconnect Exhaust Riser & Hose from Exhaust Manifold

Best practice is to disconnect the exhaust riser from the engine's exhaust manifold, in order to prevent rusting caused by water vapour from the water-lift muffler and exhaust thruhull. This is especially important in hot and humid environments.

See page 144, *Maintenance – Breathing*

4   Drain Water-Lift Muffler

Drain the muffler to keep humidity out of the engine's exhaust manifold, especially if the exhaust riser is not disconnected.

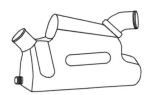

See page 145, *Maintenance – Breathing*

5   Prevent Rodents Entering via Exhaust Thruhull

Depending on local conditions and the length of time a vessel is to be laid-up, it may be necessary to plug up the exhaust thruhull (and the vessel's other thruhulls) to prevent rodents, such as muskrats, rats etc., gaining access to the hoses – which they may eat!

On larger vessels, birds may build their nest and rear young inside the shelter and security of wider diameter hoses.

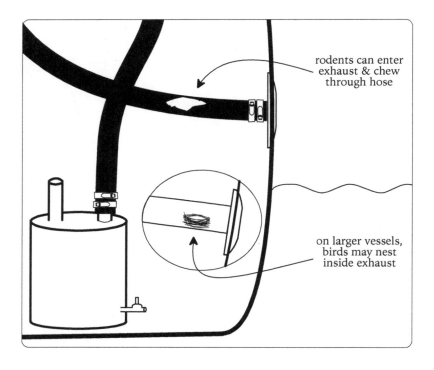

rodents can enter exhaust & chew through hose

on larger vessels, birds may nest inside exhaust

16 Lay-up – Electrical

Main Concerns
- batteries self discharge over time allowing sulphation to harden
- hard sulphation leading to early battery death
- freezing causing battery death

Task List

	Description	Page
1	clean battery top and terminals	85
2	check electrolyte levels	87
3	add distilled water to unsealed wet-cell battery	89
4	charge battery	83
5	load test questionable battery	92
6	trickle charge battery(s)	154
7	disconnect terminals from battery	154

Most of the tasks to be done to lay-up a vessel should also be being completed as part of regular, ongoing maintenance. See page 187 for all the Lay-Up Task Lists.

Battery Self Discharge
All batteries loose their electrical energy over time, even if no load is connected. The warmer the temperature, the quicker this process of self-discharge takes place. And, as the voltage falls, the battery becomes more susceptible to sulphation and to freezing (in winter conditions). It's therefore important to:
- service and fully charge batteries before putting them into storage
- if possible, start a trickle charge to keep the batteries fully charged over time

Self-Discharge of Lead Acid Battery from Fully Charged

Percent of Remaining Charge (% discharged)									
Temperature		4 weeks		8 weeks		3 months		4 months	
5°C	41°F	95%	(5%)	91%	(9%)	86%	(14%)	82%	(18%)
25°C	77°F	87%	(13%)	73%	(27%)	60%	(40%)	41%	(59%)
30°C	86°F	77%	(23%)	57%	(43%)	35%	(65%)	14%	(86%)

SOURCE: Trojan Battery Company and calculations

In tropical climates, the temperature inside the engine room can rapidly rise above 40°C (104°F) if the cockpit (typically the roof of the engine room) is exposed to direct sunshine — accelerating self-discharge causing lead sulphates on the plates to harden, effectively killing the battery. Best practice is to trickle charge batteries or to re-locate them to the coolest, driest place on or off the vessel. Batteries that are not trickle-charged will self-discharge to 0 volts. See *Sulphation*, page 82.

Lead Acid Battery Freezing

A fully-charged lead acid battery in top condition should not freeze until the temperature reaches -68°C (-92°F). However, a battery only 50% charged will freeze at just -10°C (+14°F). Freezing effectively kills a battery - acid is forced out of the casing, which may crack and internal damage cause a short-circuit. A battery that has been frozen must be replaced.

Lithium-Iron (FLP) batteries contain no water and are not affected by freezing, but should not be charged in freezing conditions. (Heat pads are available).

Wet Cell Battery State of Charge and Electrolyte Freezing

state of charge	open circuit voltage	temperature electrolyte freezes		specific gravity @ 27°C / 80°F	specific gravity @ 16°C / 60°F
		°C	°F		
0%	11.23V	+15°C	+59°F	1.120	1.128
25%	11.73V	+5°C	+41°F	1.155	1.163
50%	12.10V	-10°C	+14°F	1.190	1.198
75%	12.43V	-45°C	-49°F	1.225	1.233
100%	12.73V	-68°C	-90°F	1.265	1.273

SOURCE: Trojan Battery Company, Rolls Battery Company and calculations

1 Clean Battery Top and Terminals

Dirt attracts moisture and promotes corrosion on battery terminals.
See page 85, *Maintenance – Electrical*

2 Check Electrolyte Levels

See page 87, *Maintenance – Electrical*

Marine 12 volt START BATTERY

3 Add Water to Unsealed Wet-Cell Battery

See page 89, *Maintenance – Electrical*

battery water only

4 Charge Battery(s)

See page 83, *Maintenance – Electrical*

epoxy sealed
MARINE BATTERY CHARGER
3 banks

5 Load Test a Questionable Battery

If a battery is suspect, because it does not seem to be holding a charge, or if different cells are consuming unequal amounts of water, it can be worthwhile to load test the battery to determine whether it is likely to survive a lay-up. A battery

that is already questionable may not be worth the effort of charging and storing; it can be replaced before recommissioning. Load testing a battery gives a more accurate picture of a battery's state of health than simply using a multimeter to check voltage (open circuit voltage test). A load tester applies an actual load on the battery and measures how stable the voltage remains.
See page 92, *Maintenance – Electrical*.

6   Trickle Charge Battery

Batteries can be left connected to trickle charge during the lay-up period, using a marine battery charger or solar panels; however, batteries and charger should never be left unattended for long periods. In hot climates, lead acid batteries will self-discharge to 0 volts within weeks if they are not trickle-charged, eg. by solar cells. (See *Self-Discharge Table*, page 152). During prolonged trickle charging, unsealed wet-cell batteries will require topping up with water.

CAUTION: An unattended wind generator is not recommended because of the potential for overcharging batteries in high winds, which can destroy the regulator and potentially cause the batteries to explode. Wind generators must always be connected to a load and will not progressively "self-disconnect" (unlike solar cells) as batteries approach full charge.

7   Disconnect Terminals from Battery
Storage in Freezing or Cold Conditions

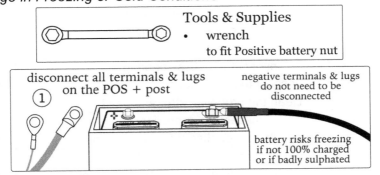

Tools & Supplies
- wrench
  to fit Positive battery nut

disconnect all terminals & lugs on the POS + post
(1)

negative terminals & lugs do not need to be disconnected

battery risks freezing if not 100% charged or if badly sulphated

Lay-Up Lithium-Iron Batteries (LFP batteries)

Best practice for lay-up is to **charge to 50 - 70% state of charge (SOC)**. Batteries should **not** be charged to 100% SOC. Trickle charging beyond 100% SOC can damage batteries. If any load (such as bilge pump, light or alarm) is left connected, be sure the battery cannot fall below it's low-capacity cut off (varies with manufacturer and settings). LFP batteries self-discharge very slowly. They contain no water, so will not be damaged by freezing, but LFP batteries should not be charged while frozen. (Heating pads are available).

Where to Store Lead Acid Batteries

Lead acid batteries are best stored as cold as possible to minimize self-discharge. (See *Self-Discharge Table* on page 152). They must be disconnected from all loads but do not need to be removed from the vessel, provided the battery is in good condition, topped up with water and 100% charged. The freezing temperature of a fully-charged battery is -68°C (-92°F). Electrolyte only 50% charged freezes at -10°C (14°F). (See *Electrolyte Freezing Table* on page 153).

In very cold conditions, a battery will go into "hibernation", losing little of its charge and therefore not freezing. A battery kept in a cool place (such as a basement) will continue to self-discharge until it is flat. Even if the electrolyte does not freeze, the loss of charge can allow sulphates to harden on the battery plates, effectively killing those areas of the plates and reducing battery capacity.

17 Lay-Up – Drive Train

Main Concerns

- marine growth blocking thruhull(s) and encrusting anodes, shaft and propeller on a vessel laid-up in the water
- failing to inspect equipment and leading to vibration and corrosion problems when the vessel is recommissioned

Task List

	Description	Page
1	check coupling between transmission & prop shaft	95
2	inspect the propeller shaft	97
3	inspect the stern gland	98
4	inspect the strut	101
5	inspect the cutlass bearing	102
6	inspect the propeller shaft anode	103
7	clean the propeller, strut and shaft	103
8	inspect the propeller	104
9	inspect the propeller nuts & cotter pin	104
10	inspect a folding propeller	105
11	inspect the anode of a feathering propeller	105
12	grease a feathering propeller	105
13	lay-up traditional stuffing box in water	157
14	protect propeller & shaft from marine growth	158

Most of the tasks to be done to lay-up a vessel should also be being completed as part of regular, ongoing maintenance to avoid future problems.

See page 187 for all the Lay-Up Task Lists.

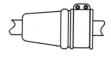

1 Check Coupling Between Transmission & Prop Shaft

See page 95, *Maintenance – Drive Train*

2 Inspect the Propeller Shaft

See page 97, *Maintenance – Drive Train*

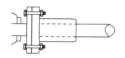

3 Inspect the Stern Gland

See page 98, *Maintenance – Drive Train*

Dripless Shaft Seals in Severe Freezing Conditions

Although these shaft seal systems are designed to be self-draining when the vessel is out of the water they should not be ignored in laying up a vessel, especially where freezing conditions may occur. If a vessel is to be left in the water in severe freezing conditions, there is risk that raw water inside the bellows may freeze, potentially rupturing the bellows. This is because the air temperature inside the vessel may be far below zero (eg. -25°C (-13°F), even when the water outside is not. Precautions may need to be taken to make sure any water in the bellows does not freeze.

4   Inspect the Strut
See page 101, *Maintenance – Drive Train*

5   Inspect the Cutlass Bearing
See page 102, *Maintenance – Drive Train*

6   Inspect the Propeller Shaft Anode
See page 103, *Maintenance – Drive Train*

7   Clean the Propeller, Strut and Shaft
See page 103, *Maintenance – Drive Train*

8   Inspect the Propeller
See page 104, *Maintenance – Drive Train*

9   Inspect the Propeller Nuts & Cotter Pin
See page 104, *Maintenance – Drive Train*

10   Inspect a Folding Propeller
See page 105, *Maintenance – Drive Train*

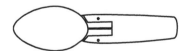

11   Inspect the Anode of a Feathering Prop
See page 105, *Maintenance – Drive Train*

12 Grease a Feathering Propeller
See page 105, *Maintenance – Drive Train*

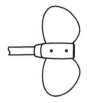

13 Lay-Up a Traditional Stuffing Box In Water
Tighten the packing gland, to prevent leaking, on any vessel lay-up in the water.

Tools & Supplies
- 2 pipe wrenches
  OR 2 adjustable square wrenches
  OR 2 packing wrenches
  to fit diameter of stuffing box glands
- Maintenance Log

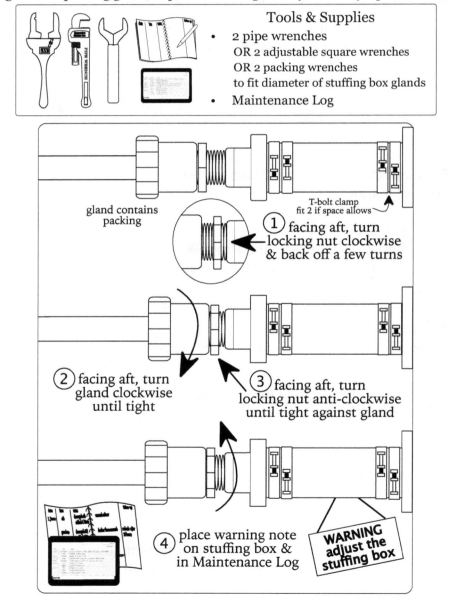

gland contains packing

T-bolt clamp
fit 2 if space allows

1) facing aft, turn locking nut clockwise & back off a few turns

2) facing aft, turn gland clockwise until tight

3) facing aft, turn locking nut anti-clockwise until tight against gland

4) place warning note on stuffing box & in Maintenance Log

WARNING adjust the stuffing box

14 Protect the Propeller & Shaft from Marine Growth

When a vessel is laid-up in warm water (ie. in tropical waters) marine growth can quickly turn a propeller into a ball of calcareous growth. This can not only be tedious to remove, requiring multiple dives, but the resulting lack of oxygen on a stainless steel shaft can cause crevice corrosion. Wrapping both the propeller and shaft in a rice bag or a strong plastic bag provides at least some protection.

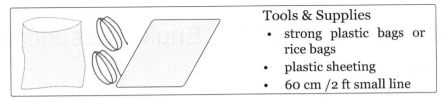

Tools & Supplies
- strong plastic bags or rice bags
- plastic sheeting
- 60 cm /2 ft small line

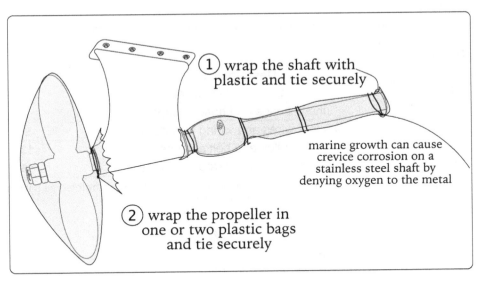

① wrap the shaft with plastic and tie securely

marine growth can cause crevice corrosion on a stainless steel shaft by denying oxygen to the metal

② wrap the propeller in one or two plastic bags and tie securely

Recommissioning

Recommissioning, sometimes called "summerizing" (in contrast to "winterizing"), is the essential second stage to the two-part process of laying-up a vessel. Completing all the necessary tasks to return a vessel to service is necessary to ensure trouble-free operation. Recommissioning should be straightforward and simple, if the necessary tasks were completed before lay-up, eg. oil change, fuel biocide, battery checks etc..

Main Concerns
- forgetting what was done/not done during lay-up (keep a good Logbook!)
- failure to complete the tasks to be done with the vessel out of the water

18 Recommission – Engine Essentials

Main Concerns
- overlooking small tasks, leading to a breakdown, potentially endangering the vessel
- forgetting to re-install or reconnect components dis-assembled during lay-up

Task List

	Description	Page
1	visual engine inspection	3
2	check hoses and hose clamps	7
3	inspect wires and wiring terminals	9
4	check pulley and belt alignment	13
5	tighten alternator and water pump belts	16

Most of the tasks to be done to lay-up a vessel should also be being completed as part of regular, ongoing maintenance to avoid future problems.
See page 187 for all the Lay-Up Task Lists.

1 Visual Engine Inspection
See page 3, *Maintenance – Engine Essentials*

2 Check Hoses and Hose Clamps
Temperature changes can loosen hose clamps so they should be checked, even if inspected before lay-up.
See page 7, *Maintenance – Engine Essentials*

3 Inspect Wires and Wiring Terminals
See page 9, *Maintenance – Engine Essentials*

4 Check Pulley and Belt Alignment
See page 13, *Maintenance – Engine Essentials*

5 Tighten Alternator and Water Pump Belts
See page 16, *Maintenance – Engine Essentials*

19 Recommission – Diesel Fuel

Main Concerns
• water and HUM growth in the fuel tank(s)
• forgetting to open all fuel lines causing engine to run out of fuel

Task List

	Description	Page
1	check diesel tank(s) for contamination	33
2	open fuel valves	160

See page 187 for all the Task Lists.

1 Check Diesel Tank(s) for Contamination
See page 33, *Maintenance – Diesel Fuel*

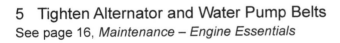

2 Open Fuel Valve(s)
Open valves in the fuel line (and between tanks, if necessary) and not forgetting
to open any valves in the fuel return line.

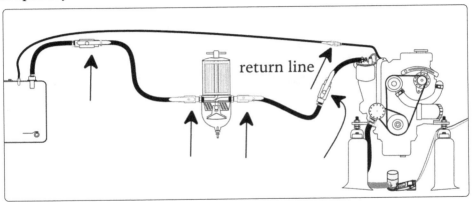

return line

20 Recommission – Lubrication

Main Concerns

* dried-out lubrication on bearings inside the engine
* failure to re-check level of transmission ATF or engine oil

Task List

	Description	Page
1	rotate engine without starting	161
2	drain transmission fluid to maximum level on dipstick	162

Most of the tasks to properly recommission the diesel system should have been completed as part of regular, ongoing maintenance to avoid problems.
See page 187 for all the Task Lists.

1 Rotate Engine Without Starting

Rotating the engine before actually starting the engine helps lubricate dry bearings before they get hot from combustion. This can help prolong engine life - *hot* bearings with no lubrication will definitely have a short life!

After a prolonged lay-up (more than one year) the valve cover should also be removed and a cup of fresh engine oil poured carefully over the valves and tappets. Be sure to re-secure the valve cover and its gasket before cranking.

Almost all diesel engines are Standard Rotation (ie. the engine rotates clockwise from the front and anti-clockwise at the flywheel). If the engine is to be rotated manually, use a large socket wrench on the crankshaft pulley nut and turn clockwise. After the engine has been rotated manually about 12 times, the engine can then be cranked electrically *without starting* to help distribute more oil.

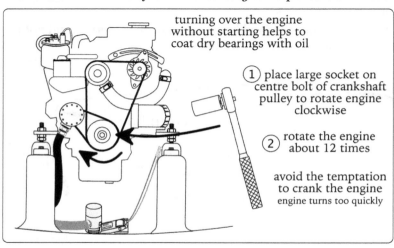

turning over the engine
without starting helps to
coat dry bearings with oil

(1) place large socket on
centre bolt of crankshaft
pulley to rotate engine
clockwise

(2) rotate the engine
about 12 times

avoid the temptation
to crank the engine
engine turns too quickly

2 Drain Transmission Fluid to Maximum Level on Dipstick

If the transmission/gearbox was filled with ATF or oil before lay-up (according to manufacturer's instructions), the fluid should be pumped down to the maximum level on the dipstick.

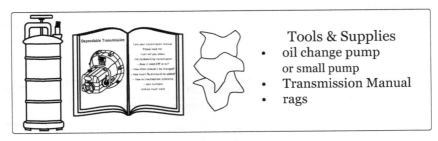

Tools & Supplies
- oil change pump or small pump
- Transmission Manual
- rags

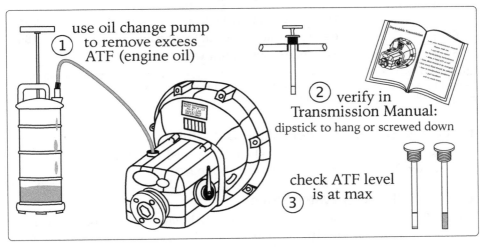

① use oil change pump to remove excess ATF (engine oil)

② verify in Transmission Manual: dipstick to hang or screwed down

③ check ATF level is at max

21 Recommission – Raw Water Cooling

Main Concerns
- forgetting to open the raw water seacock
- omitting to check all the raw water circuit before launch and engine start-up

Task List

	Description	Page
1	check seacocks open/close smoothly	62
2	check the raw water strainer	163
3	check engine and heat exchanger anodes	164
4	re-install raw water pump impeller & face plate	164
5	open raw water seacock for engine	166
6	remove plugs from exhaust & raw water intake thruhulls	166

Most of the tasks to properly recommission the diesel system should have been completed as part of regular, ongoing maintenance to avoid future problems.
See page 187 for all the Task Lists.

1 Check Seacocks Open/Close Smoothly

Seacocks serve a vital purpose and should be tested regularly.
See page 62, *Maintenance – Raw Water Cooling*

2 Check the Raw Water Strainer

The basket should be inserted and the top tightened before boat launch; air trapped in the top of the strainer may need to be "burped" after boat has been launched and the engine is started - check for this if there is no raw water flow after engine start-up.

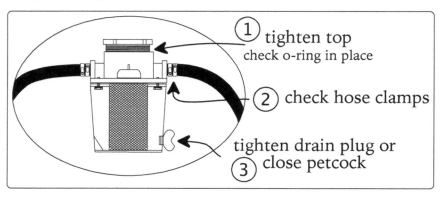

① tighten top
check o-ring in place

② check hose clamps

tighten drain plug or
③ close petcock

3   Check Engine and Heat Exchanger Anodes

Anodes continue to be consumed during lay-up if the engine block or heat exchanger(s) are flooded with antifreeze or coolant/antifreeze. Check anodes and replace if 50% consumed. For more information about anodes see page 68, *Maintenance – Raw Water Cooling.*

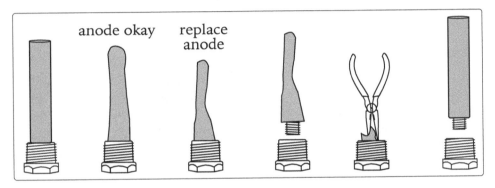

4   Re-Install the Raw Water Pump Impeller & Face Plate

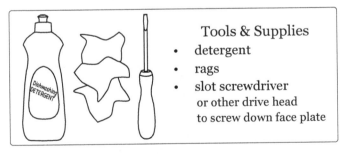

Re-Install the Raw Water Pump Impeller & Face Plate

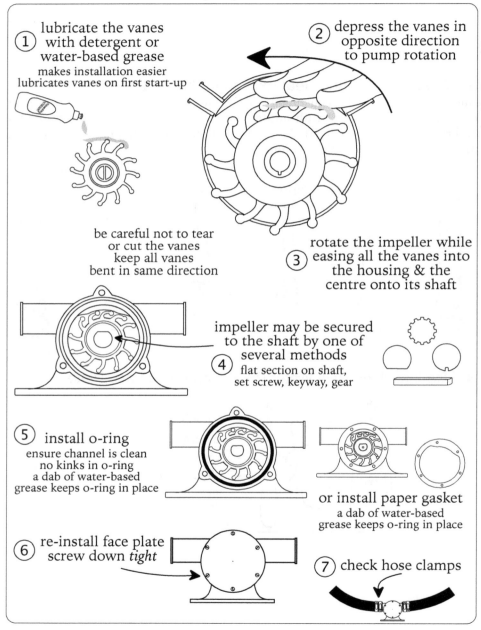

(1) lubricate the vanes with detergent or water-based grease
makes installation easier
lubricates vanes on first start-up

(2) depress the vanes in opposite direction to pump rotation

be careful not to tear or cut the vanes
keep all vanes bent in same direction

(3) rotate the impeller while easing all the vanes into the housing & the centre onto its shaft

impeller may be secured to the shaft by one of several methods
(4) flat section on shaft, set screw, keyway, gear

(5) install o-ring
ensure channel is clean
no kinks in o-ring
a dab of water-based grease keeps o-ring in place

or install paper gasket
a dab of water-based grease keeps o-ring in place

(6) re-install face plate screw down *tight*

(7) check hose clamps

5 Open Raw Water Seacock for Engine

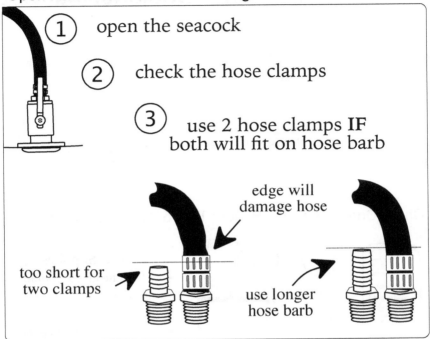

① open the seacock

② check the hose clamps

③ use 2 hose clamps **IF** both will fit on hose barb

edge will damage hose

too short for two clamps

use longer hose barb

6 Remove Plugs from Exhaust & Raw Water Intake Thruhulls

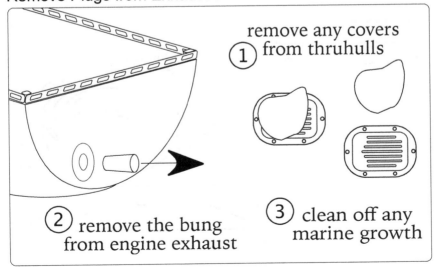

① remove any covers from thruhulls

② remove the bung from engine exhaust

③ clean off any marine growth

22 Recommission – Coolant/Antifreeze

Main Concerns
* loss of coolant/antifreeze

Task List

	Description	Page
1	check coolant level in header tank or overflow bottle	167

See page 187 for all the Task Lists.

1 Check Coolant Level in Header Tank or Overflow Bottle

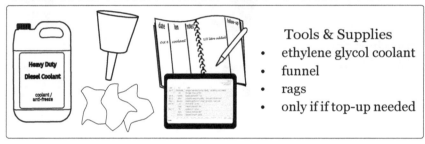

Tools & Supplies
* ethylene glycol coolant
* funnel
* rags
* only if if top-up needed

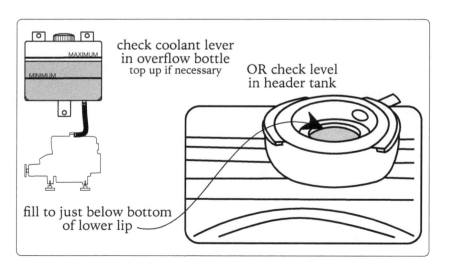

check coolant lever
in overflow bottle
top up if necessary

OR check level
in header tank

fill to just below bottom
of lower lip

23   Recommission – Breathing

Main Concerns
* air intake or engine room ventilation remains closed or blocked

Task List

	Description	Page
1	open engine room ventilation	168
2	unseal air filter/air intake on engine	168
3	re-connect exhaust riser and hoses	169
4	close drain on water-lift muffler or reconnect hose	169

See page 187 for all the Task Lists.

1   Open Engine Room Ventilators

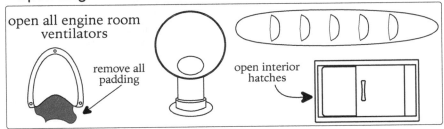

open all engine room ventilators

remove all padding

open interior hatches

2   Unseal Air Intake on Engine

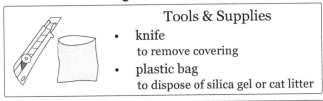

Tools & Supplies
* knife
  to remove covering
* plastic bag
  to dispose of silica gel or cat litter

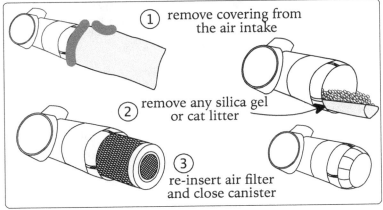

① remove covering from the air intake

② remove any silica gel or cat litter

③ re-insert air filter and close canister

3 Re-Connect Exhaust Riser and Hoses

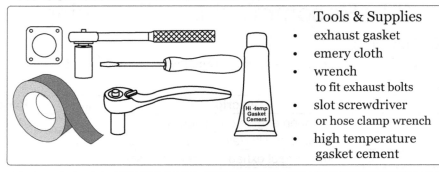

Tools & Supplies

- exhaust gasket
- emery cloth
- wrench
  to fit exhaust bolts
- slot screwdriver
  or hose clamp wrench
- high temperature
  gasket cement

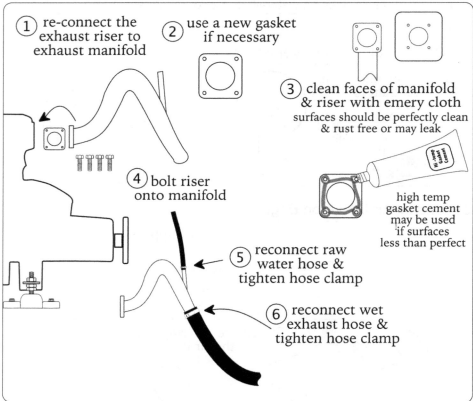

(1) re-connect the exhaust riser to exhaust manifold

(2) use a new gasket if necessary

(3) clean faces of manifold & riser with emery cloth
surfaces should be perfectly clean & rust free or may leak

(4) bolt riser onto manifold

high temp gasket cement may be used if surfaces less than perfect

(5) reconnect raw water hose & tighten hose clamp

(6) reconnect wet exhaust hose & tighten hose clamp

4 Close Drain on Water-Lift Muffler or Reconnect Hose

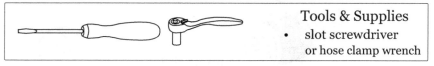

Tools & Supplies

- slot screwdriver
  or hose clamp wrench

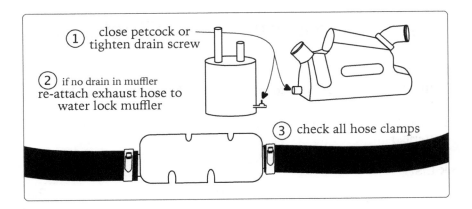

1. close petcock or tighten drain screw
2. if no drain in muffler re-attach exhaust hose to water lock muffler
3. check all hose clamps

Cautionary Tale

Everything seemed normal aboard the 65-foot boat, after the winter lay-up and spring recommissioning – except that the engine would not come up to its normal rpm. Every time the skipper opened the throttle, rpm picked up then stalled and black smoke poured from the exhaust. This was a clear sign of too much fuel and too little oxygen.

When the air filter was checked, it was found to be thick with black soot. But where was this soot coming from? Even after the air filter was cleaned and re-installed, the engine still refused to reach its normal rpm. "Maybe the turbocharger is the problem," thought the skipper. The turbo was opened and everything was found to be operating normally. No problem there. Unfortunately, not enough care was taken when the turbo was closed up, resulting in a slight misalignment of the casing. Soon as the engine was restarted, the air intake blades in the turbo rubbed inside the housing, creating a terrible clatter and bending the tips of several blades! This would cost several thousand dollars to repair.

The source of the soot in the air filter was eventually discovered to be coming from a pinhole in the vessel's dry stack exhaust; the turbocharger was sucking so hard that the soot was being sucked out between the insulation! A diesel engine will suck air from anywhere it can. But what was making the turbocharger work so hard?

A step-by-step investigation eventually revealed the cause of the trouble. When the vessel had been laid-up for the winter, a batt of fibreglass insulation had been stuffed into the engine room's air intake vent. This was not recorded in the Maintenance Log and no-one had remembered during the spring recommissioning to remove the batt to allow air flow into the engine room - so the engine was being starved for air (oxygen). Once the batt was removed – and the turbocharger came back from its expensive repairs – the engine came up to its normal rpm with no trouble at all.

24 Recommission – Electrical

Main Concerns

- battery(s) may be dead due to freezing or 100% discharged and hard sulphation
- low electrolyte levels in wet-cell trickle-charged battery(s) (not sealed batteries)

Task List

	Description	Page
1	check exterior condition of battery	171
2	check battery electrolyte level & top up, if needed	87
3	charge battery(s)	172
4	load test a 12 volt battery	92
5	reconnect battery terminals (lugs)	172

See page 187 for all the Task Lists.

1   Check Exterior Condition of Battery – Signs of a Frozen Battery

cracks in casing

bulge in side

white crystals or "water" (sulphuric acid!) on battery top or inside battery box

Marine 12 volt START BATTERY

Lithium-iron (LFP) batteries contain no water and are not damaged by being frozen, but should not be charged when below 0°C (32°F). Heating pads are available.

2   Top-up Battery Water Levels (unsealed wet-cell only)

Even in cool or cold conditions, a battery that has been trickle-charged will lose some water through evaporation (the electrolyte warms during charging). This water needs to be replaced, to ensure the plates do not become exposed during regular charging and discharging. See pages 87 – 89, *Maintenance – Electrical*.

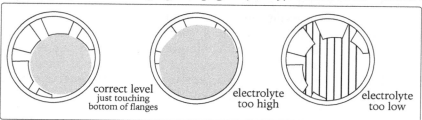

correct level
just touching
bottom of flanges

electrolyte
too high

electrolyte
too low

3   Charge Battery(s)

Do NOT attempt to charge a lead acid battery that has been frozen – replace it!

Any battery that was not trickle-charged during the lay-up will be partially discharged and should be recharged as soon as possible. This can be done using:

- marine battery charger
- wind generator
- solar panels
- run the engine (if battery has enough power to crank the engine)

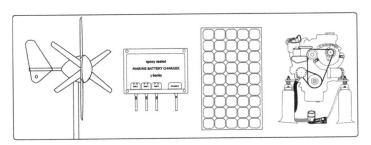

4   Load Test a 12 Volt Battery

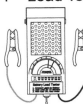

This is an important test to determine how well a battery has survived the lay-up period. A battery may show 12.65 volts (fully charged) with an open voltage test yet have become heavily sulphated and unable to perform the work expected of it.

See *Test Battery with Load Tester*, page 92.

5   Reconnect Battery Terminals (Lugs)

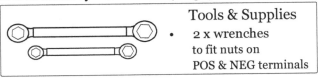

Tools & Supplies

- 2 x wrenches to fit nuts on POS & NEG terminals

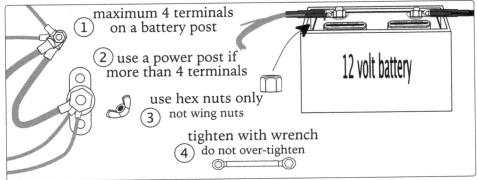

① maximum 4 terminals on a battery post

② use a power post if more than 4 terminals

③ use hex nuts only not wing nuts

④ tighten with wrench do not over-tighten

12 volt battery

25 Recommission – Drive Train

Main Concerns

- linkage controls may have rusted or seized
- failure to "burp" dripless shaft seal or adjust stuffing box (in water)

Task List

	Description	Page
1	check control cable ends are secure	173
2	check throttle cable movement	174
3	check transmission control cable	174
4	check stop cable or solenoid	175
5	grease rubber cup on dripless shaft seal	176
6	hand tighten & lock gland on traditional stuffing box	177
7	check hose(s) on dripless stuffing box	177

See page 187 for all the Task Lists.

1 Check Control Cables are Securely Attached to Levers

Cotter (split) pins break or fall out, wire rusts, nuts unscrew themselves – take a minute to double-check that the control cables are securely attached to the gear/throttle/stop lever — it may save a vessel and its skipper from disaster. Loss of control is more likely to happen when the controls are being used rapidly (eg. in & out of gear manoeuvring in a marina or harbour, ie. close to objects to hit!)

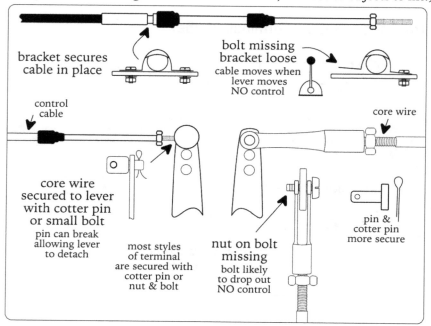

2 Check Throttle Cable Movement

Rust, dust or salt crystals can cause the control cable to become stiff or have no movement at all. Greasing cable ends and ensuring that the plastic cable end covers are in position and in good repair can prevent cable problems.

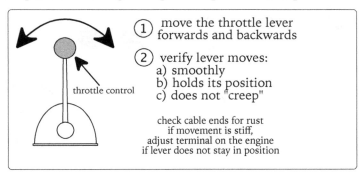

Single Lever Dual Action   <u>Pin may stick after a lay-up</u>

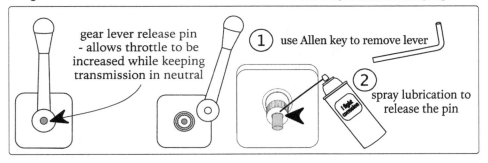

3 Check Transmission Control Cable

A) check transmission lever moves smoothly

B) check lever on transmission moves fully into position

A) Check Transmission Lever Moves Smoothly

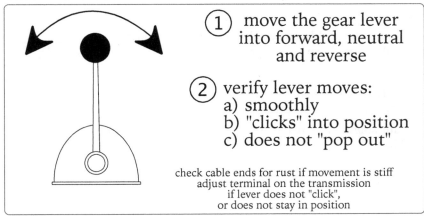

B) Check Lever on Transmission Moves Fully into Position

This check should be made when recommissioning and any time the movement of the gear lever or performance of the transmission does not "feel right".

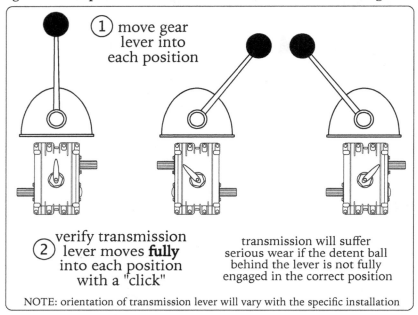

① move gear lever into each position

② verify transmission lever moves **fully** into each position with a "click"

transmission will suffer serious wear if the detent ball behind the lever is not fully engaged in the correct position

NOTE: orientation of transmission lever will vary with the specific installation

4   Check Stop Cable or Stop Solenoid Button

Never start an engine without knowing how to stop it – either by pulling the stop cable or pushing the stop button on the engine instrument panel. In both cases, best practice is to hang a large red label on the stop lever on the engine making it very easy for anyone to quickly and correctly identify the correct lever to pull in the event of the cable or solenoid failing to operate.

In an emergency, the engine could be stopped by blocking off the air intake.

Cable

1.   check the stop cable moves smoothly and pulls out the normal distance
2.   check the stop cable terminal is securely attached to the fuel control lever on the governor

Solenoid

1.   check that the wires on the solenoid are in good condition and securely attached
2.   operate solenoid — listen for "click" (on the engine) to check solenoid is working

5   Grease Rubber Cup on Dripless Shaft Seal

This specific design of shaft seal needs to be greased every year. See manual.

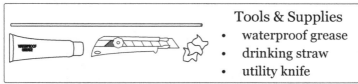

Tools & Supplies
- waterproof grease
- drinking straw
- utility knife

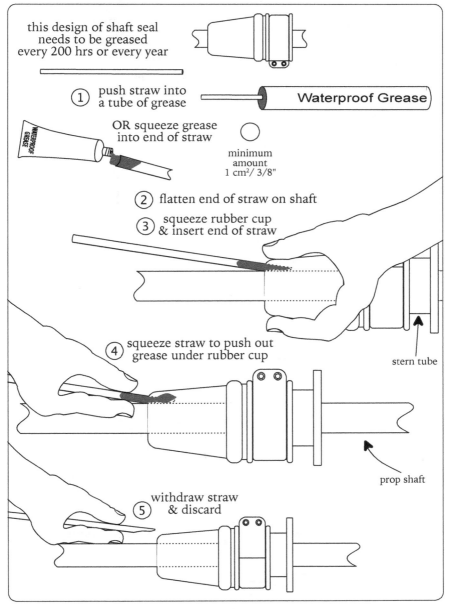

this design of shaft seal needs to be greased every 200 hrs or every year

① push straw into a tube of grease

Waterproof Grease

OR squeeze grease into end of straw

minimum amount 1 cm²/ 3/8"

② flatten end of straw on shaft

③ squeeze rubber cup & insert end of straw

stern tube

④ squeeze straw to push out grease under rubber cup

prop shaft

⑤ withdraw straw & discard

6   Hand Tighten & Lock Packing Gland on Traditional Stuffing Box

The packing gland can unscrew when the prop shaft turns if the locking nut is not tight. Best practice is to check that the gland is engaged on the threads and hand tight, then tighten the locking nut; this makes sure the packing gland will not unscrew itself when the propeller shaft turns. Leave final adjustment of the packing gland until the vessel is in the water and the prop shaft has been turning. This is essential if new packing has been installed, to allow the new packing to "seat" itself. See *Re-adjust Packing in Traditional Stuffing Box*, page 184.

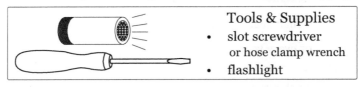

Tools & Supplies
* slot screwdriver
   or hose clamp wrench
* flashlight

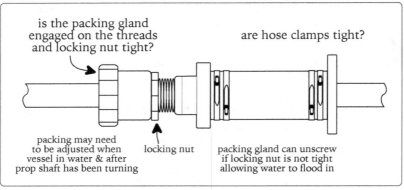

is the packing gland engaged on the threads and locking nut tight?

are hose clamps tight?

packing may need to be adjusted when vessel in water & after prop shaft has been turning

locking nut

packing gland can unscrew if locking nut is not tight allowing water to flood in

7   Check Hose(s) on Dripless Shaft Seal

Tools & Supplies
* slot screwdriver
   or hose clamp wrench
* flashlight

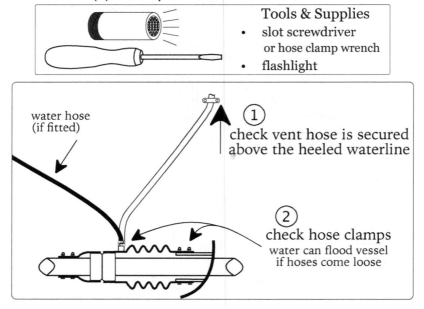

water hose
(if fitted)

① check vent hose is secured above the heeled waterline

② check hose clamps
water can flood vessel if hoses come loose

26 Recommission – In Water

Main Concerns

- forgetting routine engine start procedures
- forgetting to adjust the stern gland (adjust packing or burping bellows)

Task List

	Description	Page
1	remove protection from propeller and shaft	178
2	prime raw water strainer	179
3	start engine procedure	17
4	check raw water being expelled with exhaust	180
5	burp raw water strainer to release trapped air	181
6	check oil pressure is normal	181
7	check alternator is charging	182
8	check seacocks, raw water strainer & exhaust for leaks	182
9	check vessel moves when in gear	183
10	re-adjust packing in traditional stuffing box	184
11	burp air from dripless stuffing box	185

Most of the tasks to properly recommission the diesel system should have been completed as part of lay-up and regular, ongoing maintenance to avoid future problems. See page 187 for all the Task Lists.

1 Remove Wrap Around Propeller and Shaft

For a vessel that was laid-up in the water, protection around the propeller and shaft should be removed and any marine growth scrapped from areas that were not protected.

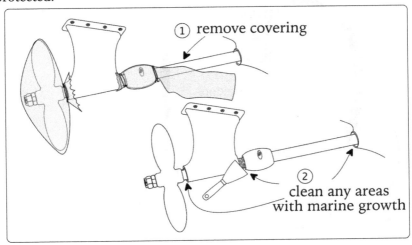

① remove covering

② clean any areas with marine growth

2   Prime Raw Water Strainer

If the raw water strainer is above the waterline, it should be primed; if not, the rubber impeller in the raw water pump will run dry and may be destroyed before water flows from the seacock, fills the strainer and finally reaches the pump.

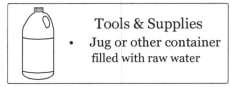

Tools & Supplies
- Jug or other container filled with raw water

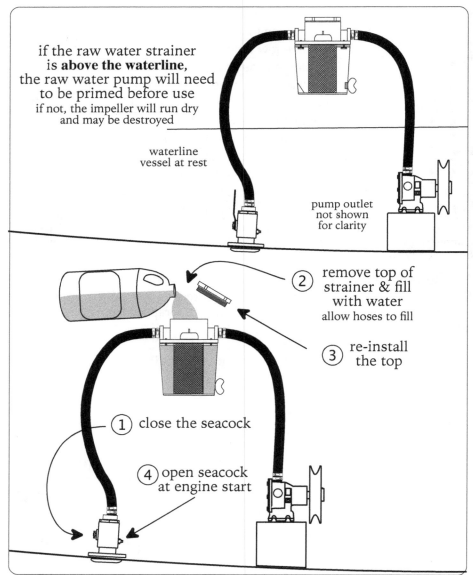

if the raw water strainer is **above the waterline**, the raw water pump will need to be primed before use
if not, the impeller will run dry and may be destroyed

waterline
vessel at rest

pump outlet
not shown
for clarity

② remove top of strainer & fill with water
allow hoses to fill

③ re-install the top

① close the seacock

④ open seacock at engine start

3   Start Engine Procedure

See page 17, *Maintenance – Engine Essentials*

The engine should start almost immediately if the Start battery is fully charged and in good condition. In cooler weather or where the engine is cold (even if the day is warm), use glow plugs to warm the pre-combustion chamber, or the in-line heater to warm incoming air in direct injection engines:

- do not crank for more than 15 seconds
- if the engine does not start, find out why not – fuel, air supply, exhaust
- allow the Starter to cool for at least 60 seconds before cranking engine again

CAUTION: raw water is pumped into the water-lift muffler when the engine is being cranked. This can fill the muffler (because the water is not being expelled by the exhaust gases) and flood back into the engine's exhaust manifold. The water-lift muffler may need to be drained, or disconnected if the water-lift muffler is small, or the exhaust hose long and there is a danger of hydro-lock.

4   Check Raw Water Being Expelled with Exhaust

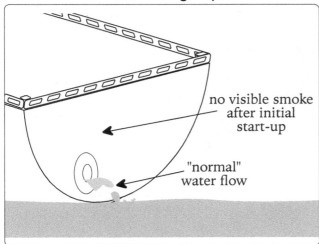

no visible smoke after initial start-up

"normal" water flow

If no water is being expelled **check**:

- raw water seacock open
- strainer air-locked
- all hoses connected
- raw water pump belt tight
- impeller installed correctly

5   Burp Raw Water Strainer to Release Trapped Air

Air trapped in the top of the strainer can prevent water flow, even with the seacock open and impeller working correctly. "Burp" the strainer by slowly unscrewing the top until water flows out.

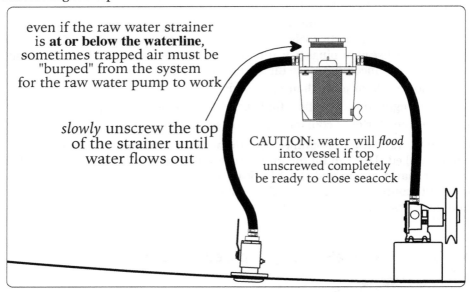

even if the raw water strainer is **at or below the waterline**, sometimes trapped air must be "burped" from the system for the raw water pump to work

slowly unscrew the top of the strainer until water flows out

CAUTION: water will *flood* into vessel if top unscrewed completely be ready to close seacock

6   Check Oil Pressure Is Normal

The engine alarm (low oil pressure alarm) should stop within seconds of the engine starting, and oil pressure should rise to "normal" within 5-10 seconds. If not, turn off the engine immediately and investigate the reason.

What is "normal" oil pressure varies from one engine to another, and also depends on operating conditions. Pressure will fall a little when the oil gets hot. Best practice is to note what is "normal" for both cold and hot running on the gauge of the specific engine.

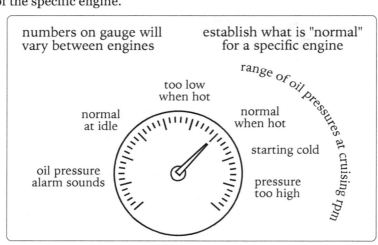

numbers on gauge will vary between engines

establish what is "normal" for a specific engine

range of oil pressures at cruising rpm

too low when hot

normal at idle

normal when hot

oil pressure alarm sounds

starting cold

pressure too high

7   Check Alternator is Charging

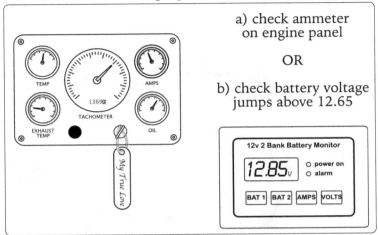

a) check ammeter
on engine panel

OR

b) check battery voltage
jumps above 12.65

8   Check Seacocks, Raw Water Strainer & Exhaust for Leaks

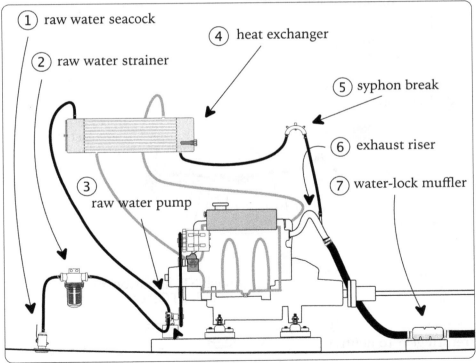

① raw water seacock

④ heat exchanger

② raw water strainer

⑤ syphon break

⑥ exhaust riser

③ raw water pump

⑦ water-lock muffler

9   Check Vessel Moves in Gear

Checking that the transmission and throttle controls are working smoothly will take only a few seconds, yet can prevent a potentially expensive accident.

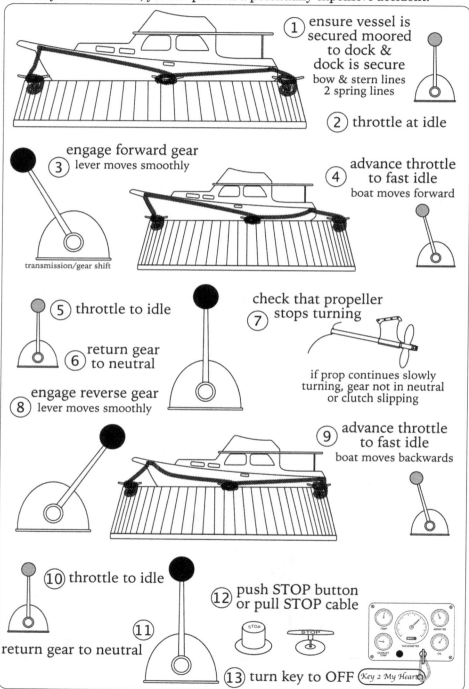

(1) ensure vessel is secured moored to dock & dock is secure
bow & stern lines
2 spring lines

(2) throttle at idle

engage forward gear
(3) lever moves smoothly

(4) advance throttle to fast idle
boat moves forward

transmission/gear shift

(5) throttle to idle

(6) return gear to neutral

(7) check that propeller stops turning

if prop continues slowly turning, gear not in neutral or clutch slipping

(8) engage reverse gear lever moves smoothly

(9) advance throttle to fast idle
boat moves backwards

(10) throttle to idle

(11) return gear to neutral

(12) push STOP button or pull STOP cable

(13) turn key to OFF   Key 2 My Heart

10 Re-adjust Packing in Traditional Stuffing Box

Packing in a traditional stuffing box will need adjusting if the packing gland was unscrewed (eg. to check the condition of the packing, install new packing, check propeller shaft for wear and corrosion, replace stuffing box hose etc.). Only tighten the packing gland in stages — to avoid initially overtightening. Overtightening can cut a grove in the shaft (score) making leak-proof adjustment more difficult to achieve.

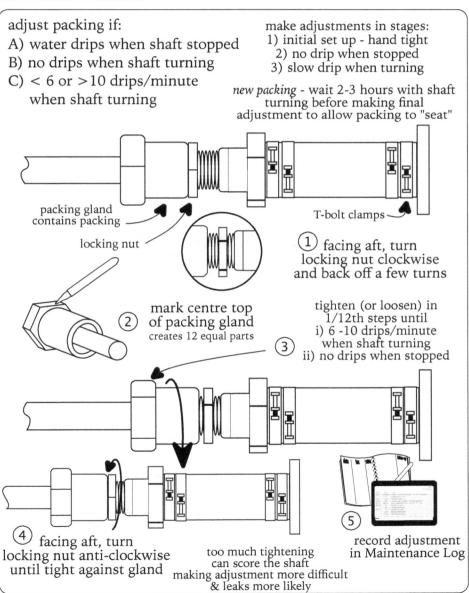

adjust packing if:
A) water drips when shaft stopped
B) no drips when shaft turning
C) < 6 or >10 drips/minute
   when shaft turning

make adjustments in stages:
1) initial set up - hand tight
2) no drip when stopped
3) slow drip when turning

new packing - wait 2-3 hours with shaft turning before making final adjustment to allow packing to "seat"

packing gland contains packing

locking nut

T-bolt clamps

① facing aft, turn locking nut clockwise and back off a few turns

② mark centre top of packing gland
creates 12 equal parts

③ tighten (or loosen) in 1/12th steps until
i) 6 -10 drips/minute when shaft turning
ii) no drips when stopped

④ facing aft, turn locking nut anti-clockwise until tight against gland

too much tightening can score the shaft making adjustment more difficult & leaks more likely

⑤ record adjustment in Maintenance Log

11   Burp Air from Dripless Shaft Seal

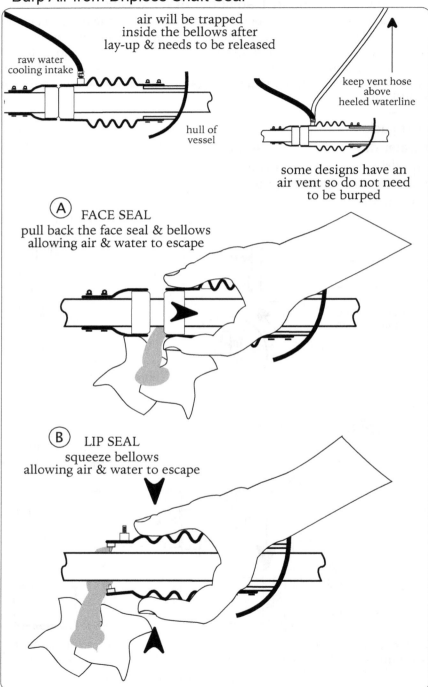

air will be trapped
inside the bellows after
lay-up & needs to be released

raw water
cooling intake

keep vent hose
above
heeled waterline

hull of
vessel

some designs have an
air vent so do not need
to be burped

(A)   FACE SEAL
pull back the face seal & bellows
allowing air & water to escape

(B)   LIP SEAL
squeeze bellows
allowing air & water to escape

Burp Air from Alternative Style Dripless Seal

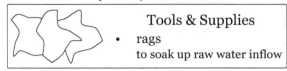

Tools & Supplies
- rags
  to soak up raw water inflow

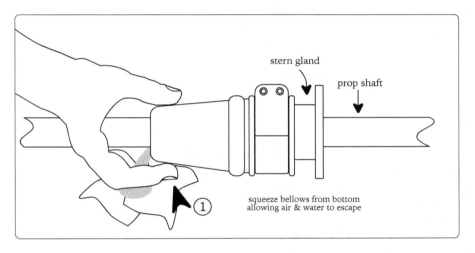

stern gland

prop shaft

① squeeze bellows from bottom
allowing air & water to escape

Task Lists

Maintenance 187

Lay-Up 189

Recommissioning 193

Tasks by Topics 194

Schedule for Maintenance Tasks 199

Saildrives 202

• Illustrated Task Lists available free
• Technical Word Lists in multiple languages
available free
www.marinedieselbasics.com

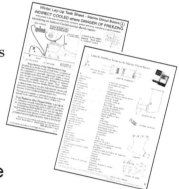

Maintenance

Engine Essentials
- ☐ visual engine room inspection
- ☐ check engine oil level
- ☐ check belt tension
- ☐ check coolant/antifreeze & top up as needed
- ☐ check transmission fluid level
- ☐ inspect belts – alternator, coolant & raw water pump
- ☐ inspect pulleys (sheaves)
- ☐ check alignment of belts & pulleys
- ☐ adjust pulley alignment
- ☐ tighten alternator and water pump belts

Diesel Fuel
- ☐ inspect fuel deck fill
- ☐ add biocide to the fuel tank(s)
- ☐ change the primary fuel filter
- ☐ change the secondary fuel filter
- ☐ bleed the diesel system
- ☐ check diesel tank(s) for contamination
- ☐ inspect injection pump and injectors

Lubrication
- ☐ check engine oil level
- ☐ dipstick diagnostics – engine oil

- ☐ check transmission fluid
- ☐ dipstick diagnostics – transmission fluid
- ☐ change the engine oil & filter
- ☐ change the transmission fluid (engine oil)
- ☐ grease the control cable ends and engine mount threads
- ☐ lubricate ignition key slot
- ☐ check injection pump & governor dipsticks

Raw Water Cooling
- ☐ clean thruhull of anti-foul paint and marine growth
- ☐ check emergency plug tied to every seacock
- ☐ check seacock opens/closes smoothly
- ☐ inspect raw water strainer
- ☐ inspect raw water pump & impeller
- ☐ check and change heat exchanger anode(s)
- ☐ flush and clean the syphon break

Coolant/Antifreeze
- ☐ check coolant/antifreeze level in header tank or overflow bottle
- ☐ inspect condition of coolant
- ☐ drain and replace worn-out coolant/antifreeze

Breathing – Air Intake & Exhaust
- ☐ clean the air filter
- ☐ check the crankcase breather (and filter)
- ☐ check adequate air flow through engine room
- ☐ inspect & repair sound insulation

Electrical
- ☐ keep battery(s) charged
- ☐ check battery open circuit voltage with a multimeter
- ☐ clean battery tops & terminals
- ☐ check electrolyte levels in wet-cell batteries
- ☐ add water to unsealed wet cell battery
- ☐ check specific gravity of a wet-cell battery
- ☐ load testing a 12 volt battery

Drive Train
- ☐ check coupling between transmission & prop shaft
- ☐ inspect the propeller shaft
- ☐ inspect the strut
- ☐ inspect the cutlass bearing
- ☐ inspect the propeller anode
- ☐ scrape the propeller, strut & shaft
- ☐ inspect the propeller
- ☐ inspect the propeller nuts and cotter pin
- ☐ inspect a folding propeller

☐ inspect the anode on a feathering propeller
☐ grease a feathering propeller

Lay-Up

Engine Essentials
☐ change engine oil & filter
☐ change transmission fluid
☐ slacken tension off belts
☐ clean the bilge
☐ wipe down the engine
☐ protect engine mounts
☐ write up good notes in Maintenance Log

Diesel Fuel
☐ add biocide to last fuel fill
☐ check deck fill fuel cap is closed
☐ change primary fuel filter
☐ bleed fuel system
☐ close all fuel valves – supply & return
☐ check fuel vent cannot back flood

Lubrication (Oil, Filter & ATF)
☐ change engine oil & filter
☐ change transmission fluid
☐ grease control cable ends & engine mount threads
☐ lubricate ignition key slot
☐ check ignition pump & governor dipsticks, if fitted
☐ fill the transmission with ATF (or engine oil)

Raw Water Cooling
Indirect Cooling – Winter Protection
☐ check all hoses & replace, if needed
☐ add antifreeze to circuit
☐ run engine & antifreeze through entire raw water circuit
☐ drain antifreeze from hose to seacock, if not filled with antifreeze
☐ drain strainer, if not filled with antifreeze
☐ service raw water pump & impeller
☐ check heat exchanger anode
☐ service exhaust riser
☐ clean the raw water syphon break
☐ drain water-lift muffler, if not filled with antifreeze

Indirect Cooling – Tropical Storage (Heat & Humidity)
☐ check all hoses & replace if needed
☐ drain all raw water hoses
☐ drain strainer
☐ service raw water pump & impeller
☐ drain heat exchanger
☐ check heat exchanger anode

☐ protect thruhull from marine growth
☐ service exhaust riser
☐ clean syphon break
☐ drain water-lift muffler

Direct Cooling – Winter Protection

☐ inspect hoses & hose clamps
☐ drain raw water from engine block
☐ check & change engine anode
☐ remove engine thermostat
☐ fill engine block with antifreeze
☐ re-install engine thermostat
☐ add antifreeze to header tank
☐ add antifreeze to circuit
☐ run engine to flush circuit
☐ drain raw water hoses, if not filled with antifreeze
☐ drain strainer, if not filled with antifreeze
☐ service raw water pump & impeller
☐ service exhaust riser
☐ clean syphon break
☐ drain water-lift muffler, if not filled with antifreeze

Direct Cooling – Tropical Storage

☐ inspect hoses & hose clamps
☐ check & change engine anode
☐ drain all raw water hoses
☐ drain strainer
☐ service raw water pump & impeller
☐ protect thruhull from marine growth
☐ service exhaust riser
☐ clean syphon break
☐ drain water-lift muffler

Coolant/Antifreeze

☐ check coolant level in header tank or overflow bottle
☐ drain and refill coolant/antifreeze
☐ test frost protection of coolant/antifreeze

Breathing (Air Intake & Exhaust)

☐ clean air filter/air intake
☐ seal air intake with plastic
☐ disconnect exhaust hose from exhaust manifold
☐ drain water-lift muffler
☐ prevent rodents entering via exhaust thruhull

Electrical

☐ clean battery top and terminals
☐ check electrolyte levels
☐ add water to unsealed wet-cell battery

☐ charge battery
☐ load test a questionable battery
☐ trickle charge battery
☐ disconnect terminals from battery

Drive Train (Coupling, Shaft Seal, Propeller etc.)

☐ check coupling between transmission & prop shaft
☐ inspect the propeller shaft
☐ inspect the stuffing box
☐ inspect the cutlass bearing
☐ inspect the propeller shaft anode
☐ clean the propeller, strut and shaft
☐ inspect the propeller
☐ inspect the propeller nuts & cotter pin
☐ inspect a folding propeller
☐ inspect the anode of a feathering prop
☐ grease a feathering propeller
☐ lay-up a traditional stuffing box in water
☐ protect the propeller & shaft from marine growth

Winter Protection   *minimum to avoid damage due to freezing*
Indirect Cooling

☐ prevent fuel contamination by water
☐ add antifreeze to circuit
☐ run engine & antifreeze through entire raw water circuit
☐ drain antifreeze from hose to seacock, if not filled with antifreeze
☐ drain strainer, if not filled with antifreeze
☐ service raw water pump & impeller
☐ drain water lock muffler, if not filled with antifreeze
☐ drain and replace coolant/antifreeze if more than 2 years old
☐ top up coolant/antifreeze in engine's header tank or overflow bottle
☐ verify the engine is fully protected against maximum frost conditions
☐ block engine air intake with plastic sheet and tape
☐ disconnect exhaust hose from exhaust manifold or drain water-lift muffler
☐ check electrolyte levels in wet-cell batteries add water to wet cell batteries
☐ charge batteries – charger, solar, wind or engine alternator
☐ check battery voltage with a multimeter
☐ disconnect positive leads from all batteries

Direct Cooling

☐ drain engine block
☐ remove thermostat
☐ fill engine block with antifreeze
☐ re-install thermostat
☐ add antifreeze to raw water circuit
☐ run engine & antifreeze through entire raw water circuit

- ☐ drain antifreeze from hose to seacock, if not filled with antifreeze
- ☐ drain strainer, if not filled with antifreeze
- ☐ service raw water pump & impeller
- ☐ drain water-lift muffler (if not filled with antifreeze)
- ☐ block engine air intake with plastic sheet and tape
- ☐ disconnect exhaust hose from exhaust manifold or drain water-lift muffler
- ☐ check electrolyte levels in wet-cell batteries
- ☐ add water to wet cell batteries
- ☐ charge batteries – charger, solar, wind or engine alternator
- ☐ check battery voltage with a multimeter
- ☐ disconnect positive leads from all batteries

Tropical Storage minimum to avoid damage due to high heat and humidity

Indirect Cooling
- ☐ prevent fuel contamination by water
- ☐ drain all raw water hoses
- ☐ drain strainer
- ☐ service raw water pump & impeller
- ☐ drain heat exchanger
- ☐ protect thruhull from marine growth
- ☐ service exhaust riser
- ☐ drain water-lift muffler
- ☐ drain and replace coolant/antifreeze if more than 2 years old
- ☐ top up coolant/antifreeze in engine's header tank or overflow bottle
- ☐ block engine air intake with plastic sheet and tape
- ☐ disconnect exhaust hose from exhaust manifold or drain water-lift muffler
- ☐ check electrolyte levels in wet-cell batteries
- ☐ add water to wet cell batteries
- ☐ charge batteries – charger, solar, wind or engine alternator
- ☐ check battery voltage with a multimeter
- ☐ disconnect positive leads from all batteries
- ☐ protect the propeller & shaft from marine growth

Direct Cooling
- ☐ drain all raw water hoses
- ☐ drain strainer
- ☐ service raw water pump & impeller
- ☐ protect thruhull from marine growth
- ☐ service exhaust riser
- ☐ drain water-lift muffler
- ☐ block engine air intake with plastic sheet and tape
- ☐ disconnect exhaust hose from exhaust manifold or drain water-lift muffler
- ☐ check electrolyte levels in wet-cell batteries
- ☐ add water to wet cell batteries
- ☐ charge batteries – charger, solar, wind or engine alternator
- ☐ check battery voltage with a multimeter
- ☐ disconnect positive leads from all batteries
- ☐ protect the propeller & shaft from marine growth

Recommissioning

Engine Essentials
- ☐ visual engine inspection
- ☐ check hoses and hose clamps
- ☐ inspect wires and wiring terminals
- ☐ check pulley and belt alignment
- ☐ tighten alternator and water pump belts

Diesel Fuel
- ☐ check diesel tank(s) for contamination
- ☐ open fuel valve(s)

Lubrication
- ☐ rotate engine without starting
- ☐ drain transmission fluid to maximum level on dipstick

Raw Water Cooling
- ☐ check seacocks open/close smoothly
- ☐ check the raw water strainer
- ☐ check engine and heat exchanger anodes
- ☐ re-install the raw water pump impeller & face plate
- ☐ open raw water seacock for engine
- ☐ remove plugs from exhaust & raw water intake thruhulls

Coolant/Antifreeze
- ☐ check coolant level in header tank or overflow bottle

Breathing
- ☐ open engine room ventilators
- ☐ open air intake on engine
- ☐ re-connect exhaust riser and hoses
- ☐ close drain on water-lift muffler or reconnect hose

Electrical
- ☐ check exterior condition of battery – signs of a frozen battery
- ☐ charge battery(s)
- ☐ reconnect battery terminals (lugs)

Drive Train
- ☐ check control cables are securely attached to lever
- ☐ check throttle cable movement
- ☐ check transmission control cable
- ☐ check stop cable or solenoid
- ☐ grease rubber cup on dripless shaft seal
- ☐ remove wrap around propeller and shaft

In Water

- ☐ prime raw water strainer
- ☐ start engine
- ☐ check oil pressure is normal
- ☐ check raw water being expelled with exhaust
- ☐ burp raw water strainer to release trapped air
- ☐ check alternator is charging
- ☐ check seacocks, raw water strainer & exhaust for leaks
- ☐ check vessel moves in gear
- ☐ re-adjust packing in traditional stuffing box
- ☐ burp air from dripless shaft seal

Tasks by Topics

Engine Essentials

Maintenance

- ☐ visual engine room inspection
- ☐ check engine oil level
- ☐ check belt tension
- ☐ check coolant/antifreeze & top-up as needed
- ☐ check transmission fluid level
- ☐ inspect belts - alternator, coolant & raw water pump
- ☐ inspect pulleys (sheaves)
- ☐ check alignment of belts & pulleys
- ☐ adjust pulley alignment
- ☐ tighten alternator and water pump belts

Lay-up

- ☐ change engine oil & filter
- ☐ change transmission fluid
- ☐ slacken tension off belts
- ☐ clean the bilge
- ☐ wipe down the engine
- ☐ protect engine mounts
- ☐ write up good notes in maintenance log

Recommission

- ☐ visual engine inspection
- ☐ check hoses and hose clamps
- ☐ inspect wires and wiring terminals
- ☐ check pulley and belt alignment
- ☐ tighten alternator and water pump belts

Diesel Fuel

Maintenance

- ☐ inspect fuel deck fill
- ☐ add biocide to the fuel tank(s)
- ☐ change the primary fuel filter

- ☐ change the secondary fuel filter
- ☐ bleed the diesel system
- ☐ check diesel tank(s) for contamination
- ☐ inspect injection pump and injectors

Lay-up

- ☐ add biocide to last fuel fill
- ☐ check deck fill fuel cap is closed
- ☐ change primary fuel filter
- ☐ bleed fuel system
- ☐ close all fuel valves – supply & return
- ☐ check fuel vent cannot back flood

Recommission

- ☐ check diesel tank(s) for contamination
- ☐ open fuel valve(s)

Lubrication

Maintenance

- ☐ check engine oil level
- ☐ dipstick diagnostics – engine oil
- ☐ check transmission fluid
- ☐ dipstick diagnostics – transmission fluid
- ☐ change the engine oil & filter
- ☐ change the transmission fluid (engine oil)
- ☐ grease the control cable ends and engine mount threads
- ☐ lubricate ignition key slot
- ☐ check injection pump & governor dipsticks

Lay-up

- ☐ change engine oil & filter
- ☐ change transmission fluid
- ☐ grease control cable ends & engine mount threads
- ☐ lubricate ignition key slot
- ☐ check ignition pump & governor dipsticks, if fitted
- ☐ fill the transmission with ATF (or engine oil)

Recommission

- ☐ rotate engine without starting
- ☐ drain transmission fluid to maximum level on dipstick

Raw Water Cooling

Maintenance

- ☐ clean thruhull of anti-foul paint and marine growth
- ☐ check emergency plug tied to every seacock
- ☐ check seacock opens/closes smoothly
- ☐ inspect raw water strainer
- ☐ inspect raw water pump & impeller
- ☐ check and change heat exchanger anode(s)
- ☐ flush and clean the syphon break

Lay-up

Indirect Cooling – Winter Protection

- ☐ check all hoses & replace, if needed
- ☐ add antifreeze to circuit
- ☐ run engine & antifreeze through entire raw water circuit
- ☐ drain antifreeze from hose to seacock, if not filled with antifreeze
- ☐ drain strainer, if not filled with antifreeze
- ☐ service raw water pump & impeller
- ☐ check heat exchanger anode
- ☐ service exhaust riser
- ☐ clean the raw water syphon break
- ☐ drain water-lift muffler, if not filled with antifreeze

Indirect Cooling – Tropical Storage (Heat & Humidity)

- ☐ check all hoses & replace, if needed
- ☐ drain all raw water hoses
- ☐ drain strainer
- ☐ service raw water pump & impeller
- ☐ drain heat exchanger
- ☐ check heat exchanger anode
- ☐ protect thruhull from marine growth
- ☐ service exhaust riser
- ☐ clean syphon break
- ☐ drain water-lift muffler

Direct Cooling – Winter Protection

- ☐ inspect hoses & hose clamps
- ☐ drain raw water from engine block
- ☐ check & change engine anode
- ☐ remove engine thermostat
- ☐ fill engine block with antifreeze
- ☐ re-install engine thermostat
- ☐ add antifreeze to header tank
- ☐ add antifreeze to circuit
- ☐ run engine to flush circuit
- ☐ drain raw water hoses, if not filled with antifreeze
- ☐ drain strainer, if not filled with antifreeze
- ☐ service raw water pump & impeller
- ☐ service exhaust riser
- ☐ clean syphon break
- ☐ drain water-lift muffler, if not filled with antifreeze

Direct Cooling – Tropical Storage

- ☐ inspect hoses & hose clamps
- ☐ check & change engine anode
- ☐ drain all raw water hoses
- ☐ drain strainer
- ☐ service raw water pump & impeller

☐ protect thruhull from marine growth
☐ service exhaust riser
☐ clean syphon break
☐ drain water-lift muffler

Recommission
☐ check seacocks open/close smoothly
☐ check the raw water strainer
☐ check engine and heat exchanger anodes
☐ re-install the raw water pump impeller & face plate
☐ open raw water seacock for engine
☐ remove plugs from exhaust & raw water intake thruhulls

Coolant/Antifreeze
Maintenance
☐ check coolant/antifreeze level in header tank or overflow bottle
☐ inspect condition of coolant
☐ drain and replace worn-out coolant/antifreeze

Lay-up
☐ check coolant level in header tank or overflow bottle
☐ drain and refill coolant/antifreeze
☐ test frost protection of coolant/antifreeze

Recommission
☐ check coolant level in header tank or overflow bottle

Breathing
Maintenance
☐ clean the air filter
☐ check the crankcase breather (and filter)
☐ check adequate air flow through engine room
☐ inspect & repair sound insulation

Lay-up
☐ clean air filter/air intake
☐ seal air intake with plastic
☐ disconnect exhaust hose from exhaust manifold
☐ drain water-lift muffler
☐ prevent rodents entering via exhaust thruhull

Recommission
☐ open engine room ventilators
☐ open air intake on engine
☐ re-connect exhaust riser and hoses
☐ close drain on water-lift muffler or reconnect hose

Electrical
Maintenance
☐ keep battery(s) charged

☐ check battery open circuit voltage with a multimeter
☐ clean battery tops & terminals
☐ check electrolyte levels in wet-cell batteries
☐ add water to unsealed wet cell battery
☐ check specific gravity of a wet-cell battery
☐ load testing a 12 volt battery

Lay-up
☐ clean battery top and terminals
☐ check electrolyte levels
☐ add water to unsealed wet-cell battery
☐ charge battery before lay-up
☐ load test a questionable battery
☐ trickle charge battery during lay-up
☐ disconnect terminals from battery

Recommission
☐ check exterior condition of battery – signs of a frozen battery
☐ charge battery(s)
☐ reconnect battery terminals (lugs)

Drive Train
Maintenance
☐ check coupling between transmission & prop shaft
☐ inspect the propeller shaft
☐ inspect the strut
☐ inspect the cutlass bearing
☐ inspect the propeller anode
☐ scrape the propeller, strut & shaft
☐ inspect the propeller
☐ inspect the propeller nuts and cotter pin
☐ inspect a folding propeller
☐ inspect the anode on a feathering propeller
☐ grease a feathering propeller

Lay-up
☐ check coupling between transmission & prop shaft
☐ inspect the propeller shaft
☐ inspect the stuffing box
☐ inspect the cutlass bearing
☐ inspect the propeller shaft anode
☐ clean the propeller, strut and shaft
☐ inspect the propeller
☐ inspect the propeller nuts & cotter pin
☐ inspect a folding propeller
☐ inspect the anode of a feathering prop
☐ grease a feathering propeller
☐ lay-up a traditional stuffing box in water
☐ protect the propeller & shaft from marine growth

Recommission
- ☐ check control cables are securely attached to lever
- ☐ check throttle cable movement
- ☐ check transmission control cable
- ☐ check stop cable or solenoid
- ☐ grease rubber cup on dripless shaft seal
- ☐ remove wrap around propeller and shaft

In Water
- ☐ prime raw water strainer
- ☐ start engine
- ☐ check raw water being expelled with exhaust
- ☐ burp raw water strainer to release trapped air
- ☐ check oil pressure is normal
- ☐ check alternator is charging
- ☐ check seacocks, 1raw water strainer & exhaust for leaks
- ☐ check vessel moves in gear
- ☐ re-adjust packing in traditional stuffing box
- ☐ burp air from dripless shaft seal

Schedule for Maintenance Tasks

Most engine and other operator manuals provide a schedule for maintenance

Daily

Engine Essentials
- ☐ visual engine room inspection
- ☐ check engine oil level
- ☐ check belt tension
- ☐ check coolant/antifreeze & top up as needed

Lubrication
- ☐ check engine oil level

Electrical
- ☐ keep battery fully charged or trickle charge

Weekly

Engine Essentials
- ☐ check transmission fluid
- ☐ inspect hoses and hose clamps
- ☐ fit & inspect anti-chafe protection
- ☐ inspect wires & terminals
- ☐ inspect belt(s)

Lubrication
- ☐ dipstick diagnostics – engine oil
- ☐ check transmission fluid level
- ☐ dipstick diagnostics – transmission

Coolant/Antifreeze
- ☐ check coolant level in header tank or overflow bottle
- ☐ inspect condition of coolant

Electrical
- ☐ check battery open circuit voltage with multimeter

Drive Train
- ☐ scrape the propeller, strut & shaft, as needed

Monthly

Engine Essentials
- ☐ inspect pulleys (sheaves)
- ☐ inspect alignment of belts & pulleys
- ☐ adjust pulley alignment (as needed)
- ☐ tighten alternator & water pump belt(s), as needed
- ☐ inspect & repair sound insulation

Diesel Fuel
- ☐ inspect injection pump & injectors

Electrical
- ☐ keep battery terminal connections tight
- ☐ clean battery tops and terminals
- ☐ check electrolyte levels in unsealed wet-cell batteries
- ☐ check specific gravity of cells in wet-cell battery
- ☐ add distilled water to wet-cell battery, when necessary

Raw Water Cooling
- ☐ flush syphon break in fresh water

Breathing
- ☐ check and clean air filter

100 hours

Lubrication
- ☐ change engine oil & filter

3 Months

Diesel Fuel
- ☐ inspect fuel deck fill
- ☐ add biocide to the fuel tank(s) (on filling tank)

Breathing
- ☐ ensure adequate air flow through engine room

Drive Train
- ☐ check coupling transmission/prop shaft
- ☐ inspect stern gland (stuffing box)

Seasonal

Lubrication
- ☐ change transmission fluid
- ☐ grease control cable ends & engine mount threads
- ☐ check injection pump & governor dipstick, if fitted

6 months

Raw Water Cooling
- ☐ check and change heat exchanger anode(s)

Drive Train
- ☐ inspect propeller shaft anode
- ☐ inspect the anode on a feathering propeller

Yearly

Diesel Fuel
- ☐ change the primary fuel filter
- ☐ change the secondary fuel filter
- ☐ bleed the fuel system, as needed
- ☐ check diesel tank(s) for contamination

Lubrication
- ☐ lubricate ignition key slot

Raw Water Cooling
- ☐ clean raw water intake thruhull
- ☐ check emergency plug tied to seacock
- ☐ check seacock open/closes smoothly
- ☐ service raw water strainer
- ☐ service raw water pump & impeller

Breathing
- ☐ inspect and repair sound insulation

Electrical
- ☐ test battery(s) with load tester

Drive Train
- ☐ inspect propeller shaft
- ☐ inspect strut
- ☐ inspect cutlass bearing
- ☐ inspect the propeller
- ☐ inspect propeller nuts are tight & cotter pin
- ☐ inspect a folding propeller

1 – 2 Years

Breathing
☐ check the crankcase breather (and filter)

Coolant/Antifreeze
☐ drain and replace worn-out coolant/antifreeze

Drive Train
☐ grease a feathering propeller

Saildrives

Saildrive – Daily
☐ check saildrive gear oil level & top up, as needed

Saildrive – Weekly (as needed)
☐ scrape the propeller, strut & shaft
☐ burp air from gear oil dipstick

Saildrive – Monthly
☐ inspect and repair paint protection
☐ clean raw water intake

Saildrive – 3 Months
☐ check coupling transmission/prop shaft
☐ inspect stern gland (stuffing box)

Saildrive – 100 – 250 hours
☐ change gear oil in lower unit

Saildrive – 6 Months
☐ inspect propeller shaft anode

Saildrive – Yearly
☐ inspect exterior rubber fairing flange
☐ inspect interior rubber sealing ring & water sensor alarm
☐ drain raw water from saildrive (for lay-up)
☐ inspect the propeller
☐ grease a feathering propeller (see owner's manual)

Task Lists

Technical Word Lists
in six languages

free from - *www.marinedieselbasics.com*

Tools & Supplies Required

- [ ] bottle – small, clean container easier to add water to batteries
- [ ] bucket fresh water – for emergency when working with wet-cell batteries
- [ ] charging system: engine alternator AND/OR marine battery charger
      solar panels, wind generator
- [ ] container for raw water pump face plate screws
- [ ] emery cloth
- [ ] Engine Manuals – operator's, workshop, spare parts
- [ ] flashlights – LED handheld
      – LED headlamp
- [ ] funnels – adding engine oil & transmission fluid
      – water to wet-cell batteries
      – diesel fuel filter funnel
- [ ] grease gun (grease can be smeared on with finger)
- [ ] hydrometers – for checking ethylene glycol antifreeze/coolant
      – for checking specific gravity of wet-cell batteries
- [ ] impeller remover OR 2 needlenose pliers OR 2 slot screwdrivers
- [ ] jugs to dispose of used coolant, used engine oil and used transmission fluid
- [ ] magnifying glass
- [ ] Maintenance Logbook – essential to keep record of filter changes etc.
- [ ] mirror – easier to inspect underside of hoses etc.
- [ ] needlenose pliers – to remove raw water impeller
      – may be needed to remove anode stub from plug
- [ ] new gasket or o-ring
- [ ] oil change pump – large or small
- [ ] oil filter wrench
- [ ] pens – ballpoint pen for Maintenance log
- [ ] permanent marker – to make change date on new oil filter mark position of thermostat in housing (direct housing)
- [ ] plastic bags – for safe disposal of acid soaked rags etc.
- [ ] plastic patch, to cover thruhull (tropical in-water storage) (e. g. cut from coolant jug)
- [ ] rubber hammer
- [ ] safety glasses – wear when working around wet-cell batteries
- [ ] screwdrivers – slot (hose clamps) OR mini-socket wrench
      – various - Phillips, Robertson etc.
- [ ] scrub pad
- [ ] scrubbing brush or used toothbrush, for cleaning air filter (depends on type)
- [ ] scuba goggles (tropical in-water storage)
- [ ] shop vacuum cleaner

- ☐ soft wood plug or rubber cones (tropical in-water storage)
- ☐ stiff wire – helpful to clean out exhaust riser
- ☐ toothbrush – used, scrubbing tool or scrubbing brush
- ☐ Transmission Manuals – operator's, workshop, spare parts
- ☐ tube of caulking
- ☐ utility blade or gasket scraper – to clean surfaces, eg. thermostat housing
- ☐ wash basin – washing air filter
  - catch-all for used oil filter, fuel filter, used oil
  (can be made by cutting side out of empty oil/coolant container)
- ☐ wrenches – 2 open-ended or flare-nut wrench
  - 2 pipe wrenches OR 2 adjustable square wrenches
    OR 2 packing wrenches to fit diameter of stuffing box glands
  - to fit top & bottom nuts of fuel injectors (if needed to bleed)
  - un-tighten battery lugs (terminals)
  - sized for thermostat housing bolts (direct cooling)
  - hose clamp mini-socket wrench or use slot screwdriver
  - bleed nut on 2nd fuel filter
  - sized for coupling bolts and nuts

SUPPLIES

- ☐ anodes – zinc, aluminum, or magnesium
  - to fit propeller shaft – pencil-type for heat exchanger
  - feathering or folding propeller (if fitted)
- ☐ ATF (automatic transmission fluid) see Transmission Manual for type and quantity. Some transmission use engine oil, not ATF
- ☐ baking soda – neutralizes battery acid
- ☐ biocide – to prevent HUM growth in diesel fuel
- ☐ corrosion inhibitor OR use engine oil
- ☐ cotter pins sized for propeller nuts, control cables
- ☐ detergent – for clean up
- ☐ disposable gloves – non-sterile or Nitrile,
- ☐ distilled water OR low mineral, boiled water for battery top-up
- ☐ engine oil (see Engine Manual for type and quantity)
- ☐ *ethylene coolant*/antifreeze for indirect-cooled diesel engines
- ☐ exhaust gasket, new gasket may be needed if riser is unbolted
- ☐ fuel filters – 10µ & 2µ (micron), with o-rings (supplied with new filter)
- ☐ gasket cement – if needed
- ☐ grease – protect control cables and engine mounts from corrosion (oxidation) – feathering or folding propeller (if fitted)
- ☐ oil filters – new, see Engine Manual for thread size
- ☐ *propylene glycol* antifreeze – for raw water cooling circuit
- ☐ rags
- ☐ thermostat gasket or thermostat o-ring (depending on model type) if needed

Acknowledgements

No-one is born a sailor or a mechanic. For a fortunate few, the skills and experience may come easily; for most people, these skills are hard gained through the university of hard knocks, big bills, gut-wrenching adventures and more than a few disappointments. No-one learns alone. We all depend on other sailors to show us the way, teach by example, share experiences, inspire us, correct our mistakes, and provide support. And we owe an enormous debt to sailors of yester-years.

This book would never have come to fruition without the support and encouragement of many people. In particular, I would like to express my respect and deep gratitude to Peter Jarrett, master marine engineer who has been teaching, explaining and answering all my questions since the day I went aboard my first boat (a Roberts 36) in Langkawi, Malaysia; Peter gamely read the first draft and made many invaluable suggestions and corrections. Michele Pippen, sailor and yacht broker, another friend in Langkawi, has also taught me much about boats. She also sold my first boat when it was time to move on and sold to me my third boat, SV *Oceans Five*.

Craig Morley, of Aquafacts Marine Surveyors in West Lorne, Ontario, diesel & marine master mechanic and sailing instructor, has been generous in sharing his knowledge and experience on all matters nautical after taking me on for a work placement that became both employment and training. Kong Njo has been generous with his time and expertise in designing the book covers for the series.

Denbigh Patton and Gillie Davies have been unstinting with their practical support and encouragement. My projects (sailing and non-sailing) would have been impossible without the close friendship and generosity of Jiri and Simone Skopek and Magdalena Krondl. Arie Agniyadis and Gearoid O'Croinin have been patient and listening friends through many adventures. These friendships are among the great blessings of my life.

After endless mechanical problems and a crisis of confidence aboard SV *Kuan Yin* on the remote coast of Labrador, Canada, I was fortunate to choose the Midland Campus of Georgian College in Ontario, for my first formal mechanical training. Rob Davidson (head of the Marine Engine Mechanic's course) and faculty did their best to impart their knowledge and experience. My thanks to them for providing all the students with a solid technical foundation on which we have all had the opportunity to develop as marine mechanics.

My thanks to Chris Callahan, Ron Koopman, Jacques Leonard-Etienne and many others who wrote to me with their comments and corrections.

And thank you to Commodore Ed Hill and all the members and staff of the Tanga Yacht Club, Tanzania, for their welcome and hospitality.

MDB Series

Purpose of the Series

The Marine Diesel Basics series of books are visual guides to the complete diesel systems on recreational vessels - motor, sail and canal boats. Whether prospective boatowner, new boatowner or experienced skipper, these books are packed with clear information:

- first principles and how things work
- what to look for when buying new equipment
- installation components to avoid problems and failures
- visual instructions *in detail* on 144+ maintenance, winterizing tasks
- why and how to inspect engine system components
- troubleshooting - identifying root causes of a problem, not just symptoms
- best practices and international standards and codes
- mechanic's know-how - techniques, tools, corrosion, advanced maintenance
- 1000s of drawings

The Marine Diesel Basics books are available in:
- paperback
- spiral bound softcover
- hardcover
- larger print hardcover
- ebook

MDB1 - Maintenance, Lay-up, Winter Protection, Tropical Storage, Spring Recommission
- paperback
- spiral bound softcover
- hardcover
- larger print hardcover
- ebook

Maintenance Logbook - 228 pages with 50+ drawings and checklists
- eLogbook – click & edit pdf for iPad and tablet
- spiral bound
- softcover
- hardcover

Future titles

MDB2 How Things Work, Installation Guidelines - coming summer 2022

MDB3 Troubleshooting – identify & solve problems, not symptoms

MDB4 Marine Mechanic's Know-How – tools, techniques, corrosion etc.

MDB Vessel Logbook - value-added logbook for short trips and ocean passages

About the Author

I started sailing almost by accident, after a family visit led to a day's sailing in Toronto Harbour, Canada, in 2000. I was immediately hooked, began crewing on clubs' race nights and taking formal training. In 2002, I bought a Roberts 36 sailboat on the Andaman Sea in Langkawi, Malaysia.

My second boat, *Kuan Yin*, was a 32-foot steel Tahitiana ketch, which I refitted in Toronto and sailed down the St. Lawrence River to Labrador & Newfoundland. For five challenging summers I sailed singlehanded north in sub-Arctic waters attempting to retrace a voyage made in 1811 by an Inuk captain and his family who took two Moravian missionaries along the Atlantic coast of Labrador into the remotest wilderness of Ungava Bay.

However, endless mechanical troubles delayed every summer's attempts to go north and get south again before the fall gales began on the majestic, desolate 1000-mile coastline. Sailing in Labrador is spectacular and enthralling, and the people welcoming and generous. For me, it was also a time of frustration, disappointment and great anxiety. Eventually, I decided that I must either give up the boat or train as a marine mechanic. So I went to school, trained as a marine mechanic, worked for a very experienced mechanic and sailor and applied myself to thoroughly learn this business.

The result is the Marine Diesel Basics books – everything I wish I'd known when I started and which I hope can help other sailors enjoy their vessels without anxiety or extra expenses. Visual information is so much easier to understand!

After a failed attempt to cross the Atlantic Ocean from Newfoundland to the Azores I sold *Kuan Yin* to focus on the new books. However, I missed sailing and boats so much it was only 8 months before I bought a 36-foot steel Chevrier sloop, built in 1982 and in need of repairs (26 rust holes!), also in Malaysia.

In 2021, I finally fulfilled a great ambition - to cross an ocean singlehanded - when I sailed *Oceans Five* across the Indian Ocean from Thailand to Tanzania, pausing in the Maldives and the Seychelles. A total distance of 5400 nautical miles.

Dennison

SV *Oceans Five*, Tanga Yacht Club, Tanzania, March 2022

Other books by Dennison Berwick:
Staycation, How to Get Away without Going Away
Savages, The Life and Killing of the Yanomami Indians
Amazon
A Walk Along the Ganges
Canadian Retreat Guide (out of print)

Index

A

Air Filter 77
  Clean the Air Filter 78
  Why Clean the Air Filter? 77
Air Intake/Air Cleaners 77
  Keep Humidity Out of the Air Intake 150
  Seal Air Intake with Plastic 149
  Unseal Air Intake on Engine 168
Alternator
  Check Alternator is Charging 182
  Inspect Belts - Alternator, Coolant & Raw Water Pump 11
Anode(s) 68
  See also Corrosion
  aluminum 68
  Check and Change Engine Block Anode(s) 133
  Check Engine and Heat Exchanger Anodes 164
  Check Heat Exchanger Anode 142
  magnesium 68
  Propeller Anode 103
  Saildrive Anodes 115
  zinc 68
Anti-Foul Paint 61
ATF (Automatic Transmission Fluid)
  Check Transmission Fluid Level 41
  Fill the Transmission with ATF (or Engine Oil) 128
Axial fans 80
  See also Ventilation

B

Batteries
  See also Lithium-iron batteries
  Add Water to Unsealed Wet-Cell Battery 89
  Adjust Specific Gravity Readings for Temperature 92
  Battery Freezing 153
  Battery Self Discharge 152
  Check Battery Open Circuit Voltage 84
  Check Specific Gravity of a Wet-Cell Battery 90
  Check the Electrolyte Levels of Wet-Cell Batteries 87
  Clean Battery Tops & Terminals 85
  Keep Battery Terminal Connections Tight 84
  Keep Battery(s) Charged 83
  Load Test a Questionable Battery 153
  Load Testing a 12 Volt Battery 92
  Reconnect Battery Terminals (Lugs) 172
  Self-Discharge of Lead Acid Battery 152
  Signs of a Frozen Battery 171
  Time Required to Charge a 12-Volt Wet-Cell Battery 83
  Top-up Battery Water Levels 171
  Trickle Charging Batteries 83
  Understanding Battery Load Test Results 93
  Where to Store Batteries 154
Belts & Pulleys
  Adjust Pulley Alignment 15
  Alternator, Coolant & Raw Water Pump Belts 11
  Check Alignment of Belts & Pulleys 13
  Inspect Pulleys (Sheaves) 12
  Tighten Alternator and Water Pump Belts 16
Biocide 20, 22
  Biocide - add before lay-up 126
Bleed the Diesel System 29
Breathing
  See also Air Filter
  See also Air Intake/Air Cleaners
  See also Exhaust Manifold
  See also Exhaust Riser
  See also Ventilation

C

Cables & Cabling 94
  See also Wires & Wiring
Cautionary Tale 18, 35, 56, 71, 76, 81, 94, 107, 145, 170
Cavitation 73
  See also Corrosion
Chafe Protection 8
Checklists 187
Condensation and Filling the Fuel Tank(s) 126
Control Cables 54
  Check Control Cables are Securely Attached to Levers 173
  Check Stop Cable or Stop Solenoid Button 175

Check Throttle Cable Movement 174
Check Transmission Control Cable 174
Check Vessel Moves in Gear 183
Single Lever Dual Action 174
Coolant/Antifreeze 147
brands of coolant/antifreeze 6
Check Coolant Level in Header Tank or
Overflow Bottle 167
Check Coolant/Antifreeze Level 73
Critical Functions of Coolant/Antifreeze 73
Drain and Replace Worn-out Coolant/
Antifreeze 74
Ethylene Glycol Coolant/Antifreeze 72
Freezing Point of Ethylene Glycol Coolant/
Antifreeze 148
IAT and OAT coolants 72
Inspect Condition of Coolant 74
Test Frost Protection 147
Testing Coolant/Antifreeze with
Hydrometer 148
Corrosion
Crevice corrosion 97, 158
dezincification 104
Coupling 95
See also Drive Train
Crankcase Breather and Filter 79
Cutlass Bearing 102
Cutless or Cutlass? 102
Inspect the Cutlass Bearing 102

D

Dezincification 104
Diesel Fuel
3 Ways to Contaminate Diesel Fuel & Tanks 20
Add Biocide to the Fuel Tank(s) 22
Bacteria, Fungi & Yeasts 20
best practices 23
Bleed the Diesel System 29
Bleed the High Pressure Fuel Lines 32
Bleed the Suction & Low Pressure Fuel Lines 31
Condensation & Filling the Fuel Tank(s) 126
Filter Funnel 22
Fuel Tank(s) 33
Fuel Tank in the Keel 33
Fuel Tank with no Drain 33
Grit, Sand & Dirt 21
HUM (Hydrocarbon Utilizing
Microorganisms) 19, 20
Importance of Very Clean Fuel 19
Inspect Fuel Deck Fill Fitting 21
microns - size comparisons 23

Preventing Fuel Contamination 21
ULSD Ultra Low Sulphur Diesel 19
Water 20
Dipstick Diagnostics – Engine Oil 38
Colour of Oil & Consistency of Oil 40
Oil Level and Change in Oil Level 39
Smell of the Oil 41
Dipstick Diagnostics – Transmission Fluid 41
ATF Level & Change in Level 42
Colour and Consistency 43
Smell 44
Direct Cooling 59
See also Raw Water Cooling
Disclaimer xi
Dripless Shaft Seal 100
See also Stern Gland
Burp Air from Alternative Style Dripless Seal
186
Burp Air from Dripless Shaft Seal 185
Check Hose(s) on Dripless Shaft Seal 177
Dripless Shaft Seals in Severe Freezing
Conditions 156
Face Seal 100
Grease Rubber Cup on Dripless Shaft Seal 176
Inspect a Dripless Shaft Seal 100
Lip seal 100
Drive Train 95
See Coupling
See Stern Gland
See Cutlass Bearing
See Propeller Shaft
Clean the Propeller, Strut & Shaft 103
Inspect the Strut 101

E

Electrolyte 87
See also Batteries
Engine
Check Belt Tension 4
Check Stop Cable or Stop Solenoid Button 175
Heat of Combustion 57
Inspect Hoses and Hose Clamps 7
Rotate Engine Without Starting 161
Start Engine Procedure 17, 180
Check Raw Water Being Expelled with
Exhaust 180
Engine Coolant/Antifreeze
Check Coolant/Antifreeze 6
Engine Lubrication
Check Engine Oil Level 4
Engine Mount 54

Grease Engine Mounts 125
Engine Oil - see Lubrication - Engine Oil
Engine Room
    Check Adequate Air Flow Through Engine
        Room 80
    Clean the Bilge 124
    Good Engine Room Ventilation 80
    Inspect & Repair Sound Insulation 81
    Open Engine Room Ventilators 168
    Visual Engine Room Inspection 3
Ethylene Glycol Coolant/Antifreeze 72
    Disposal 75
    Freezing Point of Ethylene Glycol Coolant/
        Antifreeze 148
Exhaust Manifold 150
    Exhaust Thruhull 151
Exhaust Muffler - see Water-Lift Muffler
Exhaust Riser 143
    Disconnect Exhaust Riser 150
    Re-Connect Exhaust Riser and Hoses 169
    Service the Exhaust Riser 144

F

Feathering Propeller 105
    See also Propeller
Filter Funnel 22
Flexible Coupling 95–96
Folding Propeller 105
    See also Propeller
Fresh-water cooled - see Raw Water Cooling
Fuel - see Diesel Fuel
Fuel Deck Fill Fitting 21
Fuel Pump
    electric fuel pump 29
    Mechanical Fuel Pump 29
Fuel Tank(s) 33
Fuel Vent 127
    See also Diesel Fuel

G

Galvanic corrosion 68
    See also Corrosion
Gearbox - see Transmission
Glow plugs 17, 180
Governor - engine speed 55

H

Header Tank 73, 137
Heat Exchanger 69
    See also Raw Water Cooling
    Check Heat Exchanger Anode 142
    Drain the Heat Exchanger(s) 141

Hoses and Hose Clamps 7
    hose clamps - correct sizing 166
Hydro-lock 29

I

Ignition Key Slot 55
Impeller 63
    See also Raw Water Pump
    Inspect a Rubber/Nitrile Impeller 65
Indirect Cooling (Fresh-Water Cooled) 58
    See also Raw Water Cooling
Injection Pump and Injectors 32
    Check Injection Pump & Governor Dipsticks 55
    Inspect Injection Pump and Injectors 34

J

Jubilee Clips 8
    See also Hoses & Hose Clamps

K

Keel Cooling 60

L

Lay-up
    Breathing 149
    Coolant/Antifreeze 147
    Diesel Fuel 126
    Drive Train 155
    Electrical 152
    Engine Essentials 122
    Lubrication 128
    Raw Water Cooling 129
    Winter Protection & Tropical Storage 121
Lip Seal 100
Lithium-iron batteries 171
    See also Batteries
    Lay-Up Lithium-Iron Batteries 154
    Maintaining Lithium-Iron (LiFePo4)
        Batteries 85
    Lithium-iron batteries 83
    recommissioning 171
Load Testing 92
    See also Batteries
    Understanding Battery Load Test Results 93
Lubrication
    Check Injection Pump & Governor Dipsticks 55
    Grease the Control Cable Ends and Engine
        Mount Threads 54
    Lubricate Ignition Key Slot 55
Lubrication - Engine Oil
    See also Oil Pressure
    best practices 37

Change the Engine Oil & Filter 45
Check Engine Oil Level 38
Dipstick Diagnostics – Engine Oil 38
Oil Change Procedure 46
Oil Filter Buyer's Guide 45
Oil Is An Engine's Life Blood 37
Warm Oil Flows More Easily 46
Lubrication - Transmission
Change the Transmission Fluid 52
Check Transmission Fluid Level 41
Dipstick Diagnostics – Transmission Fluid 41

M

Maintenance
Breathing 77
Coolant/Antifreeze 72
Diesel Fuel 19
Drive Train 95
Electrical 82
Engine Essentials 2
Lubrication 36
Purpose of Maintenance - Reliable and Robust 1
Raw Water Cooling 57
Water Words 58
Maintenance Logbook
eLogbook 1
Value of the Maintenance Logbook 1
Marine Growth 61, 103, 142, 158
Microns 23

O

Oil Change Procedure 46
Oil Filter Buyer's Guide 45
Oil Pressure 181
Check Oil Pressure Is Normal 181
Overflow Bottle 147

P

Potable water - not covered 121
Primary Fuel Filter 23
best practices 23
Propeller 103
Grease a Feathering Propeller 105
Inspect a Folding Propeller 105
Inspect the Anode on a Feathering Propeller 105
Inspect the Propeller 104
Inspect the Propeller Anode 103
Inspect the Propeller Nuts and Cotter Pin 104
Protect the Propeller & Shaft from Marine Growth 158

Remove Wrap Around Propeller and Shaft 178
Propeller Shaft 95
See also Drive Train
Inspect the Propeller Anode 103
Inspect the Propeller Shaft 97
Propylene glycol antifreeze 117
See also Raw Water Cooling
3 Ways to Add Propylene Glycol Antifreeze 138
Fill the Block with Propylene Glycol Antifreeze 135
Pulley - see Belts & Pulleys
Purge the fuel system 29

R

Raw Water Cooling
See also Heat Exchanger
See also Syphon Break
See also Raw Water Pump
Add Propylene Glycol Antifreeze to Header Tank 137
Check Emergency Plug Tied to Every Seacock 61
Check for Leaks 182
Check Raw Water Being Expelled with Exhaust 180
Check Seacock Opens/Closes Smoothly 62
Direct Cooling Task List 131
Drain Raw Water Hoses 139
Drain the Heat Exchanger(s) 141
Heat of Combustion 57
Indirect Cooling Task List 130
Laying-up the Raw Water Cooling Circuit 129
no exhaust water being expelled 180
Remove the Engine Thermostat 134
Raw Water Pump 63
See also Raw Water Cooling
Find Missing Impeller Pieces 67
Hydro-lock 29
Inspect a Rubber/Nitrile Impeller 65
Re-Install the Raw Water Pump Impeller & Face Plate 164
Remove and Inspecting the Rubber/Nitrile Impeller 65
Recommissioning 159
Breathing 168
Coolant/Antifreeze 167
Diesel Fuel 160
Drive Train 173
Electrical 171
Engine Essentials 159

In Water 178
Lubrication 161
Raw Water Cooling 163
Rodents 151

S

Saildrives
Anodes 115
Burp Air 112
Exterior Rubber Fairing Flange 113
Gear Oil 109
Lay-up 117
Maintenance 108
Paint Protection 116
Raw Water Intakes 116
Recommission 119
Saildrive Oil Seals 109
Water Sensor Alarm 114
Watertight Seal 113
Seacock 61
See also Raw Water Cooling
Check Seacock Opens/Closes Smoothly 62
Seacock OPEN or CLOSED? 140
Secondary Fuel Filter 26
Sheaves - see Belts & Pulleys
Single Lever Dual Action Lever 174
Solenoid Button (Stop) 175
Sound Insulation 17
Inspect & Repair Sound Insulation 17, 81
Specific Gravity 92
See also Batteries
Squirrel cage fans 80
See also Ventilation
Stern Gland 98, 100
Burp Air from Dripless Shaft Seal 185
Dripless Shaft Seals in Severe Freezing Conditions 156
Grease Rubber Cup on Dripless Shaft Seal 176
Importance of the Stuffing Box Hose 98
Inspect a Dripless Shaft Seal 100
Strainer 62
See also Raw Water Cooling
Burp Raw Water Strainer to Release Trapped Air 181
Check the Raw Water Strainer 163
Drain the Raw Water Strainer 140
Prime Raw Water Strainer 179
Strut 101
Inspect the Strut 101
Stuffing Box 98

See also Drive Train
See also Stern Gland
Hand Tighten & Lock Packing Gland on Traditional Stuffing Box 177
Inspect a Traditional Stuffing Box 98
Lay-Up a Traditional Stuffing Box In Water 157
Packing 184
Re-adjust Packing in Traditional Stuffing Box 184
Sulphation 82
See also Batteries
Syphon Break 70
See also Raw Water Cooling
Clean the Raw Water Syphon Break 145
Flush and Clean the Syphon Break 70

T

Task Lists 187
Technical Word Lists xii
Thermostat 134
Re-install the Engine Thermostat 136
Thruhulls 61
Remove Plugs from Exhaust & Raw Water Intake Thruhulls 166
Transmission
Check Transmission Fluid Level 7
Check Vessel Moves in Gear 183
Drain Transmission Fluid to Maximum Level 162
Trickle Charge Battery 154
Turbocharger 44
Best Practices 44
importance of oil changes 52

V

Ventilation
Active 80
Good Engine Room Ventilation 80
Passive 80

W

Water Words 58
Water-Lift Muffler 145
Drain Water-Lift Muffler 150
Wet Cell Batteries - see Batteries
Wires & Wiring
See also Cables & Cabling
Inspect Wires and Wiring Terminals 9
Wiring 94
Words - Canadian, American, Australian & British Equivalents xii

CPSIA information can be obtained
at www.ICGtesting.com
Printed in the USA
BVHW011055180922
647326BV00003B/31